Chemical Interactions

PRENTICE HALL Science Explorer

PEARSON

Boston, Massachusetts
Glenview, Illinois
Shoreview, Minnesota
Upper Saddle River, New Jersey

Chemical Interactions

Book-Specific Resources

Student Edition
StudentExpress™ CD-ROM
Interactive Textbook Online
Teacher's Edition
All-in-One Teaching Resources
Color Transparencies
Guided Reading and Study Workbook
Student Edition in MP3 Audio
Discovery Channel School® Video
Consumable and Nonconsumable Materials Kits

Program Print Resources

Integrated Science Laboratory Manual
Computer Microscope Lab Manual
Inquiry Skills Activity Books
Progress Monitoring Assessments
Test Preparation Workbook
Test-Taking Tips With Transparencies
Teacher's ELL Handbook
Reading Strategies for Science Content

Differentiated Instruction Resources

Adapted Reading and Study Workbook
Adapted Tests
Differentiated Instruction Guide for Labs and Activities

Program Technology Resources

TeacherExpress™ CD-ROM
Interactive Textbooks Online
PresentationExpress™ CD-ROM
ExamView®, Test Generator CD-ROM
Lab zone™ Easy Planner CD-ROM
Probeware Lab Manual With CD-ROM
Computer Microscope and Lab Manual
Materials Ordering CD-ROM
Discovery Channel School® DVD Library
Lab Activity Video Library—DVD and VHS
Web Site at PearsonSchool.com

Spanish Print Resources

Spanish Student Edition
Spanish Guided Reading and Study Workbook
Spanish Teaching Guide With Tests

Acknowledgments appear on page 198, which constitutes an extension of this copyright page.

Cover
Spectacular fireworks and golden, roasted marshmallows both result from chemical reactions.

13-digit ISBN 978-0-13-365112-6
10-digit ISBN 0-13-365112-6
6 7 8 9 10 VO63 12 11

Program Authors

Michael J. Padilla, Ph.D.
Associate Dean and Director
Eugene T. Moore School of Education
Clemson University
Clemson, South Carolina

Michael Padilla is a leader in middle school science education. He has served as an author and elected officer for the National Science Teachers Association and as a writer of the National Science Education Standards. As lead author of Science Explorer, Mike has inspired the team in developing a program that meets the needs of middle grades students, promotes science inquiry, and is aligned with the National Science Education Standards.

Ioannis Miaoulis, Ph.D.
President
Museum of Science
Boston, Massachusetts

Originally trained as a mechanical engineer, Ioannis Miaoulis is in the forefront of the national movement to increase technological literacy. As dean of the Tufts University School of Engineering, Dr. Miaoulis spearheaded the introduction of engineering into the Massachusetts curriculum. Currently he is working with school systems across the country to engage students in engineering activities and to foster discussions on the impact of science and technology on society.

Martha Cyr, Ph.D.
Director of K–12 Outreach
Worcester Polytechnic Institute
Worcester, Massachusetts

Martha Cyr is a noted expert in engineering outreach. She has over nine years of experience with programs and activities that emphasize the use of engineering principles, through hands-on projects, to excite and motivate students and teachers of mathematics and science in grades K–12. Her goal is to stimulate a continued interest in science and mathematics through engineering.

Book Authors

David V. Frank, Ph.D.
Head, Department of
Physical Sciences
Ferris State University
Big Rapids, Michigan

John G. Little
Science Teacher
St. Mary's High School
Stockton, California

Steve Miller
Science Writer
State College, Pennsylvania

Contributing Writers

Linda Blaine
Science Teacher
Millbrook High School
Raleigh, North Carolina

Mary Sue Burns
Science Teacher
Pocahontas County
High School
Dunmore, West Virginia

Thomas L. Messer
Science Teacher
Foxborough Public Schools
Foxborough, Massachusetts

Thomas R. Wellnitz
Science Teacher
The Paideia School
Atlanta, Georgia

Consultants

Reading Consultant

Nancy Romance, Ph.D.
Professor of Science
Education
Florida Atlantic University
Fort Lauderdale, Florida

Mathematics Consultant

William Tate, Ph.D.
Professor of Education and
Applied Statistics and
Computation
Washington University
St. Louis, Missouri

Reviewers

Teacher Reviewers

David R. Blakely
Arlington High School
Arlington, Massachusetts

Jane E. Callery
Two Rivers Magnet Middle
School
East Hartford, Connecticut

Melissa Lynn Cook
Oakland Mills High School
Columbia, Maryland

James Fattic
Southside Middle School
Anderson, Indiana

Dan Gabel
Hoover Middle School
Rockville, Maryland

Wayne Goates
Eisenhower Middle School
Goddard, Kansas

Katherine Bobay Graser
Mint Hill Middle School
Charlotte, North Carolina

Darcy Hampton
Deal Junior High School
Washington, D.C.

Karen Kelly
Pierce Middle School
Waterford, Michigan

David Kelso
Manchester High School Central
Manchester, New Hampshire

Benigno Lopez, Jr.
Sleepy Hill Middle School
Lakeland, Florida

Angie L. Matamoros, Ph.D.
ALM Consulting, Inc.
Weston, Florida

Tim McCollum
Charleston Middle School
Charleston, Illinois

Bruce A. Mellin
Brooks School
North Andover, Massachusetts

Ella Jay Parfitt
Southeast Middle School
Baltimore, Maryland

Evelyn A. Pizzarello
Louis M. Klein Middle School
Harrison, New York

Kathleen M. Poe
Fletcher Middle School
Jacksonville, Florida

Shirley Rose
Lewis and Clark Middle School
Tulsa, Oklahoma

Linda Sandersen
Greenfield Middle School
Greenfield, Wisconsin

Mary E. Solan
Southwest Middle School
Charlotte, North Carolina

Mary Stewart
University of Tulsa
Tulsa, Oklahoma

Paul Swenson
Billings West High School
Billings, Montana

Thomas Vaughn
Arlington High School
Arlington, Massachusetts

Susan C. Zibell
Central Elementary
Simsbury, Connecticut

Safety Reviewers

W. H. Breazeale, Ph.D.
Department of Chemistry
College of Charleston
Charleston, South Carolina

Ruth Hathaway, Ph.D.
Hathaway Consulting
Cape Girardeau, Missouri

Douglas Mandt, M.S.
Science Education Consultant
Edgewood, Washington

Activity Field Testers

Nicki Bibbo
Witchcraft Heights School
Salem, Massachusetts

Rose-Marie Botting
Broward County Schools
Fort Lauderdale, Florida

Colleen Campos
Laredo Middle School
Aurora, Colorado

Elizabeth Chait
W. L. Chenery Middle School
Belmont, Massachusetts

Holly Estes
Hale Middle School
Stow, Massachusetts

Laura Hapgood
Plymouth Community
Intermediate School
Plymouth, Massachusetts

Mary F. Lavin
Plymouth Community
Intermediate School
Plymouth, Massachusetts

James MacNeil, Ph.D.
Cambridge, Massachusetts

Lauren Magruder
St. Michael's Country
Day School
Newport, Rhode Island

Jeanne Maurand
Austin Preparatory School
Reading, Massachusetts

Joanne Jackson-Pelletier
Winman Junior High School
Warwick, Rhode Island

Warren Phillips
Plymouth Public Schools
Plymouth, Massachusetts

Carol Pirtle
Hale Middle School
Stow, Massachusetts

Kathleen M. Poe
Fletcher Middle School
Jacksonville, Florida

Cynthia B. Pope
Norfolk Public Schools
Norfolk, Virginia

Anne Scammell
Geneva Middle School
Geneva, New York

Karen Riley Sievers
Callanan Middle School
Des Moines, Iowa

David M. Smith
Eyer Middle School
Allentown, Pennsylvania

Gene Vitale
Parkland School
McHenry, Illinois

Contents

Chemical Interactions

Reference Section

VIDEO

Enhance understanding through dynamic video.

Preview Get motivated with this introduction to the chapter content.

Field Trip Explore a real-world story related to the chapter content.

Assessment Review content and take an assessment.

Get connected to exciting Web resources in every lesson.

SCI **LINKS.** NSTA Find Web links on topics relating to every section.

Active Art Interact with selected visuals from every chapter online.

Planet Diary® Explore news and natural phenomena through weekly reports.

Science News® Keep up to date with the latest science discoveries.

Experience the complete text-book online and on CD-ROM.

Activities Practice skills and learn content.

Videos Explore content and learn important lab skills.

Audio Support Hear key terms spoken and defined.

Self-Assessment Use instant feedback to help you track your progress.

Activities

Saving the Ozone Layer

Dr. Mario Molina uses a mass spectrometer to analyze chemical reactions.

As a child growing up in Mexico, long before he won a Nobel prize in Chemistry, Mario Molina enjoyed experimenting with science. "I was always interested in chemistry sets or toy microscopes. With the microscope in front of me, I'd take a piece of lettuce, put it in water, and let it rot and really stink. To see the life teeming in a drop of water—that for me was fascinating. Even then I realized it would be great if I could become a research scientist."

What Mario wanted to do, he decided, was "actually use science for things that affect society." Mario Molina began by looking at the chemicals people put into the air.

Career Path

Mario Molina was born in Mexico City, Mexico. He received a B.S. from Universidad Autónoma de México, and a Ph.D. from the University of California at Berkeley. In 1995, Mario Molina, Sherwood Rowland, and Paul Crutzen won the Nobel prize in Chemistry for their work on chlorofluorocarbons (CFCs) and the ozone layer. From 1989 to 2004, Mario was a professor at the Massachusetts Institute of Technology in Cambridge, Massachusetts. He is now a professor in the Department of Chemistry and Biochemistry at the University of California, San Diego.

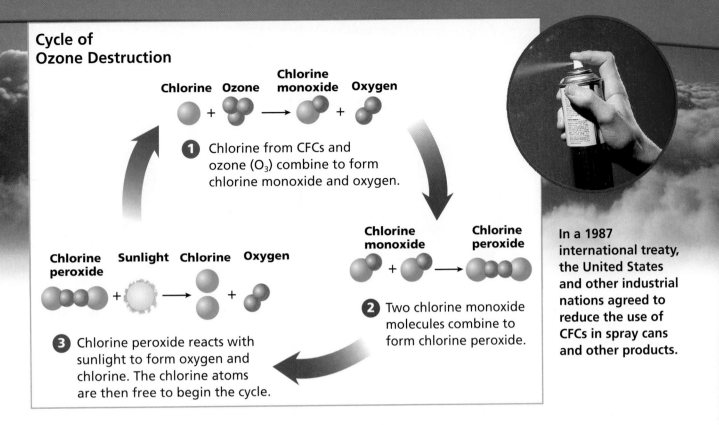

Cycle of Ozone Destruction

Chlorine + Ozone → Chlorine monoxide + Oxygen

1 Chlorine from CFCs and ozone (O_3) combine to form chlorine monoxide and oxygen.

2 Two chlorine monoxide molecules combine to form chlorine peroxide.

Chlorine monoxide + Chlorine monoxide → Chlorine peroxide

3 Chlorine peroxide reacts with sunlight to form oxygen and chlorine. The chlorine atoms are then free to begin the cycle.

Chlorine peroxide + Sunlight → Chlorine + Oxygen

In a 1987 international treaty, the United States and other industrial nations agreed to reduce the use of CFCs in spray cans and other products.

Talking With Dr. Mario Molina

Asking Simple Questions

In the early 1970s, one of Dr. Molina's co-workers, Sherwood Rowland, heard about a group of compounds called chlorofluorocarbons, or CFCs. CFCs were used in air conditioners, refrigerators, and aerosol spray cans. But they leaked into the air. "It is something that is not natural, but is now in the atmosphere all over the planet," says Mario. What happens to these compounds in the air, Rowland and Molina wondered, and what do they do to the air?

"We didn't know ahead of time if CFCs were doing damage or not," Mario explains. "So what we did was study what was going on. We learned that CFCs aren't changed much down near Earth. But we expected that if they got high enough in the atmosphere, solar radiation would destroy them."

Radiation is how energy from the sun reaches Earth. Ultraviolet (UV) rays, a form of radiation, break compounds apart and change them. "Above a certain altitude, everything falls apart. We had to learn how high CFCs went and how long it took them to get there. Then we asked: What does it mean that CFCs are up there?"

A Protective Shield in the Sky

In his laboratory, Dr. Molina studied how ultraviolet light changes CFCs. "It became clear that these molecules would be destroyed by UV rays in the stratosphere—the upper atmosphere, where the ozone layer is. At the time, I didn't even know what the ozone layer was."

Mario Molina learned fast. The ozone layer is a thin layer of the atmosphere that contains ozone, a form of oxygen. The ozone blocks out UV rays from the sun. UV rays would be dangerous to living things if they reached Earth's surface.

Dr. Molina learned something very disturbing. When the sun's rays break CFCs apart, chlorine forms. A chain of chemical changes that destroys ozone then begins. "Very small amounts of CFCs can have very big effects on ozone."

Changes in the Antarctic Ozone Layer, 1979–2001

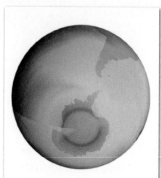

In 1979, thinning of the ozone layer was barely visible.

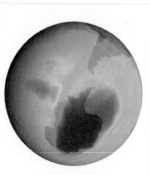

In 1986, a hole in the ozone layer was clearly visible.

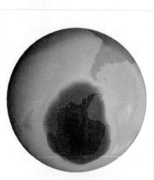

In 1994, the hole in the ozone layer was expanding.

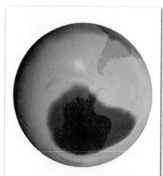

In 2001, the damage to the ozone layer was greatly increased.

These images of the South Pole, taken by satellite between 1979 and 2001, show a hole developing in the ozone layer of the atmosphere.

←——— More ozone   Less ozone ———→

A Scary Prediction Comes True

Mario Molina and his co-workers made a frightening prediction. If CFCs can reach the stratosphere, they will eventually damage the protective ozone layer. Other scientists thought Mario Molina was wrong or exaggerating. But more and more evidence came in. Researchers sent balloons up into the stratosphere with scientific instruments to measure chlorine formed by CFCs. They found that CFCs were in the stratosphere and that the sun's rays were breaking them down.

Was the ozone layer being hurt? Yes. Over Antarctica, there was an "ozone hole," an opening in the ozone layer. The hole lets in harmful radiation from the sun. "That was a surprise to us and to everybody. It was a very large effect that we hadn't predicted. Some scientists thought the ozone hole was natural, but we thought it was caused by CFCs. We checked it out by doing experiments from Antarctica. In a couple of years it became very clear that this hole was a result of the CFCs."

Scientist and Speaker

Dr. Molina now had to convince people to stop making and using CFCs. "The effect over Antarctica was so large that it was easy to measure and test. But similar effects exist everywhere. As scientists we had to inform the public and the government. If you're convinced that you're right and that something dangerous is going to happen, you need to risk speaking out."

Mario Molina went to the U.S. Senate and to other governments. He was able to show how UV radiation was causing damage. "There was damage to some crops, damage to growing fish, damage that we can already see and measure today."

Finally, the world listened. Through the United Nations, an agreement was signed by most industrial nations to stop using CFCs by the year 1995.

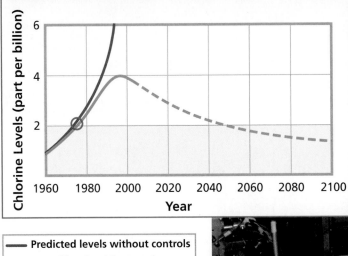

Chlorine Levels in the Atmosphere 1960–2100

y-axis: Chlorine Levels (part per billion)
x-axis: Year

—— Predicted levels without controls
—— Actual levels with controls
--- Predicted levels with controls
○ Antarctica ozone hole begins to form

The graph above shows that the level of chlorine in the atmosphere would have increased rapidly if controls on CFCs had not been passed. With controls in place, the amount of chlorine in the atmosphere should gradually decrease to levels in the light blue region of the graph. The ozone hole should then close.

In the laboratory, Mario and a graduate student investigate chemical reactions that affect the atmosphere.

Writing in Science

Career Link Mario says, "If you're convinced that you're right . . . you need to risk speaking out." After conducting a scientific investigation, a scientist's job is to communicate the results of the research. Suppose you are a scientist whose research is controversial. In a paragraph, describe the steps you might follow to convince other scientists, citizens, and governments to take action based on your research.

Work Still to Do

"Everybody has to work together," chemist Molina says. He has done more than his share. He gave $200,000 of his Nobel prize money to help train scientists from Latin America and other developing countries. "There is a need to understand our planet, and we need very good minds to work on these problems. There are big challenges out there," he says with a confident smile, "but fortunately the science is fascinating."

Go Online
PHSchool.com

For: More on this career
Visit: PHSchool.com
Web Code: cgb-2000

Atoms and Bonding

The BIG Idea
Properties of Matter

Q **How do compounds form?**

Each water molecule in this computer model consists of two hydrogen atoms (clear) bonded to one oxygen atom (red).

Lab zone™ Chapter **Project**

Models of Compounds

In this chapter, you will learn how atoms of elements react with one another to form compounds. When they form compounds, the atoms become chemically bonded to each other. In this project, you will create models of chemical compounds.

Your Goal To make models demonstrating how atoms bond in ionic compounds and in molecular compounds

To complete the project, you must

● select appropriate materials to make models of atoms
● indicate the number of bonds each atom forms
● use your model atoms to compare compounds that contain ionic bonds with compounds that contain covalent bonds
● follow the safety guidelines in Appendix A

Plan It! Brainstorm with some classmates about materials you can use to represent different atoms and chemical bonds. Look ahead in the chapter to preview ionic and covalent bonding. Think about how you will show that ionic and covalent bonding are different. You may need to find some small, but highly visible, objects to represent electrons. Be ready to display your models and explain what they show.

Elements and Atoms

Reading Preview

Key Concepts
- Why are elements sometimes called the building blocks of matter?
- How did atomic theory develop and change?

Key Terms
- matter • element
- compound • mixture • atom
- scientific theory • model
- electrons • nucleus • protons
- energy level • neutrons

Target Reading Skill

Outlining An outline shows the relationship between main ideas and supporting details. As you read, make an outline about elements and atoms. Use the red headings for the main ideas and the blue headings for the supporting ideas.

Elements and Atoms
I. The building blocks of matter
A. Elements, compounds, and mixtures
B.
II. Atomic theory and models
A.
B.

Lab zone Discover **Activity**

How Far Away Is the Electron?

1. On a piece of paper, make a small circle no bigger than a dime. The circle represents the nucleus, or center, of an atom.
2. Measure the diameter of the circle in centimeters.
3. Now predict where the outer edge of this model atom would be. For example, would the outer edge be within the edges of the paper? Your desk? The classroom? The school building?

Think It Over

Calculating The diameter of an actual atom can be 100,000 times the diameter of its nucleus. Calculate the diameter of your model atom. How close was your prediction in Step 3 to your calculation? (*Hint:* To understand the scale of your answer, change the units of measurement from centimeters to meters.)

If you take a quick look around you, you will see many examples of matter. Buildings made of wood or steel, forks and spoons made of metal, your clothing, water, the air you breathe, and all living things are matter. **Matter** is anything that has mass and takes up space. But what is matter made of? More than 2,000 years ago, the ancient Greeks believed that all matter was made up of four elements—air, earth, fire, and water. Not until much later did scientists begin to realize that matter was composed of many different elements.

The Building Blocks of Matter

Elements are the simplest pure substances, and they cannot be broken down into any other substances. You are already familiar with many elements. Aluminum, iron, copper, lead, oxygen, chlorine, neon, and helium are a few you might know. But how are elements related to the many other materials you find in your world? **Elements are often called the building blocks of matter because all matter is composed of one element or a combination of two or more elements.**

Elements, Compounds, and Mixtures Elements usually exist in combination with other elements in the form of compounds. A **compound** is a pure substance made of two or more elements that are combined chemically in a specific ratio. For example, sodium chloride (table salt) from underground mines or from seawater is always 39.3 percent sodium and 60.7 percent chlorine by mass.

Elements can also mix with other elements *without* combining chemically. The air you breathe, for example, consists mostly of nitrogen gas and oxygen gas that are separate substances. A **mixture** is two or more substances—elements, compounds, or both—that are in the same place but are not chemically combined. Air, soil, wood, gasoline, concrete, and orange juice are a few of the many mixtures in your world.

Particles of Elements If elements are the simplest forms of matter, do you wonder what the smallest piece of an element is? If you cut a copper wire in half over and over again, could you keep cutting it forever? Or would you reach a point where you have the smallest possible piece of copper?

Again, the first people to think about this question were the ancient Greeks. Around the year 430 B.C., a Greek philosopher named Democritus proposed the idea that matter is formed of small pieces that could not be cut into smaller parts. He used the word *atomos*, which means "uncuttable," for these smallest possible pieces. In modern terms, an **atom** is the smallest particle of an element. The Greek idea of atoms had to wait about 2,000 years before it became accepted.

Reading Checkpoint How is a compound different from an element?

Go Online
PHSchool.com

For: More on atomic structure
Visit: PHSchool.com
Web Code: cgd-2011

FIGURE 1
Kinds of Matter
Matter may consist of elements, compounds, or mixtures.
Inferring *What other mixture besides sand is present, but not visible, in the photo?*

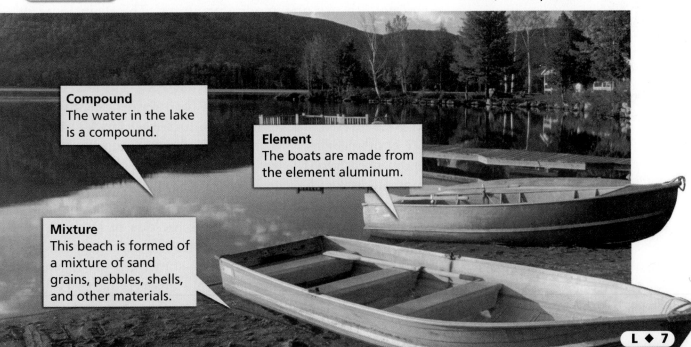

Compound
The water in the lake is a compound.

Element
The boats are made from the element aluminum.

Mixture
This beach is formed of a mixture of sand grains, pebbles, shells, and other materials.

Summary of Dalton's Ideas

- All elements are composed of atoms that cannot be divided.
- All atoms of the same element are exactly alike and have the same mass. Atoms of different elements are different and have different masses.
- An atom of one element cannot be changed into an atom of a different element. Atoms cannot be created or destroyed in any chemical change, only rearranged.
- Every compound is composed of atoms of different elements, combined in a specific ratio.

Atomic Theory and Models

The ancient Greeks did not prove the existence of atoms because they did not do experiments. In science, ideas are just ideas unless they can be tested. The idea of atoms began to develop again in the 1600s. This time, people did do experiments. As a result, atomic theory began to take shape.

A **scientific theory** is a well-tested idea that explains and connects a wide range of observations. Theories often include **models**—physical, mental, visual, and other representations of an idea to help people understand what they cannot observe directly. **Atomic theory grew as a series of models that developed from experimental evidence. As more evidence was collected, the theory and models were revised.**

Dalton's Atomic Theory Using evidence from many experiments, John Dalton, an English chemist, began to propose his atomic theory and model for atoms. The main ideas of Dalton's theory are summarized in Figure 2. With only a few changes, Dalton's atomic theory is still accepted today.

Thomson and Smaller Parts of Atoms Through a series of experiments around the start of the twentieth century, scientists discovered that atoms are made of even smaller parts. In 1897, another British scientist, J. J. Thomson, found that atoms contain negatively charged particles. Yet, scientists knew that atoms themselves had no electrical charge. So, Thomson reasoned, atoms must also contain some sort of positive charge.

Thomson proposed a model like the one in Figure 3. He described an atom that consisted of negative charges scattered throughout a ball of positive charge—something like raisins or berries in a muffin. The negatively charged particles later became known as **electrons.**

FIGURE 3
Thomson Model
Thomson suggested that atoms had negatively charged electrons embedded in a positive sphere.
Comparing and Contrasting *How is Thomson's model different from Dalton's?*

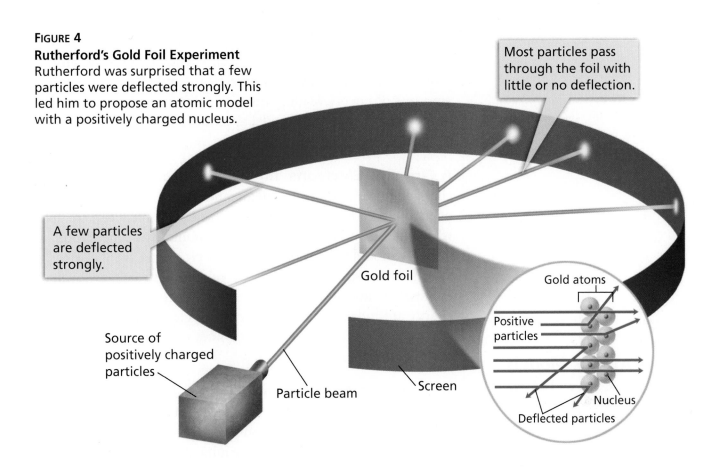

FIGURE 4
Rutherford's Gold Foil Experiment
Rutherford was surprised that a few particles were deflected strongly. This led him to propose an atomic model with a positively charged nucleus.

A few particles are deflected strongly.

Most particles pass through the foil with little or no deflection.

Gold foil

Source of positively charged particles

Particle beam

Screen

Gold atoms

Positive particles

Nucleus

Deflected particles

Rutherford and the Nucleus In 1911, one of Thomson's students, Ernest Rutherford, found evidence that countered Thomson's model. In an experiment diagrammed in Figure 4, Rutherford's research team aimed a beam of positively charged particles at a thin sheet of gold foil. They predicted that, if Thomson's model were correct, the charged particles would pass right through the foil in a straight line. The gold atoms would not have enough positive charge in any one region to strongly repel the charged particles.

Rutherford's team observed that most of the particles passed through the foil undisturbed, as expected. But, to their surprise, a few particles were deflected strongly. Since like charges repel each other, Rutherford inferred that an atom's positive charge must be clustered in a tiny region in its center, called the **nucleus** (NOO klee us). Those particles that were deflected strongly had been repelled by a gold atom's nucleus.

Scientists knew from other experiments that electrons had almost no mass. Therefore, they reasoned that nearly all of an atom's mass must also be located in the tiny, positively charged nucleus. Work by other scientists later suggested that the nucleus was made of one or more positively charged particles. Rutherford named the positively charged particles in the nucleus of an atom **protons.**

FIGURE 5
Rutherford Model
According to Rutherford's model, an atom was mostly empty space. Electrons moved around a small, positively charged nucleus in the center of the atom.

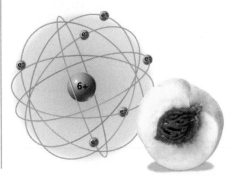

Bohr's Model In 1913, Niels Bohr, a Danish scientist and a student of both Thomson and Rutherford, revised the atomic model again. Bohr showed that electrons could have only specific amounts of energy, leading them to move in certain orbits. The series of orbits in Bohr's model resemble planets orbiting the sun or the layers of an onion.

A Cloud of Electrons In the 1920s, the atomic model changed again. Scientists determined that electrons do not orbit the nucleus like planets. Instead, electrons can be anywhere in a cloudlike region around the nucleus. The "cloud" is a visual model. It symbolizes where electrons are likely to be found. An electron's movement is related to its **energy level,** or the specific amount of energy it has. Electrons having higher energy are more loosely held by the nucleus than are electrons having lower energy. These differences affect the way the atom reacts with other atoms.

The Modern Atomic Model In 1932, British scientist James Chadwick discovered another particle in the nucleus of atoms. His discovery completed the modern atomic model. This new particle was hard to detect because it has no electrical charge even though it has nearly the same mass as a proton. Because the particle was electrically neutral, it was called a **neutron.**

FIGURE 6
Later Atomic Models

Through the first part of the twentieth century, atomic models continued to change.
Interpreting Diagrams How does the cloud model differ from the modern atomic model?

◀ **Bohr Model**
Niels Bohr suggested that electrons move in specific orbits around the nucleus of an atom.

6+

◀ **Cloud Model**
According to the cloud model, electrons move rapidly in every direction around the nucleus.

6+

6e⁻

Modern Atomic Model ▶
The nucleus, which contains both protons and neutrons, is surrounded by a cloudlike region of electrons.

6e⁻

New research continues to provide data that support this model of a small nucleus surrounded by a cloudlike region of electrons. The nucleus contains protons and neutrons that together make up nearly all of an atom's mass. The only exception is the nucleus of the hydrogen atom, which usually consists of a single proton. A cloud of rapidly moving electrons occupies most of the volume of an atom.

If you did the Discover activity at the beginning of this section, you learned that the size of an atom can be 100,000 times the size of its nucleus. To get a sense of the scale of an atom, look back at the answer you calculated if the nucleus were the size of a dime. An electron in your model atom could be more than 1,700 meters away!

All the atoms of a single element have the same number of protons. But different elements have different numbers of protons. For example, all hydrogen atoms have only one proton, and all carbon atoms have six protons. Atoms have no overall electric charge because each atom has the same number of electrons as protons. As you will read in Section 2, the number of electrons is key in explaining why different elements have different properties.

Reading Checkpoint **What are neutrons, and where in an atom are they found?**

FIGURE 7
Size of an Atom
If the nucleus of an atom were the size of a pencil eraser on home plate of this baseball field, its electrons could be farther away than the outfield.

Section 1 Assessment

Target Reading Skill Outlining Use the information in your outline about elements and atoms to help you answer the questions below.

Reviewing Key Concepts

1. a. **Defining** What is matter? What is an element?
   b. **Explaining** Why are elements called the building blocks of matter?
   c. **Inferring** Water is a compound. Does water contain elements? Explain.
2. a. **Reviewing** In general, why did atomic theory change with time?
   b. **Describing** Describe Bohr's model of the atom. What specific information did Bohr contribute to scientists' understanding of the atom?
   c. **Comparing and Contrasting** How is the modern atomic model different from Bohr's model? Why did scientists revise Bohr's model?

Writing in Science

Persuasive Letter Write a letter that Thomson might have sent to another scientist explaining why an atom must contain positive charges as well as negative charges. The letter should also explain why Thomson proposed the atomic model that he did.

Atoms, Bonding, and the Periodic Table

Reading Preview

Key Concepts
- How is the reactivity of elements related to valence electrons in atoms?
- What does the periodic table tell you about atoms and the properties of elements?

Key Terms
- valence electrons
- electron dot diagram
- chemical bond
- symbol • atomic number
- period • group • family
- noble gas • halogen
- alkali metal

Target Reading Skill
Building Vocabulary After you read this section, reread the paragraphs that contain definitions of Key Terms. Use all the information you have learned to write a definition of each Key Term in your own words.

Lab zone Discover Activity

What Are the Trends in the Periodic Table?

1. Examine the periodic table of the elements that your teacher provides. Look in each square for the whole number located above the symbol of the element. As you read across a row from left to right, what trend do you see?
2. Now look at a column from top to bottom. What trend do you see in these numbers?

Think It Over
Interpreting Data Can you explain why one row ends and a new row starts? Why are certain elements in the same column?

Why isn't the world made only of elements? How do the atoms of different elements combine to form compounds? The answers to these questions are related to electrons and their energy levels. And the roadmap to understanding how electrons determine the properties of elements is the periodic table.

Valence Electrons and Bonding

In Section 1 you learned about electrons and energy levels. An atom's **valence electrons** (VAY luns) are those electrons that have the highest energy level and are held most loosely. **The number of valence electrons in an atom of an element determines many properties of that element, including the ways in which the atom can bond with other atoms.**

FIGURE 8
Valence Electrons
Skydivers in the outer ring are less securely held to the group than are members of the inner ring. Similarly, valence electrons are more loosely held by an atom than are electrons of lower energy.

Electron Dot Diagrams Each element has a specific number of valence electrons, ranging from 1 to 8. Figure 9 shows one way to depict the number of valence electrons in an element. An **electron dot diagram** includes the symbol for the element surrounded by dots. Each dot stands for one valence electron.

Chemical Bonds and Stability Most atoms are more stable—less likely to react—when they have eight valence electrons. For example, atoms of neon, argon, krypton, and xenon all have eight valence electrons and are very unreactive. These elements do not easily form compounds. Some small atoms, such as helium, are stable with just two valence electrons.

Atoms usually react in a way that makes each atom more stable. One of two things can happen: Either the number of valence electrons increases to eight (or two, in the case of hydrogen). Or, the atom gives up loosely held valence electrons. Atoms that react this way can become chemically combined, that is, bonded to other atoms. A **chemical bond** is the force of attraction that holds two atoms together as a result of the rearrangement of electrons between them.

Chemical Bonds and Chemical Reactions When atoms bond, electrons may be transferred from one atom to another, or they may be shared between the atoms. In either case, the change results in a chemical reaction—that is, new substances form. Later in this chapter, you will learn which elements are likely to gain electrons, which are likely to give up electrons, and which are likely to share electrons. You will also learn how the periodic table of the elements can help you predict how atoms of different elements react.

Reading Checkpoint What information does an electron dot diagram show?

FIGURE 9
Electron Dot Diagrams
An atom's valence electrons are shown as dots around the symbol of the element. Notice that oxygen atoms have 6 valence electrons. **Predicting** *How many more electrons are needed to make an oxygen atom stable?*

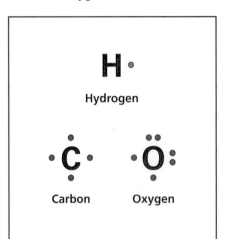

Hydrogen

Carbon   Oxygen

The Periodic Table

The periodic table is a system used worldwide for organizing elements into categories. The way the elements are organized gives you important information about the arrangement of the electrons in their atoms. If you know the number of valence electrons that atoms of different elements have, you have a clue as to which elements combine and how.

Organizing the Elements Look at the periodic table in Figure 10. Each element is represented by a **symbol,** usually consisting of one or two letters. Above the symbol is the element's atomic number. The **atomic number** of an element is the number of protons in the nucleus of an atom. Notice that the elements are arranged in order of increasing atomic number.

FIGURE 10
The Periodic Table

Elements are organized into rows and columns based on their atomic number. **Interpreting Tables** *What other element is in the same period as hydrogen? What is the next element in the same group as oxygen?*

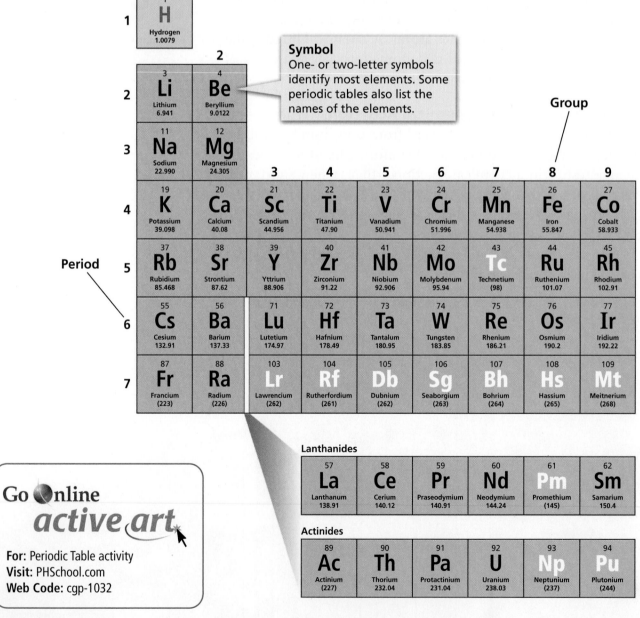

Symbol
One- or two-letter symbols identify most elements. Some periodic tables also list the names of the elements.

Periods and Groups A row of elements across the periodic table is called a **period.** Hydrogen and helium make up the first period. The second period starts with lithium (Li) and continues across to neon (Ne). Notice that the atomic number increases one at a time across a period of elements. Because the number of protons in an atom is equal to its number of electrons, it is also true that the number of electrons increases one at a time across a period.

Elements in the same column are called a **group** or **family.** Notice the numbers across the tops of the columns of the periodic table. These numbers identify the group to which an element belongs. For example, carbon (C) is in Group 14 and oxygen (O) is in Group 16.

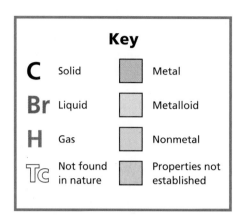

Key

C Solid		Metal
Br Liquid		Metalloid
H Gas		Nonmetal
Tc Not found in nature		Properties not established

Atomic Number
The atomic number is the number of protons in an atom's nucleus.

Atomic Mass
Atomic mass is the average mass of an element's atoms. Atomic masses in parentheses are those of the most stable isotope.

18

2
He
Helium
4.0026

13	14	15	16	17	
5 **B** Boron 10.81	6 **C** Carbon 12.011	7 **N** Nitrogen 14.007	8 **O** Oxygen 15.999	9 **F** Fluorine 18.998	10 **Ne** Neon 20.179
13 **Al** Aluminum 26.982	14 **Si** Silicon 28.086	15 **P** Phosphorus 30.974	16 **S** Sulfur 32.06	17 **Cl** Chlorine 35.453	18 **Ar** Argon 39.948

10	11	12						
28 **Ni** Nickel 58.71	29 **Cu** Copper 63.546	30 **Zn** Zinc 65.38	31 **Ga** Gallium 69.72	32 **Ge** Germanium 72.59	33 **As** Arsenic 74.922	34 **Se** Selenium 78.96	35 **Br** Bromine 79.904	36 **Kr** Krypton 83.80
46 **Pd** Palladium 106.4	47 **Ag** Silver 107.87	48 **Cd** Cadmium 112.41	49 **In** Indium 114.82	50 **Sn** Tin 118.69	51 **Sb** Antimony 121.75	52 **Te** Tellurium 127.60	53 **I** Iodine 126.90	54 **Xe** Xenon 131.30
78 **Pt** Platinum 195.09	79 **Au** Gold 196.97	80 **Hg** Mercury 200.59	81 **Tl** Thallium 204.37	82 **Pb** Lead 207.2	83 **Bi** Bismuth 208.98	84 **Po** Polonium (209)	85 **At** Astatine (210)	86 **Rn** Radon (222)
110 **Ds** Darmstadtium (269)	111 **Rg** Roentgenium (272)	112 ***Uub** Ununbium (277)	113 ***Uut** Ununtrium (284)	114 ***Uuq** Ununquadium (289)	115 ***Uup** Ununpentium (288)	116 ***Uuh** Ununhexium (292)		118 ***Uuo** Ununoctium (294)

*Discovery not yet officially confirmed

63 **Eu** Europium 151.96	64 **Gd** Gadolinium 157.25	65 **Tb** Terbium 158.93	66 **Dy** Dysprosium 162.50	67 **Ho** Holmium 164.93	68 **Er** Erbium 167.26	69 **Tm** Thulium 168.93	70 **Yb** Ytterbium 173.04

95 **Am** Americium (243)	96 **Cm** Curium (247)	97 **Bk** Berkelium (247)	98 **Cf** Californium (251)	99 **Es** Einsteinium (252)	100 **Fm** Fermium (257)	101 **Md** Mendelevium (258)	102 **No** Nobelium (259)

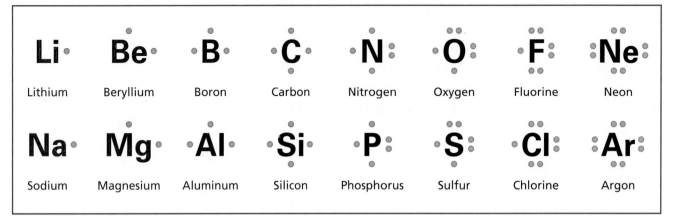

| Li Lithium | Be Beryllium | B Boron | C Carbon | N Nitrogen | O Oxygen | F Fluorine | Ne Neon |
| Na Sodium | Mg Magnesium | Al Aluminum | Si Silicon | P Phosphorus | S Sulfur | Cl Chlorine | Ar Argon |

FIGURE 11

Patterns of Valence Electrons
After the number of valence electrons reaches 8, a new period begins.
Comparing and Contrasting *How does the number of valence electrons in elements within the same group compare?*

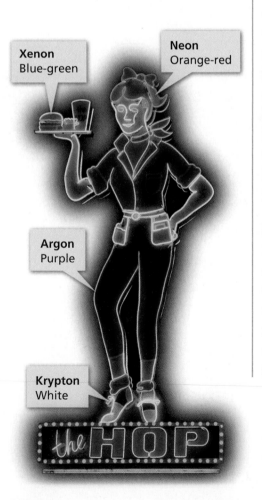

Xenon
Blue-green

Neon
Orange-red

Argon
Purple

Krypton
White

How the Periodic Table Works The periodic table is based on the structure of atoms, especially the arrangement of electrons. Think of how atoms change from left to right across a period. **As the number of protons—or atomic number— increases, the number of electrons also increases. As a result, the properties of the elements change in a regular way across a period.** Figure 11 compares the electron dot diagrams of the elements in Periods 2 and 3 from left to right across the table. Notice that each element has one more valence electron than the element to its left.

Except for Period 1, a period ends when the number of valence electrons reaches eight. The next period begins with atoms having valence electrons of higher energy than those in the period before it. This repeating pattern means the elements within a group always have the same number of valence electrons. For example, all the Group 1 elements have one valence electron, and all the Group 2 elements have two. Elements in Group 17 have seven valence electrons. The elements within a group have similar properties because they all have the same number of valence electrons in their atoms.

Noble Gases The Group 18 elements are known as the **noble gases.** Atoms of these elements have eight valence electrons, except for helium, which has two. Recall that when atoms have the maximum number of valence electrons, they become stable. This is already the case with the noble gases. As a result, noble gases do not react easily with other elements. Even so, chemists have been able to make noble gases form compounds with a few other elements.

FIGURE 12

"Neon" Signs
The variety of colors in a "neon" sign results from passing an electric current through sealed glass tubes containing different noble gases.

Reactive Nonmetals and Metals Now look at the elements in the column just to the left of the noble gases. The elements in Group 17 are called the **halogens.** Atoms in the halogen family have seven valence electrons. A gain of just one more electron gives these atoms the stable number of eight electrons, as in the noble gases. As a result, elements in the halogen family react easily with other elements whose atoms can give up or share electrons.

At the far left side of the periodic table is Group 1, called the **alkali metal** family. Atoms of the alkali metals have only one valence electron. Except for lithium, losing this electron leaves a Group 1 atom with a stable set of eight electrons that have lower energy. (Lithium atoms are left with a stable set of two electrons.) Therefore, alkali metal atoms can become chemically more stable by losing their one valence electron. This property makes the alkali metals very reactive.

 Reading Checkpoint **Where on the periodic table are the halogens found?**

FIGURE 13
Reactive Elements
Elements in Group 17 (the halogens) and Group 1 (the alkali metals) are highly reactive.
Relating Cause and Effect *Why are elements in these two groups so reactive?*

▼ Sodium, an alkali metal, reacts vigorously with bromine, a halogen.

▲ Steel wool burns when exposed to the halogen chlorine.

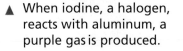

▲ When iodine, a halogen, reacts with aluminum, a purple gas is produced.

Atoms and Bonding

Video Preview
▶ Video Field Trip
Video Assessment

Other Metals Look at the elements in Groups 2 through 12 of the periodic table. Like the Group 1 elements, these elements are metals. Most have one, two, or three valence electrons. They react by losing these electrons, especially when they combine with oxygen or one of the halogens.

How reactive a metal is depends on how easily its atoms lose valence electrons. Some metals, such as those in Group 2 (the alkaline earth metals), lose electrons easily and are almost as reactive as the alkali metals of Group 1. Other metals, such as platinum (Pt) in Group 10 and gold (Au) in Group 11, are unreactive. Mercury (Hg) is the only metal that is a liquid at room temperature. All the other metals are solids, although gallium (Ga) melts just above room temperature.

Science and **History**

Discovery of the Elements
In 1869, Dmitri Mendeleev published the first periodic table. At that time, 63 elements were known. Since then, scientists have discovered or created about 50 new elements.

1894
Argon, Neon, Krypton, and Xenon
British chemist William Ramsay discovered an element he named argon, after the Greek word for "lazy." The name fits because argon does not react with other elements. Ramsay looked for other nonreactive gases and discovered neon, krypton, and xenon.

1875
Gallium
The French chemist Paul-Émile Lecoq de Boisbaudran discovered an element that he called gallium. It had properties predicted by Mendeleev for an unknown element that would fit directly below aluminum in the periodic table.

1898
Polonium and Radium
Polish chemist Marie Curie started with three tons of uranium ore before she eventually isolated a few grams of two new elements. She named them polonium and radium.

1830   1865   1900

18 ◆ L

Other Nonmetals Elements in the green section of the periodic table are the nonmetals. Carbon (C), phosphorus (P), sulfur (S), selenium (Se), and iodine (I) are the only nonmetals that are solids at room temperature. Bromine (Br) is the only liquid. All of the nonmetals have four or more valence electrons. Like the halogens, other nonmetals become stable when they gain or share enough electrons to have a set of eight valence electrons.

The nonmetals combine with metals usually by gaining electrons. But nonmetals can also combine with other nonmetals by sharing electrons. Of the nonmetals, oxygen and the halogens are highly reactive. In fact, fluorine is the most reactive element known. It even forms compounds with some of the noble gases.

Writing in Science

Research and Write Select three elements that interest you and find out more about them. Who identified or discovered the elements? How did the elements get their names? How are the elements used? To answer these questions, look up the elements in reference books.

**1941
Plutonium**
American chemist Glenn Seaborg was the first to isolate plutonium, which is found in small amounts in uranium ores. Plutonium is used as fuel in certain nuclear reactors. It has also been used to power equipment used in space exploration.

**1997
Elements 101 to 109**
The International Union of Pure and Applied Chemists (IUPAC) agreed on names for elements 101 to 109. Many of the names honor scientists, such as Lise Meitner, shown here in 1946. All of the new elements were created in laboratories, and none is stable enough to exist in nature.

**2003 to Present
More New Elements**
Darmstadtium (110) and roentgenium (111) are named. Reasearch to produce and study new synthetic elements continues.

**1939
Francium**
Although Mendeleev predicted the properties of an element he called "eka-cesium," the element was not discovered until 1939. French chemist Marguerite Perey named her discovery francium, after the country France.

| 1935 | 1970 | 2005 |

The quartz movement of the watch

FIGURE 14
A Metalloid at Work
This quartz-movement watch keeps time with a small quartz crystal, a compound made of the metalloid silicon and the nonmetal oxygen. The crystal vibrates at about 32,000 vibrations per second when a voltage is applied.

Metalloids Several elements known as metalloids lie along a zigzag line between the metals and nonmetals. Depending on the conditions, these elements can behave as either metals or nonmetals. The metalloids have from three to six valence electrons and can either lose or share electrons when they combine with other elements.

Hydrogen Notice that hydrogen is considered to be a nonmetal. It is located above Group 1 in the periodic table because it has only one valence electron. However, even though hydrogen is a reactive element, its properties differ greatly from those of the alkali metals.

✔ Reading Checkpoint **Why is hydrogen grouped above the Group 1 elements even though it is not a metal?**

Section 2 Assessment

🎯 **Target Reading Skill** Building Vocabulary Use your definitions to help you answer the questions below.

Reviewing Key Concepts
1. a. **Defining** What are valence electrons?
   b. **Reviewing** What role do valence electrons play in the formation of compounds from elements?
   c. **Comparing and Contrasting** Do oxygen atoms become more stable or less stable when oxygen forms compounds? Explain.
2. a. **Summarizing** Summarize how the periodic table is organized. Use the words *period* and *group*.
   b. **Explaining** Why do the properties of elements change in a regular way across a period?
   c. **Relating Cause and Effect** How reactive are the elements in Group 18? Explain this reactivity in terms of the number of valence electrons.

Lab zone At-Home **Activity**

Looking for Elements Find some examples of elements at home. Then locate the elements on the periodic table. Show your examples and the periodic table to your family. Point out the positions of the elements on the table and explain what the periodic table tells you about the elements. Include at least two nonmetals in your discussion. (*Hint:* The nonmetals may be invisible.)

Comparing Atom Sizes

Problem

How is the radius of an atom related to its atomic number?

Skills Focus

making models, graphing, interpreting data

Materials

- drawing compass
- metric ruler
- calculator
- periodic table of the elements (Appendix D)

Procedure ✂

1. Using the periodic table as a reference, predict whether the size (radius) of atoms will increase, remain the same, or decrease as you go from the top to the bottom of a group, or family, of elements.

2. The data table lists the elements in Group 2 in the periodic table. The atomic radius of each element is given in picometers (pm). Copy the data table into your notebook.

3. Calculate the relative radius of each atom compared to beryllium, the smallest atom listed. Do this by dividing each radius by the radius of beryllium. (*Hint:* The relative radius of magnesium would be 160 pm divided by 112 pm, or 1.4.) Record these values, rounded to the nearest tenth, in your data table.

4. Using a compass, draw a circle for each element with a radius that corresponds to the relative radius you calculated in Step 3. Use centimeters as your unit for the radius of each circle. **CAUTION:** *Do not push the sharp point of the compass against your skin.*

5. Label each model with the symbol of the element it represents.

Data Table			
Atomic Number	Element	Radius (pm)*	Relative Radius
4	Be	112	1
12	Mg	160	
20	Ca	197	
38	Sr	215	
56	Ba	222	

A picometer (pm) is one billionth of a millimeter.

Analyze and Conclude

1. **Making Models** Based on your models, was your prediction in Step 1 correct? Explain.

2. **Graphing** Make a bar graph of the data given in the first and third columns of the data table. Label the horizontal axis *Atomic Number.* Mark the divisions from 0 to 60. Then label the vertical axis *Radius* and mark its divisions from 0 to 300 picometers.

3. **Interpreting Data** Do the points on your graph fall on a straight line or on a curve? What trend do the data show?

4. **Predicting** Predict where you would find the largest atom in any group, or family, of elements. What evidence would you need to tell if your prediction is correct?

5. **Communicating** Write a paragraph explaining why it is useful to draw a one- to two-centimeter model of an atom that has an actual radius of 100 to 200 picometers.

More to Explore

Look up the atomic masses for the Group 2 elements. Devise a plan to model their relative atomic masses using real-world objects.

Ionic Bonds

Reading Preview

Key Concepts
- What are ions, and how do they form bonds?
- How are the formulas and names of ionic compounds written?
- What are the properties of ionic compounds?

Key Terms
- ion • polyatomic ion
- ionic bond • ionic compound
- chemical formula • subscript
- crystal

Target Reading Skill

Previewing Visuals Before you read, preview Figure 17. Then write two questions that you have about the diagram in a graphic organizer like the one below. As you read, answer your questions.

Formation of an Ionic Bond

Q. What is an ionic bond?
A.
Q.

Discover **Activity**

How Do Ions Form?

1. Place three pairs of checkers (three red and three black) on your desk. The red represent electrons and the black represent protons.
2. Place nine pairs of checkers (nine red and nine black) in a separate group on your desk.
3. Move a red checker from the smaller group to the larger group.
4. Count the number of positive charges (protons) and negative charges (electrons) in each group.
5. Now sort the checkers into a group of four pairs and a group of eight pairs. Repeat Steps 3 and 4, this time moving two red checkers from the smaller group to the larger group.

Think It Over

Inferring What was the total charge on each group before you moved the red checkers (electrons)? What was the charge on each group after you moved the checkers? Based on this activity, what do you think happens to the charge on an atom when it loses electrons? When it gains electrons?

You and a friend walk past a market that sells apples for 40 cents each and pears for 50 cents each. You have 45 cents and want an apple. Your friend also has 45 cents but wants a pear. You realize that if you give your friend a nickel, she will have 50 cents and can buy a pear. You will have 40 cents left to buy an apple. Transferring the nickel gets both of you what you want. Your actions model, in a simple way, what can happen between atoms.

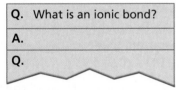

If you transfer a nickel to your ▶ friend, both of you will have the money you need.

FIGURE 15
How Ions Form
When an atom loses one of its electrons, it becomes a positively charged ion. The atom that gains the electron becomes a negatively charged ion.

Ions and Ionic Bonds

Atoms with five, six, or seven valence electrons usually become more stable when this number increases to eight. Likewise, most atoms with one, two, or three valence electrons can lose electrons and become more stable. When these two types of atoms combine, electrons are transferred from one type of atom to the other. The transfer makes both types of atoms more stable.

How Ions Form An **ion** (EYE ahn) is an atom or group of atoms that has an electric charge. **When an atom loses an electron, it loses a negative charge and becomes a positive ion. When an atom gains an electron, it gains a negative charge and becomes a negative ion.** Figure 16 lists some ions you will often see in this book. Use this table as a reference while you read this section and other chapters.

Polyatomic Ions Notice in Figure 16 that some ions are made of several atoms. For example, the ammonium ion is made of nitrogen and hydrogen atoms. Ions that are made of more than one atom are called **polyatomic ions** (pahl ee uh TAHM ik). The prefix *poly* means "many," so *polyatomic* means "many atoms." You can think of a polyatomic ion as a group of atoms that reacts as a unit. Like other ions, polyatomic ions have an overall positive or negative charge.

Reading Checkpoint How does an ion with a charge of 2+ form?

FIGURE 16
Ions are atoms that have lost or gained electrons. **Interpreting Tables** *How many electrons does a sulfur atom gain when it becomes a sulfide ion?*

Ions and Their Charges		
Name	**Charge**	**Symbol or Formula**
Lithium	1+	Li^+
Sodium	1+	Na^+
Potassium	1+	K^+
Ammonium	1+	NH_4^+
Calcium	2+	Ca^{2+}
Magnesium	2+	Mg^{2+}
Aluminum	3+	Al^{3+}
Fluoride	1–	F^-
Chloride	1–	Cl^-
Iodide	1–	I^-
Bicarbonate	1–	HCO_3^-
Nitrate	1–	NO_3^-
Oxide	2–	O^{2-}
Sulfide	2–	S^{2-}
Carbonate	2–	CO_3^{2-}
Sulfate	2–	SO_4^{2-}
Phosphate	3–	PO_4^{3-}

Ionic Bonds Look at Figure 17 to see how sodium atoms and chlorine atoms combine to form sodium chloride (table salt). Notice that sodium has 1 valence electron and chlorine has 7 valence electrons. When sodium's valence electron is transferred to chlorine, both atoms become ions. The sodium atom becomes a positive ion (Na^+). The chlorine atom becomes a negative ion (Cl^-).

Because oppositely charged particles attract, the positive Na^+ ion and the negative Cl^- ion attract each other. An **ionic bond** is the attraction between two oppositely charged ions. **Ionic bonds form as a result of the attraction between positive and negative ions.** A compound that consists of positive and negative ions, such as sodium chloride, is called an **ionic compound.**

FIGURE 17
Formation of an Ionic Bond

Reactions occur easily between metals in Group 1 and nonmetals in Group 17. Follow the process below to see how an ionic bond forms between a sodium atom and a chlorine atom.
Relating Cause and Effect *Why is sodium chloride electrically neutral?*

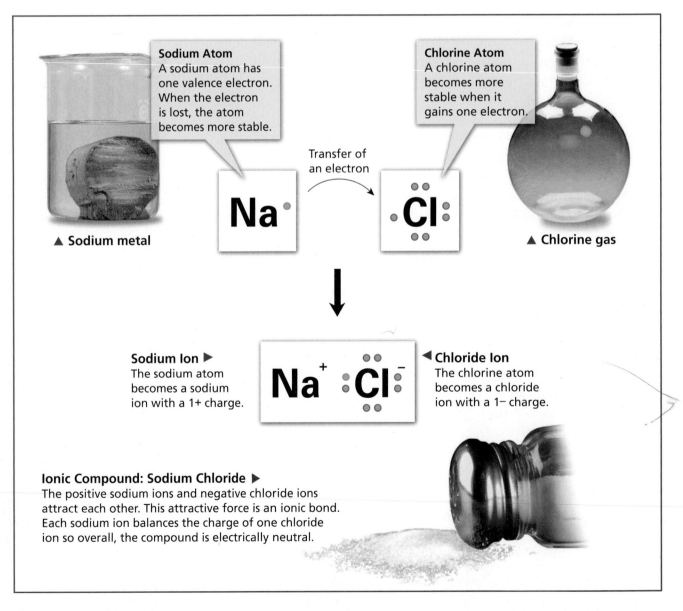

Sodium Atom
A sodium atom has one valence electron. When the electron is lost, the atom becomes more stable.

Chlorine Atom
A chlorine atom becomes more stable when it gains one electron.

Transfer of an electron

▲ Sodium metal

▲ Chlorine gas

Sodium Ion ▶
The sodium atom becomes a sodium ion with a 1+ charge.

◀ Chloride Ion
The chlorine atom becomes a chloride ion with a 1– charge.

Ionic Compound: Sodium Chloride ▶
The positive sodium ions and negative chloride ions attract each other. This attractive force is an ionic bond. Each sodium ion balances the charge of one chloride ion so overall, the compound is electrically neutral.

Chemical Formulas and Names

Compounds can be represented by chemical formulas. A **chemical formula** is a combination of symbols that shows the ratio of elements in a compound. For example, the formula for magnesium chloride is $MgCl_2$. What does the formula tell you?

Formulas of Ionic Compounds From Figure 16 you know that the charge on the magnesium ion is 2+. **When ionic compounds form, the ions come together in a way that balances out the charges on the ions. The chemical formula for the compound reflects this balance.** Two chloride ions, each with a charge of 1− will balance the charge on the magnesium ion. That's why the formula of magnesium chloride is $MgCl_2$. The number "2" is a subscript. A **subscript** tells you the ratio of elements in the compound. For $MgCl_2$, the ratio of magnesium ions to chloride ions is 1 to 2.

If no subscript is written, the number 1 is understood. For example, the formula NaCl tells you that there is a 1 to 1 ratio of sodium ions to chloride ions. Formulas for compounds of polyatomic ions are written in a similar way. For example, calcium carbonate has the formula $CaCO_3$.

Naming Ionic Compounds Magnesium chloride, sodium bicarbonate, sodium oxide—where do these names come from? **For an ionic compound, the name of the positive ion comes first, followed by the name of the negative ion.** The name of the positive ion is usually the name of a metal. But, a few positive polyatomic ions exist, such as the ammonium ion (NH_4^+). If the negative ion is a single element, as you've already seen with sodium chloride, the end of its name changes to *-ide*. For example, MgO is named magnesium oxide. If the negative ion is polyatomic, its name usually ends in *-ate* or *-ite*, as in Figure 16. The compound NH_4NO_3, named ammonium nitrate, is a common fertilizer for gardens and crop plants.

 Reading Checkpoint What is the name of the ionic compound with the formula K_2S?

FIGURE 18
Calcium Carbonate
The white cliffs of Dover, England, are made of chalk formed from the remains of tiny sea organisms. Chalk is mostly an ionic compound, calcium carbonate.

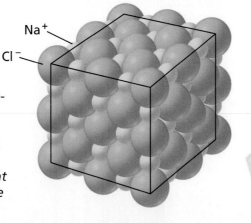

Lab zone Try This **Activity**

Crystal Clear

Can you grow a salt crystal?

1. Add salt to a jar containing about 200 mL of hot tap water and stir. Keep adding salt until no more dissolves and it settles out when you stop stirring.

2. Tie a large crystal of coarse salt into the middle of a piece of thread.

3. Tie one end of the thread to the middle of a pencil.

4. Suspend the other end of the thread in the solution by laying the pencil across the mouth of the jar. Do not allow the crystal to touch the solution.

5. Place the jar in a quiet, undisturbed area. Check the size of the crystal over the next few days.

Observing Does the salt crystal change size over time? What is its shape? What do you think is happening to the ions in the solution?

Properties of Ionic Compounds

Table salt, baking soda, and iron rust are different compounds with different properties. You wouldn't want to season your food with either iron rust or baking soda. However, these compounds are alike in some ways because they are all ionic compounds. **In general, ionic compounds are hard, brittle crystals that have high melting points. When dissolved in water or melted, they conduct electricity.**

Ionic Crystals Figure 19 shows a chunk of halite, or table salt, NaCl. Pieces of halite have sharp edges, corners, flat surfaces, and a cubic shape. Equal numbers of Na^+ and Cl^- ions in solid sodium chloride are attracted in an alternating pattern, as shown in the diagram. The ions form an orderly, three-dimensional arrangement called a **crystal.**

In an ionic compound, every ion is attracted to ions of opposite charge that surround it. It is attracted to ions above, below, and to all sides. The pattern formed by the ions remains the same no matter what the size of the crystal. In a single grain of salt, the crystal pattern extends for millions of ions in every direction. Many crystals of ionic compounds are hard and brittle, due to the strength of their ionic bonds and the attractions among all the ions.

High Melting Points What happens when you heat an ionic compound such as table salt? When you heat a substance, its energy increases. When ions have enough energy to overcome the attractive forces between them, they break away from each other. In other words, the crystal melts to a liquid. Because ionic bonds are strong, a lot of energy is needed to break them. As a result, ionic compounds have high melting points. They are all solids at room temperature. Table salt must be heated to 801°C before the crystal melts.

FIGURE 19
Ionic Crystals
The ions in ionic compounds are arranged in specific three-dimensional shapes called crystals. Some crystals have a cube shape like these crystals of halite, or sodium chloride.
Making Generalizations What holds the ions together in the crystal?

Na$^+$

Cl$^-$

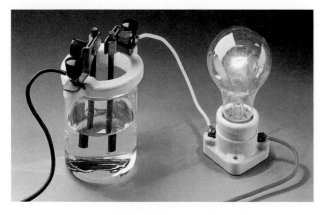

FIGURE 20
Ions in Solution
A solution of sodium chloride conducts electricity across the gap between the two black rods of a conductivity tester. As a result, the bulb lights up.

Electrical Conductivity Electric current is the flow of charged particles. When ionic crystals dissolve in water, the bonds between ions are broken. As a result, the ions are free to move about, and the solution conducts current. Likewise, when an ionic compound melts, the ions are able to move freely, and the liquid conducts current. In contrast, ionic compounds in solid form do not conduct current well. The ions in the solid crystal are tightly bound to each other and cannot move from place to place. If charged particles cannot move, there is no current.

Reading Checkpoint **What is a crystal?**

Go Online
SciLINKS

For: Links on ionic compounds
Visit: www.SciLinks.org
Web Code: scn-1213

Section 3 Assessment

Target Reading Skill Previewing Visuals Compare your questions and answers about Figure 17 with those of a partner.

Reviewing Key Concepts

1. **a. Reviewing** What are the two basic ways in which ions form from atoms?
   b. Comparing and Contrasting Contrast sodium and chloride ions, including how they form. Write the symbol for each ion.
   c. Relating Cause and Effect What holds the ions together in sodium chloride? Indicate the specific charges that are involved.

2. **a. Identifying** What information is given by the formula of an ionic compound?
   b. Explaining The formula for sodium sulfide is Na_2S. Explain what this formula means.
   c. Applying Concepts Write the formula for calcium chloride. Explain how you determined this formula.

3. **a. Listing** List three properties of ionic compounds.
   b. Making Generalizations Relate each property that you listed to the characteristics of ionic bonds.

Writing in Science

Firsthand Account Pretend that you are the size of an atom, observing a reaction between a potassium atom and a fluorine atom. Write an account of the formation of an ionic bond as the atoms react. Tell what happens to the valence electrons on each atom and how each atom is changed by losing or gaining electrons.

Shedding Light on Ions

Problem

What kinds of compounds produce ions in solution?

Skills Focus

controlling variables, interpreting data, inferring

Materials

- 2 dry cells, 1.5 V
- small light bulb and socket ⎫
- 4 lengths of wire with alligator clips on both ends ⎬ or conductivity probe
- 2 copper strips ⎭
- distilled water
- small beaker
- small plastic spoon
- sodium chloride
- graduated cylinder, 100-mL
- sucrose
- additional materials supplied by your teacher

Procedure

1. Make a conductivity tester as described below or, if you are using a conductivity probe, see your teacher for instructions. Then make a data table in your notebook similar to the one above.

Data Table	
Sample	Observations
Tap water	
Distilled water	
Sodium chloride	
Sodium chloride in water	

2. Pour about 50 mL of tap water into a small beaker. Place the copper strips in the beaker. Be sure the strips are not touching each other. Attach the alligator clip of the free end of one wire to a copper strip. Do the same with the other wire and the other copper strip. Record your observations.

3. Disconnect the wires from the copper strips. Take the strips out of the beaker, and pour out the tap water. Dry the inside of the beaker and the copper strips with a paper towel.

4. Pour 50 mL of distilled water into the beaker. Reconnect the conductivity tester and test the water as in Step 2. Keep the copper strips about the same distance apart as in Step 2. Record your observations.

5. Use 3 spoonfuls of sodium chloride to make a small pile on a clean piece of paper. Dry off the copper strips of the conductivity tester and use it to test the conductivity of the sodium chloride. Record your observations.

Making a Conductivity Tester

A. Use wire with alligator clips to connect the positive terminal of a dry cell to a lamp socket. **CAUTION:** *The bulb is fragile and can break.*

B. Similarly connect another wire between the negative terminal of the cell and the positive terminal of the second cell.

C. Connect one end of a third wire to the negative terminal of the second dry cell.

D. Connect one end of a fourth wire to the other terminal of the lamp socket.

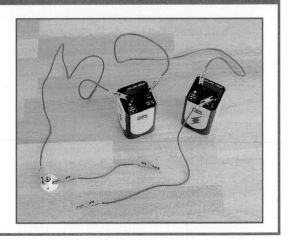

6. Add 1 spoonful of sodium chloride to the distilled water in the beaker. Stir with the spoon until the salt dissolves. Repeat the conductivity test and record your observations.

7. Disconnect the conductivity tester and rinse the beaker, spoon, and copper strips with distilled water. Dry the beaker as in Step 3.

8. Test sucrose (table sugar) in the same ways that you tested sodium chloride in Steps 4 through 7. Test additional materials supplied by your teacher.
   - If the material is a solid, mix 1 spoonful of it with about 50 mL of distilled water and stir until the material dissolves. Test the resulting mixture.
   - If the substance is a liquid, simply pour about 50 mL into the beaker. Test it as you did the other mixtures.

Analyze and Conclude

1. **Controlling Variables** Why did you test both tap water and distilled water before testing the sodium chloride solution?

2. **Interpreting Data** Could you have used tap water in your tests instead of distilled water? Explain.

3. **Drawing Conclusions** Based on your observations, add a column to your data table indicating whether each substance produced ions in solution.

4. **Inferring** Sodium chloride is an ionic compound. How can you account for any observed differences in conductivity between dry and dissolved sodium chloride?

5. **Communicating** Based on your observations, decide whether or not you think sucrose (table sugar) is made up of ions. Explain how you reached your answer, using evidence from the experiment.

Design an Experiment

Design an experiment to test the effects of varying the spacing between the copper strips of the conductivity tester. *Obtain your teacher's permission before carrying out your investigation.*

Covalent Bonds

Reading Preview

Key Concepts
- What holds covalently bonded atoms together?
- What are the properties of molecular compounds?
- How does unequal sharing of electrons occur, and how does it affect molecules?

Key Terms
- covalent bond • molecule
- double bond • triple bond
- molecular compound
- polar bond • nonpolar bond

Target Reading Skill

Asking Questions Before you read, preview the red headings. In a graphic organizer like the one below, ask a *what* or *how* question for each heading. As you read, answer your questions.

Covalent Bonds

Question	Answer
How do covalent bonds form?	Covalent bonds form when...

Lab zone Discover Activity

Can Water and Oil Mix?

1. Pour water into a small jar that has a tight-fitting lid until the jar is about a third full.
2. Add an equal amount of vegetable oil to the jar. Cover the jar tightly.
3. Shake the jar vigorously for 20 seconds. Observe the contents.
4. Allow the jar to sit undisturbed for 1 minute. Observe again.
5. Remove the top and add 3 drops of liquid detergent. Cover the jar and repeat Steps 3 and 4.

Think It Over
Forming Operational Definitions Based on your observations, write an operational definition of *detergent*. How might your observations relate to chemical bonds in the detergent, oil, and water molecules?

Uh oh, you have a big project due in English class next week! You need to write a story and illustrate it with colorful posters. Art has always been your best subject, but writing takes more effort. Luckily, you're working with a partner who writes well but doesn't feel confident in art. If you each contribute your skills, together you can produce a high-quality finished project.

FIGURE 21
Sharing Skills
One student is a skilled artist, while the other is a skilled writer. By pooling their skills, the students can complete their project.

How Covalent Bonds Form

Just as you and your friend can work together by sharing your talents, atoms can become more stable by sharing electrons. The chemical bond formed when two atoms share electrons is called a **covalent bond.** Covalent bonds usually form between atoms of nonmetals. In contrast, ionic bonds usually form when a metal combines with a nonmetal.

Electron Sharing Recall that the noble gases are not very reactive. In contrast, all other nonmetals, including hydrogen, can bond to other nonmetals by sharing electrons. Most nonmetals can even bond with another atom of the same element, as is the case with fluorine in Figure 22. When you count the electrons on each atom, count the shared pair each time. By sharing electrons, each atom has a stable set of eight. **The force that holds atoms together in a covalent bond is the attraction of each atom's nucleus for the shared pair of electrons.** The two bonded fluorine atoms form a molecule. A **molecule** is a neutral group of atoms joined by covalent bonds.

How Many Bonds? Look at the electron dot diagrams in Figure 23. Count the valence electrons around each atom. Except for hydrogen, the number of covalent bonds that nonmetal atoms can form equals the number of electrons needed to make a total of eight. Hydrogen needs only two electrons.

For example, oxygen has six valence electrons, so it can form two covalent bonds. In a water molecule, oxygen forms one covalent bond with each of two hydrogen atoms. As a result, the oxygen atom has a stable set of eight valence electrons. Each hydrogen atom can form one bond because it needs only a total of two electrons to be stable. Do you see why water's formula is H_2O, instead of H_3O, H_4O, or just HO?

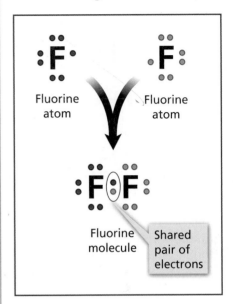

FIGURE 22
Sharing Electrons
By sharing electrons in a covalent bond, each fluorine atom has a stable set of eight valence electrons.

FIGURE 23
Covalent Bonds
The oxygen atom in water and the nitrogen atom in ammonia are each surrounded by eight valence electrons as a result of sharing electrons with hydrogen atoms.
Interpreting Diagrams *How many electrons does each hydrogen atom have as a result of sharing?*

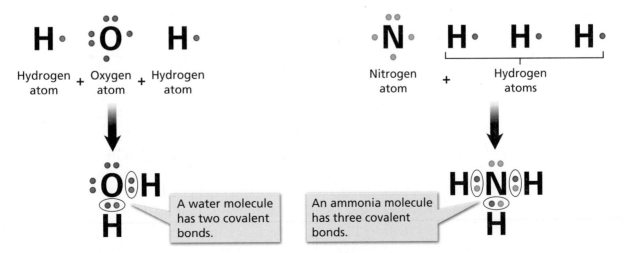

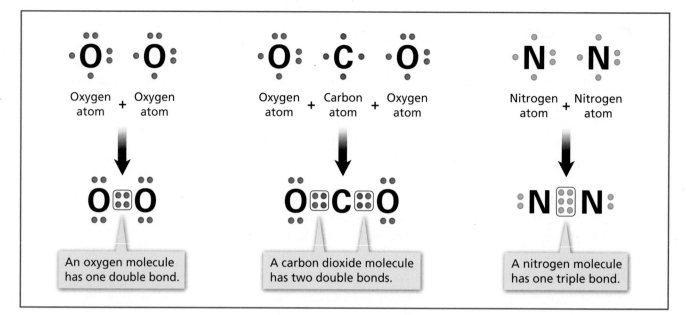

FIGURE 24
Double and Triple Bonds
Double and triple bonds can form when atoms share more than one pair of electrons.
Interpreting Diagrams *In a nitrogen molecule, how many electrons does each nitrogen atom share with the other?*

Double Bonds and Triple Bonds Look at the diagram of the oxygen molecule (O_2) in Figure 24. What do you see that's different? This time the two atoms share two pairs of electrons, forming a **double bond.** In a carbon dioxide molecule (CO_2), carbon forms a double bond with each of two oxygen atoms. Elements such as nitrogen and carbon can form **triple bonds** in which their atoms share three pairs of electrons.

Reading Checkpoint **What is the difference between a double bond and a triple bond?**

Molecular Compounds

A **molecular compound** is a compound that is composed of molecules. The molecules of a molecular compound contain atoms that are covalently bonded. Molecular compounds have very different properties than ionic compounds. **Compared to ionic compounds, molecular compounds generally have lower melting points and boiling points, and they do not conduct electricity when dissolved in water.**

Low Melting Points and Boiling Points Study the table in the Analyzing Data box on the next page. It lists the melting points and boiling points for a few molecular compounds and ionic compounds. In molecular solids, forces hold the molecules close to one another. But, the forces between molecules are much weaker than the forces between ions in an ionic solid. Compared with ionic solids, less heat must be added to molecular solids to separate the molecules and change the solid to a liquid. That is why most familiar compounds that are liquids or gases at room temperature are molecular compounds.

Go Online
sci LINKS™ NSTA

For: Links on molecular compounds
Visit: www.SciLinks.org
Web Code: scn-1214

Comparing Molecular and Ionic Compounds

The table compares the melting points and boiling points of a few molecular compounds and ionic compounds. Use the table to answer the following questions.

1. **Graphing** Create a bar graph of just the melting points of these compounds. Put the molecular compounds on the left and the ionic compounds on the right. Arrange the bars in order of increasing melting point. The *y*-axis should start at −200°C and go to 900°C.

2. **Interpreting Data** Describe what your graph reveals about the melting points of molecular compounds compared to those of ionic compounds.

3. **Inferring** How can you account for the differences in melting points between molecular compounds and ionic compounds?

4. **Interpreting Data** How do the boiling points of the molecular and ionic compounds compare?

Melting Points and Boiling Points of Molecular and Ionic Compounds			
Substance	Formula	Melting Point (°C)	Boiling Point (°C)
Methane	CH_4	−182.4	−161.5
Rubbing alcohol	C_3H_8O	−89.5	82.4
Water	H_2O	0	100
Zinc chloride	$ZnCl_2$	290	732
Magnesium chloride	$MgCl_2$	714	1,412
Sodium chloride	$NaCl$	800.7	1,465

Molecular compound ▢   Ionic compound ▢

5. **Predicting** Ammonia's melting point is −78°C and its boiling point is −34°C. Is ammonia a molecular compound or an ionic compound? Explain.

Poor Conductivity Most molecular compounds do not conduct electricity. No charged particles are available to move, so electricity cannot flow. Materials such as plastic and rubber are used to insulate wires because these materials are composed of molecular substances. Even as liquids, molecular compounds are poor conductors. Pure water, for example, does not conduct electricity. Neither does table sugar or alcohol when they are dissolved in pure water.

Unequal Sharing of Electrons

Have you ever played tug of war? If you have, you know that if both teams pull with equal force, the contest is a tie. But what if the teams pull on the rope with unequal force? Then the rope moves toward the side of the stronger team. The same is true of electrons in a covalent bond. **Atoms of some elements pull more strongly on shared electrons than do atoms of other elements. As a result, the electrons are pulled more toward one atom, causing the bonded atoms to have slight electrical charges.** These charges are not as strong as the charges on ions.

FIGURE 25
Nonpolar and Polar Bonds
Fluorine forms a nonpolar bond with another fluorine atom. In hydrogen fluoride, fluorine attracts electrons more strongly than hydrogen does, so the bond formed is polar.

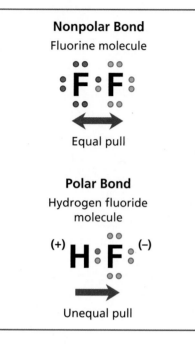

Nonpolar Bond
Fluorine molecule

Equal pull

Polar Bond
Hydrogen fluoride molecule

Unequal pull

Polar Bonds and Nonpolar Bonds The unequal sharing of electrons is enough to make the atom with the stronger pull slightly negative and the atom with the weaker pull slightly positive. A covalent bond in which electrons are shared unequally is called a **polar bond.** Of course, if two atoms pull equally on the electrons, neither atom becomes charged. A covalent bond in which electrons are shared equally is a **nonpolar bond.** Compare the bond in fluorine (F_2) with the bond in hydrogen fluoride (HF) in Figure 25.

Polar Bonds in Molecules It makes sense that a molecule with nonpolar bonds will itself be nonpolar. But a molecule may contain polar bonds and still be nonpolar overall. In carbon dioxide, the oxygen atoms attract electrons much more strongly than carbon does. So, the bonds between the oxygen and carbon atoms are polar. But, as you can see in Figure 26, a carbon dioxide molecule has a shape like a straight line. So, the two oxygen atoms pull with equal strength in opposite directions. In a sense, the attractions cancel out, and the molecule is nonpolar.

In contrast, other molecules that have polar covalent bonds are themselves polar. In a water molecule, the two hydrogen atoms are at one end of the molecule, while the oxygen atom is at the other end. The oxygen atom attracts electrons more strongly than do the hydrogen atoms. As a result, the oxygen end has a slight negative charge and the hydrogen end has a slight positive charge.

Attractions Between Molecules If you could shrink small enough to move among a bunch of water molecules, what would you find? The negatively charged oxygen ends of the polar water molecules attract the positively charged hydrogen ends of nearby water molecules. These attractions pull water molecules toward each other. In contrast, there is little attraction between nonpolar molecules, such as carbon dioxide molecules.

FIGURE 26
Nonpolar and Polar Molecules
A carbon dioxide molecule is a nonpolar molecule because of its straight-line shape. In contrast, a water molecule is a polar molecule because of its bent shape.
Interpreting Diagrams *What do the arrows in the diagram show?*

Nonpolar Molecule
Carbon dioxide

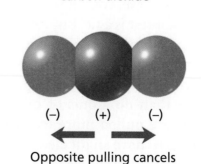

(–)   (+)   (–)

Opposite pulling cancels

Polar Molecule
Water

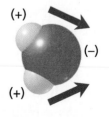

(+)

(–)

(+)

Electrons pulled toward oxygen

The properties of polar and nonpolar compounds differ because of differences in attractions between their molecules. For example, water and vegetable oil don't mix. The molecules in vegetable oil are nonpolar, and nonpolar molecules have little attraction for polar water molecules. On the other hand, the water molecules are attracted more strongly to one another than to the molecules of oil. Thus, water stays with water, and oil stays with oil.

If you did the Discover activity, you found that adding detergent helped oil and water to mix. This is because one end of a detergent molecule has nonpolar covalent bonds. The other end includes an ionic bond. The detergent's nonpolar end mixes easily with the oil. Meanwhile, the charged ionic end is attracted to polar water molecules, so the detergent dissolves in water.

FIGURE 27
Getting Out the Dirt
Most laundry dirt is oily or greasy. Detergents can mix with both oil and water, so when the wash water goes down the drain, the soap and dirt go with it.

Reading Checkpoint Why is water (H_2O) a polar molecule but a fluorine molecule (F_2) is not?

Section 4 Assessment

Target Reading Skill Asking Questions Use the answers to the questions you wrote about the headings to help you answer the questions below.

Reviewing Key Concepts

1. **a. Identifying** What is the attraction that holds two covalently bonded atoms together?
   b. Inferring A carbon atom can form four covalent bonds. How many valence electrons does it have?
   c. Interpreting Diagrams What is a double bond? Use Figure 24 to explain how a carbon dioxide molecule has a stable set of eight valence electrons for each atom.
2. **a. Reviewing** How are the properties of molecular compounds different from those of ionic compounds?
   b. Relating Cause and Effect Why are most molecular compounds poor conductors of electricity?
3. **a. Reviewing** How do some atoms in covalent bonds become slightly negative or slightly positive? What type of covalent bonds do these atoms form?

b. Comparing and Contrasting Both carbon dioxide molecules and water molecules have polar bonds. Why then is carbon dioxide a nonpolar molecule while water is a polar molecule?
c. Predicting Predict whether carbon dioxide or water would have a higher boiling point. Explain your prediction in terms of the attractions between molecules.

Lab zone **At-Home Activity**

Laundry Chemistry Demonstrate the action of soaps and detergents to your family. Pour some vegetable oil on a clean cloth and show how a detergent solution can wash the oil away better than water alone can. Explain to your family the features of soap and detergent molecules in terms of their chemical bonds.

• Tech & Design •

Bonding in Metals

Reading Preview

Key Concepts
- How are metal atoms bonded in solid metal?
- How does metallic bonding result in useful properties of metals?

Key Terms
- metallic bond • alloy
- ductile • malleable

Target Reading Skill
Relating Cause and Effect As you read, identify the properties of metals that result from metallic bonding. Write the information in a graphic organizer like the one below.

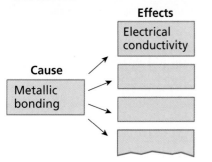

Effects

Electrical
conductivity

Cause

Metallic
bonding

Lab zone Discover **Activity**

What Do Metals Do?

1. Your teacher will give you pieces of different metals. Examine each metal and try changing its shape by bending, stretching, folding, or any other action you can think of. **CAUTION:** *Handle metal pieces with sharp edges carefully.*

2. What properties are common to these metals? What properties are different?

3. What properties make each metal suitable for its use?

Think It Over
Inferring Paper clips (made mostly of iron), aluminum foil, and copper wire are made from large chunks of metals. What properties must these metals have to be made into these products?

Why would you choose metal to cover the complex shape of the building in Figure 28? You couldn't cover the building with brittle, crumbly nonmetals such as sulfur or silicon. What physical properties make metal an ideal material for making furniture, musical instruments, electrical wire, pots and pans, eating utensils, and strong beams for buildings? Why do metals have these physical properties?

FIGURE 28
Metal in Architecture
The Guggenheim Museum in Bilbao, Spain, provides a dramatic example of some properties of metals. The museum's shiny outer "skin" is made of the lightweight metal titanium, which can be pressed into large, thin, flexible sheets.

Metallic Bonding

The properties of solid metals can be explained by the structure of metal atoms and the bonding between those atoms. Recall that most metals have 1, 2, or 3 valence electrons. When metal atoms combine chemically with atoms of other elements, they usually lose valence electrons, becoming positively charged metal ions. Metals lose electrons easily because their valence electrons are not strongly held.

The loosely held electrons in metal atoms result in a type of bonding that is characteristic of metals. Like many solids, metals exist as crystals. The metal atoms are very close together and in specific arrangements. These atoms are actually positively charged ions. Their valence electrons are free to drift among the ions. Each metal ion is held in the crystal by a **metallic bond**—an attraction between a positive metal ion and the electrons surrounding it. Look at Figure 29. **A metal consists of positively charged metal ions embedded in a "sea" of valence electrons.** The more valence electrons an atom can add to the "sea," the stronger the metallic bonds will be.

 What is a metallic bond?

FIGURE 29
Metallic Bonding
Solid metals consist of positively charged ions surrounded by a loose "sea" of valence electrons.
Problem Solving *Why would nonmetals be unlikely to have the type of bonding shown here?*

Metallic Properties

Metallic bonding explains many of the common physical properties of metals and their alloys. An **alloy** is a material made of two or more elements that has the properties of a metal.

Suppose that you placed one hand on an unheated aluminum pan and the other hand on a wooden tabletop. The aluminum pan would feel cooler than the tabletop even though both are at the same temperature. You feel the difference because aluminum conducts heat away from your hand much faster than wood does. **The "sea of electrons" model of solid metals explains their ability to conduct heat and electricity, the ease with which they can be made to change shape, and their luster.**

Heat Conductivity Heat causes particles of matter to move faster. If these particles collide with cooler particles, energy is transferred to the cooler particles. The freely moving valence electrons in a metal transfer energy to atoms and other electrons nearby. In this way, heat travels easily through the metal.

Go Online
SciLINKS NSTA

For: Links on metallic bonding
Visit: www.SciLinks.org
Web Code: scn-1215

FIGURE 30
Properties of Metals

The unique properties of metals result from the ability of their electrons to move about freely.

Interpreting Diagrams *What happens to metal ions when a metal is struck by a hammer? Why does this happen?*

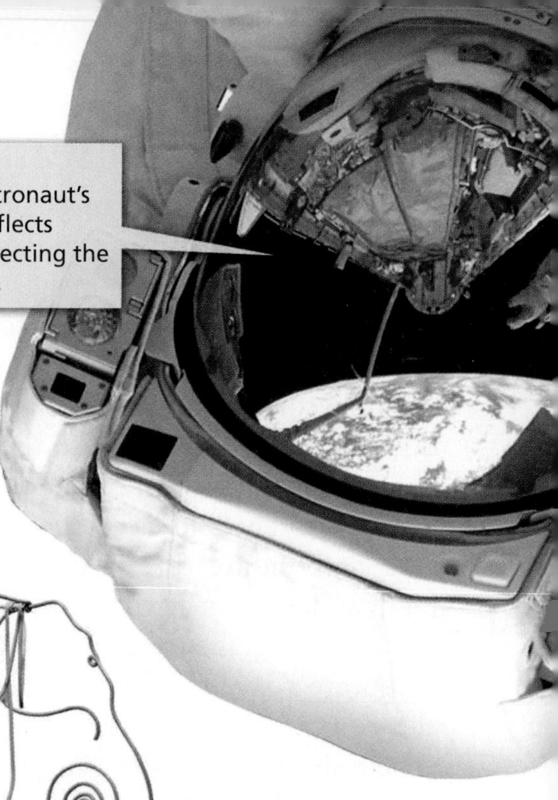

Luster
Gold in an astronaut's face shield reflects sunlight, protecting the wearer's eyes.

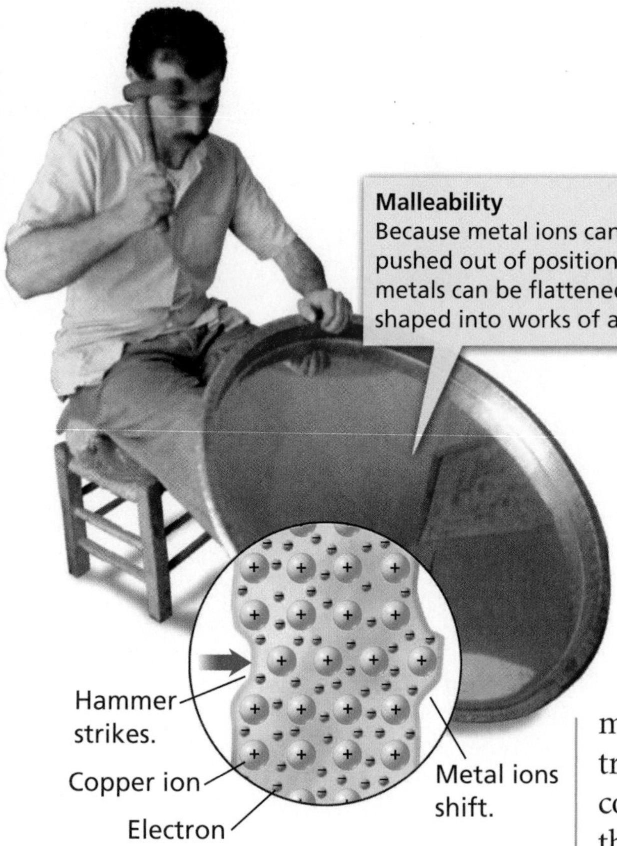

Malleability
Because metal ions can be pushed out of position, metals can be flattened and shaped into works of art.

Ductility
A wire's ability to bend but not break can lead to creative uses.

Hammer strikes.

Copper ion

Electron

Metal ions shift.

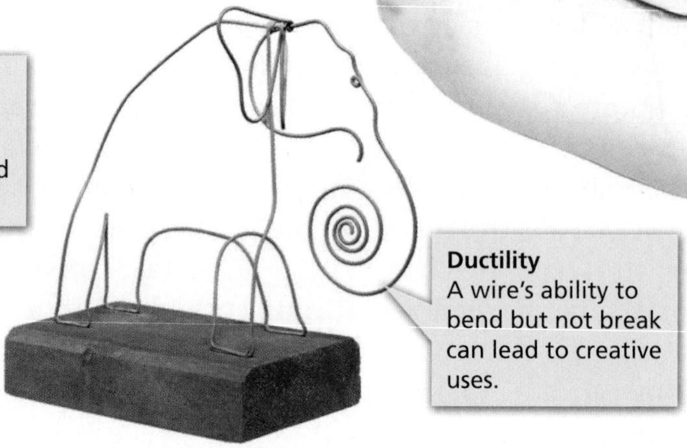

Electrical Conductivity Recall from Section 3 that electricity can flow when charged particles are free to move. Metals conduct electricity easily because the electrons in a metal can move freely among the atoms. When connected to a device such as a battery, electrons move into the metal at one point and out at another point.

Changes in Shape A metal's ability to conduct electricity would not be very useful if the metal couldn't be made into thin wires that could bend. Most metals are flexible and can be reshaped easily. They can be stretched, pushed, or compressed into different shapes without breaking. Metals act this way because the ions in metal are not attracted to the other ions. Instead, they are attracted to the loose electrons all around them. As a result, the ions can be pushed out of position, as shown in Figure 30.

Because the metal ions move easily, metals are **ductile,** which means that they can be bent easily and pulled into thin strands or wires. Metals are also **malleable**—able to be rolled into thin sheets, as in aluminum foil, or beaten into complex shapes.

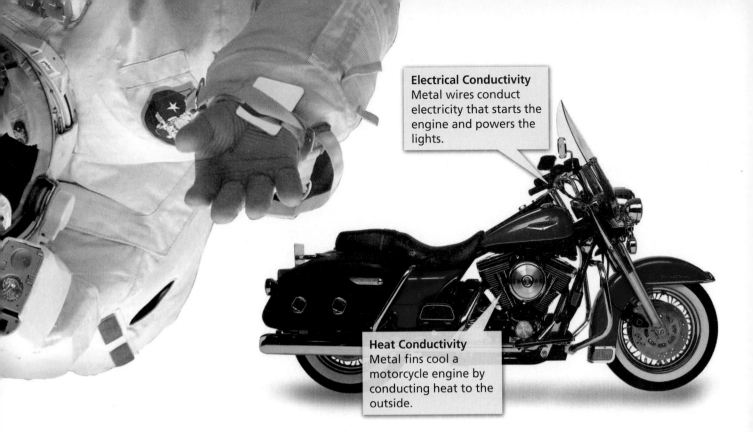

Electrical Conductivity Metal wires conduct electricity that starts the engine and powers the lights.

Heat Conductivity Metal fins cool a motorcycle engine by conducting heat to the outside.

Luster Polished metals exhibit luster, that is, they are shiny and reflective. A metal's luster is due to its valence electrons. When light strikes these electrons, they absorb the light and then give it off again. This property makes metals useful for making products as varied as mirrors, buildings, jewelry, and astronaut helmets.

 Reading Checkpoint Why do metals exhibit luster?

Section 5 Assessment

Target Reading Skill Relating Cause and Effect Refer to your graphic organizer about metallic properties to help you answer Question 2 below.

Reviewing Key Concepts

1. a. **Describing** Describe the structure of a metal.
   b. **Relating Cause and Effect** Explain how metal atoms form metallic bonds. What role do the valence electrons play?
   c. **Comparing and Contrasting** Review what you learned about ionic bonds in Section 3. How does a metallic bond differ from an ionic bond?

2. a. **Listing** Name five properties of metals. What accounts for these properties?
   b. **Explaining** Explain how heat travels through metals.
   c. **Applying Concepts** Why is it safer to use a nonmetal mixing spoon when cooking something on a stove?

Writing in Science

Product Label Choose a familiar metal object and create a "product label" for it. Your label should describe at least two of the metal's properties and explain why it exhibits those properties. You can include illustrations on your label as well.

The BIG Idea **Properties of Matter** Atoms of different elements combine to form compounds by gaining, losing, or sharing electrons.

1 Elements and Atoms

Key Concepts

- Elements are the building blocks of matter because all matter is composed of one element or a combination of two or more elements.
- Atomic theory grew as a series of models that developed from experimental evidence. As more evidence was collected, the theory and models were revised.

Key Terms

- matter • element • compound • mixture
- atom • scientific theory • model
- electrons • nucleus • protons • energy level
- neutrons

2 Atoms, Bonding, and the Periodic Table

Key Concepts

- The number of valence electrons in an atom of an element determines many properties of that element, including the ways in which the atom can bond with other atoms.
- The properties of elements change in a regular way across a period in the periodic table.

Key Terms

- valence electrons • electron dot diagram
- chemical bond • symbol • atomic number
- period • group • family • noble gas
- halogen • alkali metal

3 Ionic Bonds

Key Concepts

- When an atom loses an electron, it becomes a positive ion. When an atom gains an electron, it becomes a negative ion.
- Ionic bonds form as a result of the attraction between positive and negative ions.
- When ionic compounds form, the charges on the ions balance out.
- Ionic compounds are hard, brittle crystals that have high melting points and conduct electricity when dissolved in water.

Key Terms

- ion • polyatomic ion • ionic bond
- ionic compound • chemical formula
- subscript • crystal

4 Covalent Bonds

Key Concepts

- The force that holds atoms together in a covalent bond is the attraction of each atom's nucleus for the shared pair of electrons.
- Molecular compounds have low melting and boiling points and do not conduct electricity.
- In polar covalent bonds, the bonded atoms have slight electrical charges.

Key Terms

- covalent bond • molecule • double bond
- triple bond • molecular compound
- polar bond • nonpolar bond

5 Bonding in Metals

Key Concepts

- A metal consists of positively charged metal ions in a "sea" of valence electrons.
- Solid metals conduct heat and electricity, can change shape easily, and have luster.

Key Terms

metallic bond	ductile
alloy	malleable

Review and Assessment

Go Online
PHSchool.com

For: Self-Assessment
Visit: PHSchool.com
Web Code: cga-2010

Organizing Information

Comparing and Contrasting
Copy the graphic organizer about chemical bonds onto a separate sheet of paper. Then complete it. (For more on Comparing and Contrasting, see the Skills Handbook.)

Types of Chemical Bonds

Feature	Ionic Bond	Polar Covalent Bond	Nonpolar Covalent Bond	Metallic Bond
How Bond Forms	a. ___?___	Unequal sharing of electrons	b. ___?___	c. ___?___
Charge on Bonded Atoms?	Yes; positive or negative	d. ___?___	e. ___?___	Yes; positive
Example	f. ___?___	g. ___?___	O_2 molecule	h. ___?___

Reviewing Key Terms

Choose the letter of the best answer.

1. All compounds are made up of two or more
   a. elements.　　**b.** electrons.
   c. nuclei.　　**d.** mixtures.

2. The nucleus of an atom has a positive charge because the nucleus contains
   a. electrons.　　**b.** protons.
   c. mass.　　**d.** neutrons.

3. On the periodic table, elements with the same number of valence electrons are in the same
   a. square.　　**b.** period.
   c. block.　　**d.** group.

4. When an atom loses or gains electrons, it becomes a(n)
   a. ion.　　**b.** formula.
   c. crystal.　　**d.** subscript.

5. A covalent bond in which electrons are shared unequally is a
   a. double bond.
   b. triple bond.
   c. polar bond.
   d. nonpolar bond.

6. Because it can be pounded into thin sheets, copper is said to be
   a. an alloy.
   b. conductive.
   c. ductile.
   d. malleable.

If the statement is true, write *true*. If it is false, change the underlined word or words to make the statement true.

7. In the modern atomic model, most of the volume of an atom is occupied by its <u>nucleus</u>.

8. The <u>atomic number</u> of an element is the number of protons in the nucleus of an atom.

9. A <u>polyatomic ion</u> is made up of more than one atom.

10. An <u>alloy</u> is a mixture of elements that has the properties of a metal.

Writing in Science

Travel Brochure Pretend you have just visited a city modeled on the periodic table. Write a travelogue about how the "city" is organized. Be sure to describe some of the elements you visited and how they are related to their neighbors.

Discovery CHANNEL SCHOOL

Atoms and Bonding

Video Preview
Video Field Trip
▶ Video Assessment

Review and Assessment

Checking Concepts

11. What discoveries did Rutherford make about the atom from his team's experiments?

12. Which element is less reactive, an element whose atoms have seven valence electrons or an element whose atoms have eight valence electrons? Explain.

13. Why do ionic compounds generally have high melting points?

14. The formula of sulfuric acid is H_2SO_4. How many atoms of hydrogen, sulfur, and oxygen are in one molecule of sulfuric acid?

15. Why is the covalent bond between two atoms of the same element a nonpolar bond?

16. Explain how metallic bonding causes metals to conduct electricity.

Thinking Critically

17. **Applying Concepts** Your friend tells you that she has a theory that eating cabbage will make hair grow faster. How does your friend's use of the word theory differ from a scientist's use of the word?

18. **Making Generalizations** What information does the organization of the periodic table tell you about atoms and the bonds they form?

19. **Classifying** Classify each molecule below as either a polar molecule or a nonpolar molecule. Explain your reasoning.

Oxygen

Carbon dioxide

20. **Relating Cause and Effect** Many molecular compounds with small molecules are gases at room temperature. Water, however, is a liquid. Use what you know about polar and nonpolar molecules to explain this difference. (*Hint:* Molecules of a gas are much farther apart than molecules of a liquid.)

Applying Skills

Use the electron dot diagrams below to answer Questions 21–25.

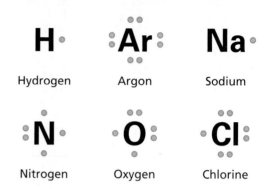

Hydrogen   Argon   Sodium

Nitrogen   Oxygen   Chlorine

21. **Predicting** When nitrogen and hydrogen combine, what will be the ratio of hydrogen atoms to nitrogen atoms in a molecule of the resulting compound? Explain.

22. **Inferring** Which of these elements can become stable by losing one electron? Explain.

23. **Drawing Conclusions** Which of these elements is least likely to react with other elements? Explain.

24. **Interpreting Diagrams** Which of these elements would react with two atoms of sodium to form an ionic compound? Explain.

25. **Classifying** What type of bond forms when two atoms of nitrogen join to form a nitrogen molecule? When two atoms of oxygen join to form an oxygen molecule?

Lab zone Chapter **Project**

Performance Assessment Present your models to the class, telling what the parts of each model represent. Explain why you chose particular items to model the atoms and chemical bonds. Which kind of bonds were easier to show? Why? What more would you like to know about bonding that could help improve your models?

Standardized Test Prep

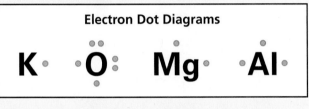
Choose the letter of the best answer.

Use the electron dot diagrams above to answer Questions 1–3.

1. Oxygen has 6 valence electrons, as indicated by the 6 dots around the letter symbol "O." Based on this information, how many covalent bonds could an oxygen atom form?
   A six
   B three
   C two
   D none

2. If a reaction occurs between potassium (K) and oxygen (O), what will be the ratio of potassium ions to oxide ions in the resulting compound, potassium oxide?
   F 1 : 1   **G** 1 : 2
   H 2 : 1   **J** 2 : 2

3. The element boron (B) is directly above aluminum (Al) on the periodic table. Which statement about boron is true?
   A Boron is in the same period as aluminum and has two valence electrons.
   B Boron is in the same group as aluminum and has two valence electrons.
   C Boron is in the same period as aluminum and has three valence electrons.
   D Boron is in the same group as aluminum and has three valence electrons.

4. The chemical formula for a glucose molecule is $C_6H_{12}O_6$. The subscripts represent the
   F mass of each element.
   G number of atoms of each element in a glucose molecule.
   H total number of bonds made by each atom.
   J number of valence electrons.

5. An ice cube (solid H_2O) and a scoop of table salt (NaCl) are left outside on a warm, sunny day. Which best explains why the ice cube melts and the salt does not?
   A The attractive forces between molecules of H_2O are much weaker than those between ions in NaCl.
   B NaCl can dissolve in H_2O.
   C The mass of the H_2O was less than the mass of the NaCl.
   D NaCl is white and H_2O is colorless.

Constructed Response

6. In a working light bulb, electricity passes through a thin tungsten wire filament that is wound in a coil. Describe two properties that make the metal tungsten a good material for the filament of a light bulb. Indicate how the type of bonding in tungsten contributes to these properties.

The BIG Idea

Chemical Changes in Matter

Q What happens during a chemical reaction?

Chapter Preview

Sparks fly as sodium metal ▶
reacts with water.

Lab zone™ Chapter **Project**

Design and Build a Closed Reaction Chamber

When water evaporates, it is not destroyed or lost. In fact, matter is never created or destroyed in either a physical change or a chemical reaction. In this chapter project, you will design and build a closed structure in which a chemical reaction can occur. You will use the chamber to confirm that matter is not created or destroyed in a chemical reaction.

Your Goal To design and build a closed chamber in which sugar can be broken down

Your structure must

- be made of materials that are approved by your teacher
- be built to specifications agreed upon by the class
- be a closed system so the masses of the reactants and products can be measured
- be built following the safety guidelines in Appendix A

Plan It! Before you design your reaction chamber, find out how sugar can be broken down. Next, brainstorm with class-mates to determine the safety features of your chamber. Then choose materials for your struc-ture and sketch your design. When your teacher has approved your design, build and test your structure.

Observing Chemical Change

Reading Preview

Key Concepts
- How can matter and changes in matter be described?
- How can you tell when a chemical reaction occurs?

Key Terms
- matter • chemistry
- physical property
- chemical property
- physical change
- chemical reaction • precipitate
- endothermic reaction
- exothermic reaction

🔄 Target Reading Skill

Asking Questions Before you read, preview the red headings. In a graphic organizer like the one below, ask a *what* or *how* question for each heading. As you read, write the answers to your questions.

Properties and Changes of Matter

Question	Answer
What are physical properties of matter?	Physical properties are . . .

Lab zone • Discover **Activity**

What Happens When Chemicals React?

1. Put on your safety goggles. Place 2 small spoonfuls of baking soda into a clear plastic cup.
2. Holding the cup over a large bowl or sink, add about 125 mL of vinegar. Swirl the cup gently.
3. Look at the material in the cup. What changes do you see? Feel the outside of the cup. What do you notice about the temperature?
4. Carefully fan the air above the liquid toward you. What do you smell?

Think It Over

Observing What changes did you detect using your senses of smell and touch?

Picture yourself toasting marshmallows over a campfire. You see the burning logs change from a hard solid to a soft pile of ash. You hear popping and hissing sounds from the fire as the wood burns. You smell smoke. You feel the heat on your skin. Finally, you taste the results. The crisp brown surface of the toasted marshmallow tastes quite different from the soft white surface of a marshmallow just out of its bag. Firewood, skin, and marshmallows are all examples of matter. **Matter** is anything that has mass and takes up space. The study of matter and how matter changes is called **chemistry.**

Chemical change can ▶ lead to a treat.

Properties and Changes of Matter

Part of studying matter is describing it. When you describe matter, you explain its characteristics, or properties, and how it changes. **Matter can be described in terms of two kinds of properties—physical properties and chemical properties. Changes in matter can be described in terms of physical changes and chemical changes.**

Properties of Matter   A **physical property** is a characteristic of a substance that can be observed without changing the substance into another substance. The temperature at which a solid melts is a physical property. For example, ice melts at a temperature of zero degrees Celsius. Color, hardness, texture, shine, and flexibility are some other physical properties of matter. The ability of a substance to dissolve in water and how well it conducts heat and electricity are examples of still more physical properties of matter.

A **chemical property** is a characteristic of a substance that describes its ability to change into other substances. To observe the chemical properties of a substance, you must change it to another substance. For example, when magnesium burns, it combines with oxygen in the air, forming a new substance called magnesium oxide. People who make objects out of magnesium must be careful because the metal can catch fire. Burning is only one type of chemical property. Other examples of chemical properties are tarnishing and rusting.

FIGURE 1
Properties of Water
This geyser gives off hot water and water vapor, which condenses into a visible cloud in the cold air. The temperatures at which water boils and freezes are physical properties of water.
Predicting *How will the snow change when spring arrives?*

Chemical Properties of Water
• Made of hydrogen atoms and oxygen atoms in a 2 to 1 ratio
• Does not burn
• Reacts with some metals

Physical Properties of Water
• Clear, colorless liquid at room temperature
• Boils at 100°C
• Freezes at 0°C

Physical Change
You can flatten and pull on a marshmallow but its composition will stay the same.

FIGURE 2
Changes in Matter
Matter can undergo both physical change and chemical change.

Chemical Change
If you toast a marshmallow, the sugars and other substances will cook or burn, producing a crust made of new substances.

Lab zone Skills **Activity**

Classifying

Classify each of the following changes as either a chemical change or a physical change. Explain your reasoning for each case.

- A piece of metal is heated to a high temperature and changes to a liquid.
- When two solutions are poured into the same container, a powdery solid forms and settles to the bottom.
- Water left in a dish overnight has disappeared by the next day.
- A blacksmith hammers a piece of red-hot iron into the shape of a knife blade.

Changes of Matter You probably have seen solid water (ice) change to liquid water. Water is the same substance, whether it is frozen or liquid. Therefore, changing from a solid to a liquid is a physical change. A **physical change** is any change that alters the form or appearance of a substance but that does not make the substance into another substance. You cause a physical change when you squash a marshmallow. The shape of the marshmallow changes but not the taste! It's still made of the same compounds that have the same properties. Other examples of physical changes are bending, crushing, breaking, cutting, and anything else that changes only the shape or form of matter. Braiding your hair is another example of a physical change.

Sometimes when a change occurs in a substance, the substance itself is changed. For example, the brown crust on a toasted marshmallow is the result of sugar changing to different substances in a mixture called caramel. A change in matter that produces one or more new substances is a chemical change, or **chemical reaction.** The burning of gasoline in a car's engine is a chemical change. The new substances formed end up as the car's exhaust.

✓ **Reading Checkpoint** What kind of change occurs when you toast the outside of a marshmallow?

Bonding and Chemical Change **Chemical changes occur when bonds break and new bonds form.** As a result, new substances are produced. You may recall that atoms form bonds when they share or transfer electrons. The reaction pictured in Figure 3 involves both the breaking of shared bonds and a transfer of electrons.

Oxygen gas (O_2) in the air consists of molecules made of two oxygen atoms that share electrons. These bonds are broken when oxygen reacts with magnesium metal (Mg). Each magnesium atom transfers two of its electrons to an oxygen atom. The oxygen atom becomes a negative ion, and the magnesium atom becomes a positive ion.

You can probably guess what happens next. You may recall that oppositely charged ions attract. An ionic bond forms between the Mg^{2+} ions and the O^{2-} ions. The ionic compound magnesium oxide (MgO) is produced, and energy is released. Magnesium oxide—a white, crumbly powder—has properties that differ from those of either shiny magnesium or oxygen gas. For example, while magnesium melts at about 650°C, it takes temperatures of more than 2,800°C to melt magnesium oxide!

Go Online
SciLINKS NSTA

For: Links on chemical changes
Visit: www.SciLinks.org
Web Code: scn-1221

FIGURE 3
Bonding and Chemical Change
As magnesium burns, bonds between atoms break and new bonds form. The reaction gives off energy. **Interpreting Diagrams** *Why does the oxygen ion have a 2– charge?*

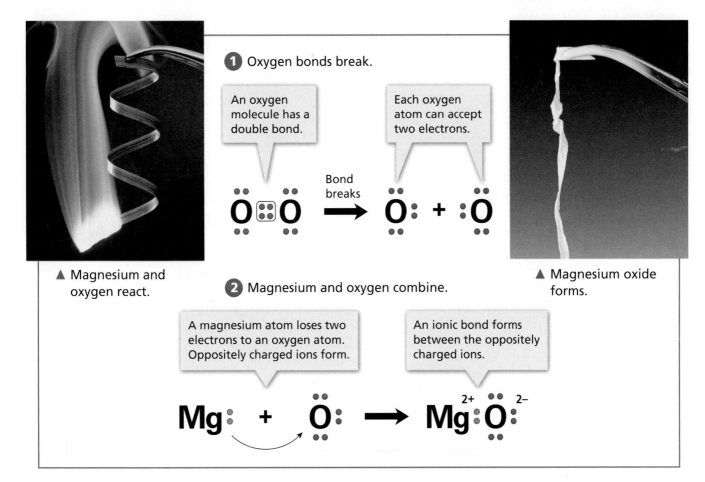

▲ Magnesium and oxygen react.

1 Oxygen bonds break.

An oxygen molecule has a double bond.

Each oxygen atom can accept two electrons.

Bond breaks

$O::O \rightarrow O: + :O$

2 Magnesium and oxygen combine.

A magnesium atom loses two electrons to an oxygen atom. Oppositely charged ions form.

An ionic bond forms between the oppositely charged ions.

$Mg: + O: \rightarrow Mg^{2+}O^{2-}$

▲ Magnesium oxide forms.

Evidence for Chemical Reactions

Look at the photograph below of the beaker. Even without reading the caption, you probably could guess it shows a chemical reaction. But how do you know? How can you tell when a chemical reaction occurs? **Chemical reactions involve two main kinds of changes that you can observe—formation of new substances and changes in energy.**

Changes in Properties One way to detect chemical reactions is to observe changes in the properties of the materials involved. Changes in properties result when new substances form. What kinds of changes should you look for? Look at Figure 4. First, a color change may signal that a new substance has formed. Second, a solid may appear when two solutions are mixed. A solid that forms from solution during a chemical reaction is called a **precipitate** (pree SIP uh tayt).

FIGURE 4
Evidence for Chemical Reactions

Many kinds of change provide evidence that a chemical reaction has occurred. **Applying Concepts** *What other evidence might tell you a chemical reaction has occurred?*

Two clear liquids react, ▲ forming a precipitate.

◀ The light green leaves of early spring slowly turn darker as chemical reactions in the leaves produce more of the green compound chlorophyll.

Third, a gas might be produced from solids or liquids. If the reaction occurs in a liquid, you may see the gas as bubbles. Finally, other kinds of observable changes in properties can also signal a chemical reaction. For example, moist bread dough forms a dry, porous solid after baking.

Although you may observe a property change in matter, the change does not always indicate that a chemical reaction has taken place. Sometimes physical changes give similar results. For example, when water boils, the gas bubbles you see are made of molecules of water, just as the original liquid was. The sign of a chemical reaction is that one or more new substances are produced. For example, when an electric current is passed through water during electrolysis, two gases are produced, hydrogen gas (H_2) and oxygen gas (O_2).

Reading Checkpoint How is a precipitate evidence for a chemical reaction?

Lab zone Try This **Activity**

Mostly Cloudy

1. Put on your safety goggles and apron.
2. Pour about 5 mL of limewater into a plastic cup.
3. Pour an equal amount of plain water into another plastic cup.
4. Add about 5 mL of carbonated water to each of the cups.

Drawing Conclusions In which cup do you think a chemical reaction occurred? What evidence supports your conclusion?

A golden loaf of bread with its crunchy crust has very different properties from the soft dough that went into the oven. ▼

Oxygen bubbles that form during photosynthesis collect on the leaves of a plant. ▼

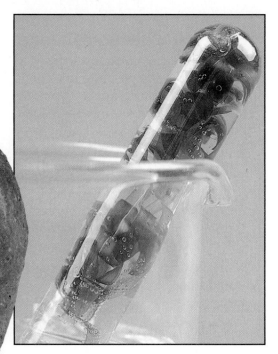

FIGURE 5

An Endothermic Reaction
Energy must be added continuously to fry an egg. **Making Generalizations** *In terms of energy, what kind of reaction usually occurs when food is cooked?*

Energy can change egg whites from a clear liquid into a white solid.

Changes in Energy From your everyday experience, you know about various types of energy, such as heat, light, and electricity. As matter changes, it can either absorb or release energy. A change in energy occurs during a chemical reaction. Some reactions absorb energy, while others release energy. One common indication that energy has been absorbed or released is a change in temperature.

If you did the Discover activity, you observed that the mixture became colder. When baking soda (sodium bicarbonate) reacts with vinegar, the reaction takes heat from the solution, making it feel cooler. This kind of reaction is an example of an endothermic reaction. An **endothermic reaction** (en doh THUR mik) is a reaction in which energy is absorbed. However, endothermic reactions do not always result in a decrease in temperature. Many endothermic reactions occur only when heat is constantly added. For example, the reactions that occur when you fry an egg are endothermic.

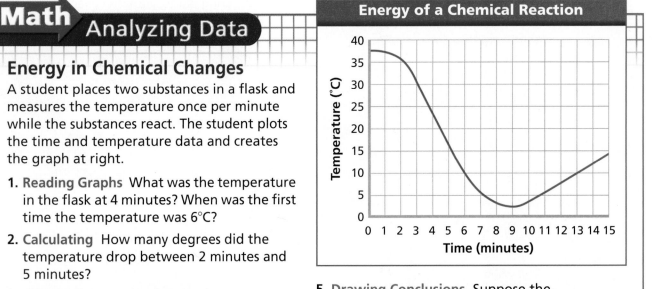

Math ▶ Analyzing Data

Energy in Chemical Changes

A student places two substances in a flask and measures the temperature once per minute while the substances react. The student plots the time and temperature data and creates the graph at right.

Energy of a Chemical Reaction

1. **Reading Graphs** What was the temperature in the flask at 4 minutes? When was the first time the temperature was 6°C?

2. **Calculating** How many degrees did the temperature drop between 2 minutes and 5 minutes?

3. **Interpreting Data** Is the reaction endothermic or exothermic? Explain.

4. **Inferring** At what temperature did the reaction stop? How can you tell?

5. **Drawing Conclusions** Suppose the temperature in the flask increased instead of decreased as the reaction occurred. In terms of energy, what kind of reaction would it be? Explain.

FIGURE 6
An Exothermic Reaction
Enough energy is released by the burning of airplane fuel to keep a plane moving fast enough to fly.

In contrast, the reaction between fuel and oxygen in an airplane engine releases energy, mostly in the form of heat. The heat causes gases in the engine to expand. The expansion and movement of the gases out of the plane exerts a force that moves the plane forward. A reaction that releases energy in the form of heat is called an **exothermic reaction** (ek soh THUR mik). You will learn more about energy and chemical changes in Section 3.

 Reading Checkpoint **What is an endothermic reaction?**

Section 1 Assessment

Target Reading Skill Asking Questions Use the answers to questions you wrote about the headings to help you answer the questions below.

Reviewing Key Concepts

1. a. **Explaining** What is the difference between the physical properties and the chemical properties of a substance?
   b. **Posing Questions** When silver coins are found in ancient shipwrecks, they are coated with a black crust. What question could you ask to help you decide whether the silver underwent a chemical change or a physical change? Explain.
   c. **Making Generalizations** In terms of chemical bonds and electrons, what kinds of changes occur between atoms when substances undergo chemical reactions?

2. a. **Listing** What are five kinds of evidence you can use to determine if a chemical reaction has occurred?
   b. **Interpreting Photographs** How do the properties of the cooked egg shown in Figure 5 differ from the properties of a raw egg?
   c. **Comparing and Contrasting** How are endothermic and exothermic reactions the same? How are they different?

Writing in Science

Persuasive Letter Imagine you have a pen pal who is studying chemistry just like you are. Your pen pal claims the change from liquid water to water vapor is a chemical change. Write a brief letter that might convince your pen pal otherwise.

Where's the Evidence?

Problem

What are some signs that a chemical reaction has taken place?

Skills Focus

observing, predicting, drawing conclusions

Materials

- 4 small plastic cups
- birthday candles
- 2 plastic spoons
- sugar
- tongs
- clay
- matches
- sodium carbonate (powdered solid)
- graduated cylinder, 10 mL
- aluminum foil, about 10-cm square
- dilute hydrochloric acid in a dropper bottle
- copper sulfate solution
- sodium carbonate solution

Procedure

Preview the steps for each reaction and copy the data table into your notebook.

PART 1

1. Put a pea-sized pile of sodium carbonate into a clean plastic cup. Record in the data table the appearance of the sodium carbonate.

2. Observe a dropper containing hydrochloric acid. Record the appearance of the acid. **CAUTION:** *Hydrochloric acid can burn you or anything else it touches. Wash spills immediately with water.*

3. Make a prediction about how you think the acid and the sodium carbonate will react when mixed. Record your prediction.

4. Add about 10 drops of hydrochloric acid to the sodium carbonate. Swirl to mix the contents of the cup. Record your observations.

PART 2

5. Fold up the sides of the aluminum foil square to make a small tray.

6. Use a plastic spoon to place a pea-sized pile of sugar into the tray.

7. Carefully describe the appearance of the sugar in your data table.

Data Table				
Reaction	Observations Before Reaction	Predictions	Observations During Reaction	Observations After Reaction
1. Sodium carbonate (powder) + hydrochloric acid				
2. Sugar + heat				
3. Copper sulfate + sodium carbonate solutions				

8. Secure a small candle on your desktop in a lump of clay. Carefully light the candle with a match only after being instructed to do so by your teacher. **CAUTION:** *Tie back long hair and loose clothing.*

9. Predict what you think will happen if you heat the sugar. Record your prediction.

10. Use tongs to hold the aluminum tray. Heat the sugar slowly by moving the tray gently back and forth over the flame. Make observations while the sugar is heating.

11. When you think there is no longer a chemical reaction occurring, blow out the candle.

12. Allow the tray to cool for a few seconds and set it down on your desk. Record your observations of the material left in the tray.

PART 3

13. Put about 2 mL of copper sulfate solution in one cup. **CAUTION:** *Copper sulfate is poisonous and can stain your skin and clothes. Do not touch it or get it in your mouth.* Put an equal amount of sodium carbonate solution in another cup. Record the appearance of both liquids.

14. Write a prediction of what you think will happen when the two solutions are mixed.

15. Combine the two solutions and record your observations. **CAUTION:** *Dispose of the solutions as directed by your teacher.*

16. Wash your hands when you have finished working.

Analyze and Conclude

1. **Predicting** How do the results of each reaction compare with your predictions?

2. **Observing** How did you know when the reaction in Part 1 was over?

3. **Interpreting Data** What was the evidence of a chemical reaction in Part 1? In Part 2?

4. **Drawing Conclusions** Was the reaction in Part 2 endothermic or exothermic? Explain.

5. **Observing** Was the product of the reaction in Part 3 a solid, a liquid, or a gas? How do you know?

6. **Drawing Conclusions** How do you know if new substances were formed in each reaction?

7. **Communicating** Make a table or chart briefly describing each chemical change in this lab, followed by the evidence for the chemical change.

More to Explore

Use your observation skills to find evidence of chemical reactions involving foods in your kitchen. Look for production of gases, color changes, and formation of precipitates. Share your findings with your classmates.

Describing Chemical Reactions

Reading Preview

Key Concepts
- What information does a chemical equation contain?
- What does the principle of conservation of mass state?
- What must a balanced chemical equation show?
- What are three categories of chemical reactions?

Key Terms
- chemical equation
- reactant • product
- conservation of mass
- open system • closed system
- coefficient • synthesis
- decomposition • replacement

Target Reading Skill
Building Vocabulary Using a word in a sentence helps you think about how best to explain the word. After you read the section, reread the paragraphs that contain definitions of Key Terms. Use all of the information you have learned to write a meaningful sentence using each Key Term.

Discover **Activity**

Do You Lose Anything?

1. Place about two dozen coins on a table. Sort them into stacks of pennies, nickels, dimes, and quarters.
2. Count and record the number of coins in each stack. Calculate and record the value of each stack and the total of all stacks combined.
3. Mix all the coins together and then divide them randomly into four unsorted stacks.
4. Again calculate the value of each stack and the total amount of money. Count the total number of each type of coin.
5. Repeat Steps 3 and 4.

Think It Over
Making Models What happened to the total value and types of coins when you rearranged them? Did rearranging the coins change the properties of any coin? If you think of the coins as each representing a different type of atom, what does this model tell you about chemical reactions?

You look at your cellular phone display and read the message "U wan2 gt pza 2nite?" You reply "No. MaB TPM. CUL8R." These messages are short for saying "Do you want to get some pizza tonight?" and "No. Maybe tomorrow afternoon (P.M.). See you later."

Cellular phone messages use symbols and abbreviations to express ideas in shorter form. A type of shorthand is used in chemistry too. "Hydrogen molecules react with oxygen molecules to form water molecules" is a lengthy way to describe the reaction between hydrogen and oxygen. And writing it is slow. Instead, chemists often use chemical equations in place of words.

◀ **A message on a cellular display**

What Are Chemical Equations?

A **chemical equation** is a short, easy way to show a chemical reaction, using symbols instead of words. Although chemical equations are shorter than sentences, they contain more information. **Chemical equations use chemical formulas and other symbols instead of words to summarize a reaction.**

Formulas in an Equation All chemical equations use formulas to represent the substances involved in a reaction. You may recall that a chemical formula is a combination of symbols that represents the elements in a compound. For example, CO_2 is the formula for carbon dioxide. The formula tells you that this compound is made up of the elements carbon and oxygen and each molecule has 1 carbon atom and 2 oxygen atoms. Figure 7 lists formulas of other compounds that may be familiar to you.

Structure of an Equation All chemical equations have a common structure. A chemical equation tells you the substances you start with in a reaction and the substances you get at the end. The substances you have at the beginning are called the **reactants.** When the reaction is complete, you have new substances called the **products.**

The formulas for the reactants are written on the left, followed by an arrow. You read the arrow as "yields." The formulas for the products are written on the right. When there are two or more reactants, they are separated by plus signs. In a similar way, plus signs are used to separate two or more products. Below is the general plan for a chemical equation.

Reactant + Reactant ⟶ Product + Product

The number of reactants and products can vary. Some reactions have only one reactant or product. Other reactions have two, three, or more reactants or products. In Figure 8, you can see the equation for a reaction that occurs when limestone ($CaCO_3$) is heated. Count the number of reactants and products, and familiarize yourself with the parts of the equation.

FIGURE 7
The formula of a compound identifies the elements in the compound and the ratios in which their atoms are present.

Formulas of Familiar Compounds	
Compound	**Formula**
Water	H_2O
Carbon dioxide	CO_2
Propane	C_3H_8
Sugar (sucrose)	$C_{12}H_{22}O_{11}$
Rubbing alcohol	C_3H_8O
Ammonia	NH_3
Sodium chloride	$NaCl$
Baking soda	$NaHCO_3$

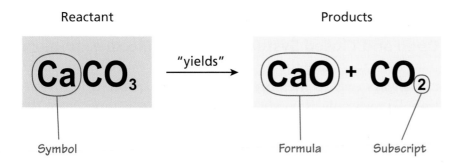

Reactant   Products

"yields"

Symbol   Formula   Subscript

FIGURE 8
A Chemical Equation
Like a building, a chemical equation has a basic structure.
Interpreting Diagrams *What does the subscript 3 in the formula for calcium carbonate tell you?*

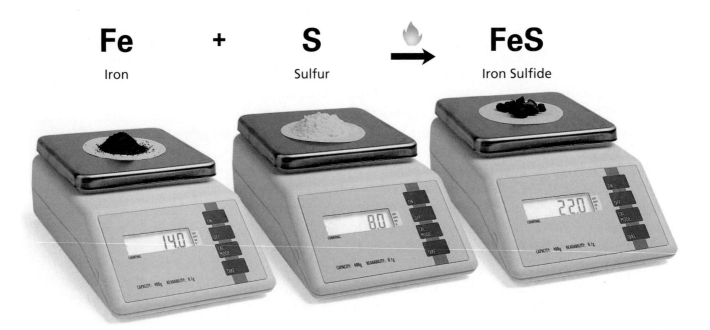

Fe   **+**   **S**   🔥➡   **FeS**

Iron   Sulfur   Iron Sulfide

FIGURE 9
Conservation of Mass
Mass is conserved in chemical reactions.

Lab zone Try This **Activity**

Still There

1. Measure the mass of a collection of bolts, each with a nut attached to it.
2. Remove all the nuts from the bolts. Measure the total mass of the nuts. Then do the same with the bolts. Add these values.
3. Rearrange your collection, putting two or three nuts on one bolt, one nut on another bolt, and so on. You can even leave a few pieces unattached.
4. Measure the total mass again. Compare this figure with the totals from Steps 1 and 2.

Making Models How does your activity model the idea of conservation of mass?

Conservation of Mass

Look closely at the values for mass in Figure 9. Iron and sulfur can react to form iron sulfide. The photograph represents a principle first demonstrated by the French chemist Antoine Lavoisier in 1774. This principle is called **conservation of mass,** and it states that during a chemical reaction, matter is not created or destroyed. All the atoms present at the start of the reaction are present at the end.

Modeling Conservation of Mass Think about what happens when classes change at your school during the day. A class is made of a group of students and a teacher together in a room. When the bell rings, people from each class move from room to room, ending up in different classes. The number of people in the school has not changed. But their arrangement has.

Now imagine that all the students and teachers are atoms, each class is a molecule, and the changing of classes is a chemical reaction. At the end of the reaction, the same atoms are present, but they are grouped together differently. The amount of matter does not change. **The principle of conservation of mass states that in a chemical reaction, the total mass of the reactants must equal the total mass of the products.**

Open and Closed Systems At first glance, some reactions may seem to violate the principle of conservation of mass. It's not always easy to measure all the matter involved in a reaction. For example, if you burn a match, oxygen comes from the surrounding air. But how much? Likewise, the products escape into the air. Again, how much?

A burning match is an example of an open system. In an **open system**, matter can enter from or escape to the surroundings. The burned out fire in Figure 10 is another example of an open system. If you want to measure all the matter before and after a reaction, you have to be able to contain it. In a **closed system**, matter is not allowed to enter or leave. The pear decaying under glass in Figure 10 is a closed system. So is a chemical reaction inside a sealed plastic bag.

 Reading Checkpoint **What is a closed system?**

FIGURE 10

Open and Closed Systems

A wood fire is an open system because gases escape into the air. A pear in a glass dome is a closed system because the reactants and products are contained inside the dome.
Problem Solving *What masses would you need to measure before and after a wood fire to show conservation of mass?*

Open System
Except for the ash, products of the wood fire have escaped up the chimney or into the room.

Closed System
The total mass of the pear and the substances produced during its decay are contained by the glass dome.

Fresh pear   Decayed pear

Balancing Chemical Equations

The principle of conservation of mass means that the same number of atoms exists in the products as in the reactants. **To describe a reaction accurately, a chemical equation must show the same number of each type of atom on both sides of the equation.** Chemists say an equation is balanced when it accurately represents conservation of mass. How can you write a balanced chemical equation?

❶ **Write the Equation** Suppose you want to write a balanced chemical equation for the reaction between hydrogen and oxygen that forms water. To begin, write the correct formulas for both reactants and product.

$$H_2 \quad + \quad O_2 \quad \longrightarrow \quad H_2O$$

Reactants   Products

Place the reactants, H_2 and O_2, on the left side of the arrow, separated by a plus sign. Then write the product, H_2O, on the right side of the arrow.

❷ **Count the Atoms** Count the number of atoms of each element on each side of the equation. You find two atoms of oxygen in the reactants but only one atom of oxygen in the product.

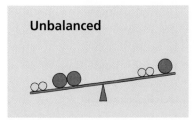

Unbalanced

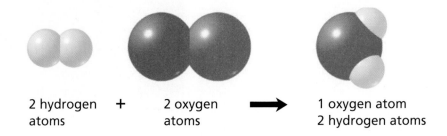

2 hydrogen   **+**   2 oxygen   ⟶   1 oxygen atom
atoms   atoms   2 hydrogen atoms

How can you get the number of oxygen atoms on both sides to be the same? You cannot change the formula for water to H_2O_2 because H_2O_2 is the formula for hydrogen peroxide, a completely different compound. So, how can you show that mass is conserved?

❸ **Use Coefficients to Balance Atoms** To balance the equation, use coefficients. A **coefficient** (koh uh FISH unt) is a number placed in front of a chemical formula in an equation. It tells you how many atoms or molecules of a reactant or a product take part in the reaction. If the coefficient is 1, you don't need to write it.

Balance the number of oxygen atoms by writing the coefficient 2 for water. That's like saying "2 × H₂O." Now there are two oxygen atoms—one in each molecule of water.

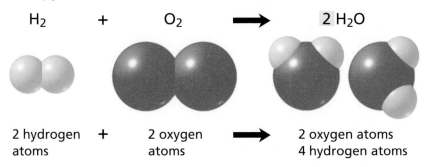

$$H_2 \quad + \quad O_2 \quad \longrightarrow \quad 2\,H_2O$$

2 hydrogen   +   2 oxygen   2 oxygen atoms
atoms   atoms   4 hydrogen atoms

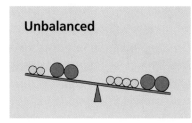

Unbalanced

Balancing the oxygen atoms throws off the hydrogen atoms. There are now two hydrogen atoms in the reactants and four in the product. How can you balance the hydrogen? Try doubling the number of hydrogen atoms on the left side of the equation by writing the coefficient 2 for hydrogen.

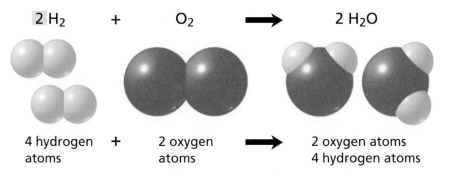

$$2\,H_2 \quad + \quad O_2 \quad \longrightarrow \quad 2\,H_2O$$

4 hydrogen   +   2 oxygen   2 oxygen atoms
atoms   atoms   4 hydrogen atoms

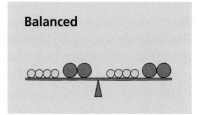

Balanced

❹ **Look Back and Check** The equation is balanced. It tells you that two molecules of hydrogen react with one molecule of oxygen to yield two molecules of water. Count the atoms in the balanced equation again to see that the equation is correct.

Math Analyzing Data

Balancing Chemical Equations

Magnesium metal (Mg) reacts with oxygen gas (O_2) forming magnesium oxide (MgO). To write a balanced equation for this reaction, first write the equation using the formulas of the reactants and products. Then, count the number of atoms of each element.

1. **Balancing Chemical Equations** Balance the equation for the reaction of sodium metal (Na) with oxygen gas (O_2), forming sodium oxide (Na_2O).
2. **Balancing Chemical Equations** Balance the equation for the reaction of tin (Sn) with chlorine gas (Cl_2), forming tin chloride ($SnCl_2$).

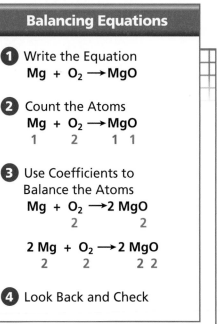

Balancing Equations

❶ Write the Equation
$$Mg + O_2 \longrightarrow MgO$$

❷ Count the Atoms
$$Mg + O_2 \longrightarrow MgO$$
1   2   1 1

❸ Use Coefficients to Balance the Atoms
$$Mg + O_2 \longrightarrow 2\,MgO$$
          2   2

$$2\,Mg + O_2 \longrightarrow 2\,MgO$$
  2   2   2 2

❹ Look Back and Check

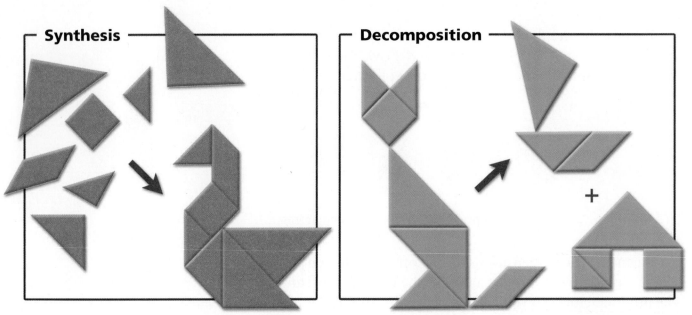

Synthesis

Decomposition

Types of Reactions

Three categories of chemical reactions are synthesis, decomposition, and replacement. **Making Models** *How do these different geometric shapes act as models for elements and compounds in reactions?*

Classifying Chemical Reactions

Substances may combine to make a more complex substance. They may break apart to make simpler substances. Or, they may even exchange parts. In each case, new substances form. **Many chemical reactions can be classified in one of three categories: synthesis, decomposition, or replacement.**

Synthesis Have you ever listened to music from a synthesizer? You can hear many different notes and types of sounds combined to make music. To synthesize is to put things together. In chemistry, when two or more elements or compounds combine to make a more complex substance, the process is called **synthesis** (SIN thuh sis). The reaction of hydrogen and oxygen to make water is a synthesis reaction.

Decomposition In contrast to a synthesis reaction, a process called **decomposition** breaks down compounds into simpler products. You may have a bottle of hydrogen peroxide (H_2O_2) in your house to clean cuts. If you keep such a bottle for a very long time, you'll have water instead. The hydrogen peroxide decomposes into water and oxygen gas.

$$2\ H_2O_2 \longrightarrow 2\ H_2O + O_2$$

Replacement When one element replaces another in a compound, or when two elements in different compounds trade places, the process is called **replacement.** Look at this example:

$$2\ Cu_2O + C \longrightarrow 4\ Cu + CO_2$$

Copper metal can be obtained by heating copper oxide with carbon. The carbon takes the place of copper.

Replacement

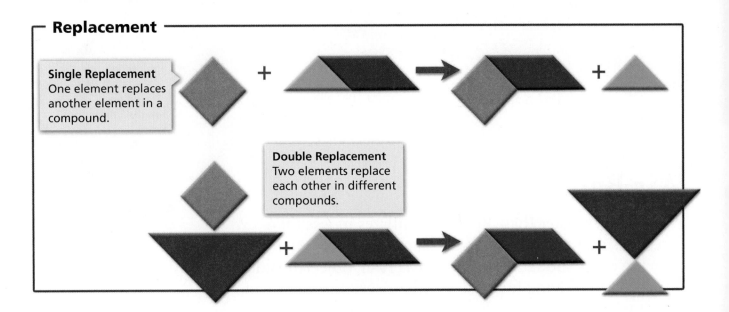

Single Replacement
One element replaces another element in a compound.

Double Replacement
Two elements replace each other in different compounds.

The reaction between copper oxide and carbon is called a *single* replacement reaction because one element, carbon, replaces another element, copper, in the compound. In a *double* replacement reaction, elements in one compound appear to "trade places" with elements in another compound. The following reaction is an example of a double replacement:

$$FeS + 2\,HCl \longrightarrow FeCl_2 + H_2S$$

Use Figure 11 to help you track what happens to elements in different types of chemical reactions.

Section 2 Assessment

🎯 **Target Reading Skill** Building Vocabulary Use your definitions to help you answer the questions.

Reviewing Key Concepts

1. a. Identifying What do the formulas, arrow, and plus signs in a chemical equation tell you?

b. Comparing and Contrasting How are reactants and products treated the same in a chemical reaction? How are they treated differently?

2. a. Summarizing In your own words, state the meaning of the principle of conservation of mass.

b. Applying Concepts If the total mass of the products of a reaction is 250 g, what was the total mass of the reactants?

3. a. Reviewing What are three types of chemical reactions?

b. Inferring What is the smallest possible number of products in a decomposition reaction?

c. Classifying Classify the following reaction:
$$P_4O_{10} + 6\,H_2O \longrightarrow 4\,H_3PO_4$$

Math Practice

Balance the following equations:

4. $Fe_2O_3 + C \longrightarrow Fe + CO_2$

5. $SO_2 + O_2 \longrightarrow SO_3$

AIR BAG &
SEAT BELT
SAFETY
CAMPAIGN

Air Bags

What moves faster than 300 km/h, inflates in less than a second, and saves lives? An air bag, of course! When a moving car is suddenly stopped in a crash, objects inside the car keep moving forward. Death or serious injury can result when passengers hit the hard parts of the car's interior. Air bags, working with seat belts, can slow or stop a person's forward motion in a crash.

How Do Air Bags Increase Safety?

Before front air bags became a requirement in the 1990s, seat belts were the only restraints for passengers in cars. Seat belts do a great job of keeping people from flying forward in a crash, but even with seat belts, some movement takes place. Air bags were designed as a second form of protection. They provide a buffer zone between a person and the steering wheel, dashboard, or windshield.

$$2\ NaN_3 \longrightarrow 2\ Na + 3\ N_2$$

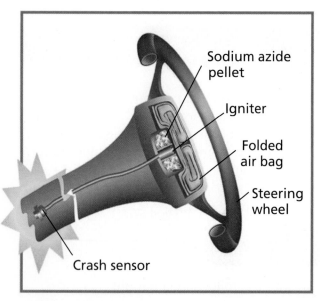

Sodium azide pellet

Igniter

Folded air bag

Steering wheel

Crash sensor

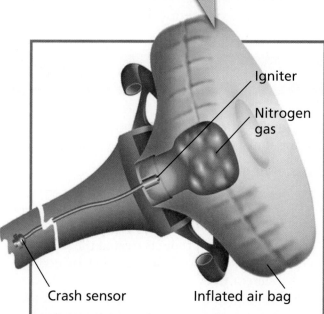

Igniter

Nitrogen gas

Crash sensor

Inflated air bag

Collision Detected
The crash sensor is located toward the front of the car. The sensor detects an impact and sends a signal to the air bag igniter to start the chemical reaction.

Air Bag Inflates
Pellets of a compound called sodium azide (NaN_3) are heated, causing a rapid decomposition reaction. This reaction releases sodium metal (Na) and nitrogen gas (N_2), which inflate the air bag in about 30 milliseconds.

During a crash test, the air bag should inflate upon impact.

Cushion or Curse?

Air bags save hundreds of lives each year. Still, if your body is too close to the air bag when it inflates, the impact of the expanding bag may do more harm than good. Front air bags are designed for adults but can pose a danger to smaller, lightweight adults and children. The risk of death to children who ride in the front seat is about one-third higher than the risk if they ride in back. That is why children should never ride in a front seat. They are safer in the back seat.

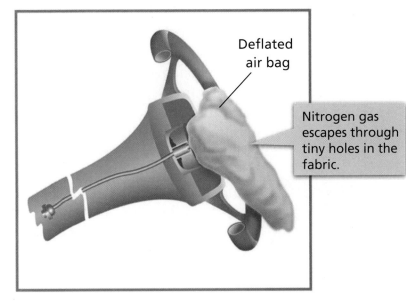

Deflated air bag

Nitrogen gas escapes through tiny holes in the fabric.

Air Bag Deflates
Tiny holes in the fabric of the air bag allow some of the nitrogen gas to escape, so the bag starts to deflate by the time a person makes contact with it. In this way, the air bag provides a deflating cushion that slows forward movement.

▲ Car manufacturers must test their vehicles to verify that they meet minimum government safety standards. New cars are required to have air bags on both the driver and passenger sides.

Weigh the Impact

1. Identify the Need
Air bags are called supplemental restraint systems. Why is it so important to restrain people in a collision?

2. Research
Use the Internet to learn how air bags are being changed, added, and redesigned to improve their safety and effectiveness.

3. Write
Choose one type of new air bag technology and summarize it in a few short paragraphs.

For: More on air bags
Visit: PHSchool.com
Web Code: cgh-2020

Controlling Chemical Reactions

Reading Preview

Key Concepts
- How is activation energy related to chemical reactions?
- What factors affect the rate of a chemical reaction?

Key Terms
- activation energy
- concentration • catalyst
- enzyme • inhibitor

Target Reading Skill
Relating Cause and Effect As you read, identify the factors that can cause the rate of a chemical reaction to increase. Write the information in a graphic organizer like the one below.

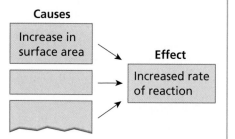

Causes

Increase in surface area	→	Effect
	→	Increased rate of reaction
	→	

Can You Speed Up or Slow Down a Reaction?
1. Put on your safety goggles and lab apron.
2. Obtain three 125-mL solutions of vitamin C and water—one at room temperature, one at about 75°C, and one chilled to between 5°C and 10°C.
3. Add 3 drops of iodine solution to each container and stir each with a clean spoon. Compare changes you observe in the solutions.
4. Clean up your work area and wash your hands.

Think It Over
Inferring What conclusion can you make about the effect of temperature on the reaction of iodine and vitamin C?

With a splintering crash, a bolt of lightning strikes a tree in the forest. The lightning splits the tree and sets fire to the leaves on the ground below it. The leaves are dry and crisp from drought. The crackling fire burns a black patch in the leaves. The flames leap to nearby dry twigs and branches on the ground. Soon, the forest underbrush is blazing, and the barks of trees start burning. Miles away in an observation tower, a ranger spots the fire and calls in the alarm—"Forest fire!"

Forest fires don't just happen. Many factors contribute to them—lightning and drought to name just two. But, in general, wood does not always burn easily. Yet, once wood does begin to burn, it gives off a steady supply of heat and light. Why is it so hard to start and maintain some chemical reactions?

◀ **Lightning can supply enough energy to ignite a forest fire.**

FIGURE 12
Modeling Activation Energy
The rock at the top of this hill cannot roll down the hill until a small push gets it going.
Making Models *How is this cartoon a kind of model for the role of activation energy in a chemical reaction?*

Energy and Reactions

To understand why it can be hard to start some chemical reactions, look at Figure 12. The rock at the top of the hill can fall over the cliff, releasing energy when it crashes into the rocks at the bottom. Yet it remains motionless until it's pushed over the small hump.

Activation Energy Every chemical reaction is like that rock. A reaction won't begin until the reactants have enough energy to push them "over the hump." The energy is used to break the chemical bonds of the reactants. Then, the atoms begin to form the new chemical bonds of the products. The **activation energy** is the minimum amount of energy needed to start a chemical reaction. **All chemical reactions need a certain amount of activation energy to get started.**

Consider the reaction in which hydrogen and oxygen form water. This reaction gives off a large amount of energy. But if you just mix the two gases together, they can remain unchanged for years. For the reaction to start, a tiny amount of activation energy is needed—even just an electric spark. Once a few molecules of hydrogen and oxygen react, the rest will quickly follow because the first few reactions provide activation energy for more molecules to react. Overall, the reaction releases more energy than it uses. Recall from Section 1 that this type of reaction is described as exothermic.

Discovery CHANNEL
SCHOOL™

Chemical Reactions

Video Preview
▶ Video Field Trip
Video Assessment

 Reading Checkpoint **What is the function of a spark in a reaction between hydrogen gas and oxygen gas?**

Exothermic and Endothermic Reactions Every chemical reaction needs activation energy to get started. Whether or not a reaction needs still more energy from the environment to keep going depends on if it is exothermic or endothermic.

Exothermic reactions follow the pattern you can see in the first diagram in Figure 13. The dotted line marks the energy of the reactants before the reaction begins. The peak in the graph shows the activation energy. Notice that at the end of the reaction, the products have less energy than the reactants. This difference results in a release of heat. The burning of fuel, such as wood, natural gas, or oil, is an example of an exothermic reaction. People can make use of the heat that is released to warm their homes and cook food.

Now look at the graph of an endothermic reaction on the right of Figure 13. Endothermic reactions also need activation energy to get started. But, in addition, they need energy to keep going. Notice that the energy of the products is higher than that of the reactants. This difference tells you that the reaction must absorb energy to continue.

When you placed baking soda in vinegar in the Discover activity in Section 1, the thermal energy already present in the solution was enough to start the reaction. The reaction continued by drawing energy from the solution, making the solution feel colder. But most endothermic reactions require a continuous source of heat to occur. For example, baking bread requires added heat until the baking process is completed.

Reading Checkpoint **In what type of reaction do the reactants have less energy than the products?**

FIGURE 13
Energy Changes in Chemical Reactions
Both exothermic and endothermic reactions need energy to get started. **Reading Graphs** *What does the peak in the curve in each graph represent?*

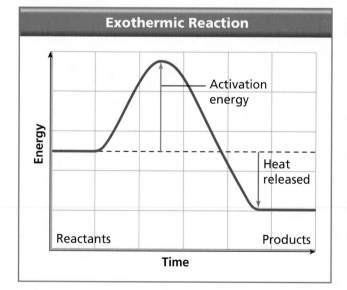

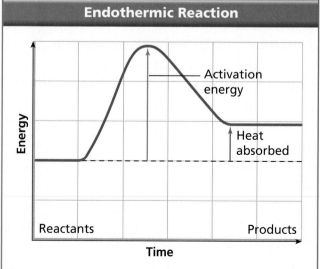

Rates of Chemical Reactions

Chemical reactions don't all occur at the same rate. Some, like explosions, are very fast. Others, like the rusting of metal, are much slower. Also, a particular reaction can occur at different rates depending on the conditions.

If you want to make a chemical reaction happen faster, you need to get more reactant particles together more often and with more energy. To slow down a reaction, you need to do the opposite. **Chemists can control rates of reactions by changing factors such as surface area, temperature, and concentration, and by using substances called catalysts and inhibitors.**

Surface Area Look at Figure 14. The wreckage used to be a grain elevator. It exploded when grain dust ignited in the air above the stored grain. Although the grain itself doesn't react violently in air, the grain dust can. This difference is related to surface area. When a chunk of solid substance reacts with a liquid or gas, only the particles on the surface of the solid come into contact with the other reactant. But if you break the solid into smaller pieces, more particles are exposed and the reaction happens faster. Sometimes, speeding up a reaction this way is dangerous. Other times, increasing surface area can be useful. For example, chewing your food breaks it into smaller pieces that your body can digest more easily and quickly.

FIGURE 14
Surface Area and Reaction Rate
Grain dust reacts explosively with oxygen. Minimizing grain dust in a grain elevator can help prevent an accident like the one shown here.

Temperature Another way to increase the rate of a reaction is to increase its temperature. When you heat a substance, its particles move faster. Faster-moving particles increase the reaction rate in two ways. First, the particles come in contact more often, which means there are more chances for a reaction to happen. Second, faster-moving particles have more energy. This increased energy causes more particles of the reactants to get over the activation energy "hump."

In contrast, reducing temperature slows down reaction rates. For example, milk contains bacteria, which carry out thousands of chemical reactions as they live and reproduce. At room temperature, those reactions happen faster and milk spoils more quickly. You store milk and other foods in the refrigerator because keeping foods cold slows down those reactions, so your foods stay fresh longer.

Concentration A third way to increase the rate of a chemical reaction is to increase the concentration of the reactants. **Concentration** is the amount of a substance in a given volume. For example, adding a small spoonful of sugar to a glass of lemonade will make it sweet. But adding a large spoonful of sugar makes the lemonade sweeter. The glass with more sugar has a greater concentration of sugar molecules.

Increasing the concentration of reactants supplies more particles to react. Compare the two reactions of acid and magnesium metal in Figure 15. The test tube on the left has a lower concentration of acid. This reaction is slower than the one on the right, where the acid concentration is higher. You see evidence for the increased rate of reaction in the greater amount of gas bubbles produced.

✓ Reading Checkpoint **Why may an increase in temperature affect the rate of a chemical reaction?**

FIGURE 15
Concentration and Reaction Rate
Bubbles of hydrogren gas form when magnesium reacts with acid.
Relating Cause and Effect *What makes the reaction faster in the test tube on the right?*

Catalysts Another way to control the rate of a reaction is to change the activation energy needed. A **catalyst** (KAT uh list) is a material that increases the rate of a reaction by lowering the activation energy. Although catalysts affect a reaction's rate, they are not permanently changed by a reaction. For this reason catalysts are not considered reactants.

Many chemical reactions happen at temperatures that would kill living things. Yet, some of these reactions are necessary for life. The cells in your body (as in all living things) contain biological catalysts called **enzymes** (EN zymz). Your body has thousands of different enzymes. Each one is specific—it affects only one chemical reaction.

As shown in Figure 16, enzymes provide a surface on which reactions can take place. By bringing reactant molecules close together, the enzyme lowers the activation energy needed. In this way, enzymes make chemical reactions that are necessary for life happen at a low temperature.

Inhibitors Sometimes a reaction is more useful when it can be slowed down rather than speeded up. A material used to decrease the rate of a reaction is an **inhibitor.** Most inhibitors work by preventing reactants from coming together. Usually they combine with one of the reactants either permanently or temporarily. Inhibitors include preservatives added to food products to prevent them from becoming stale or spoiling.

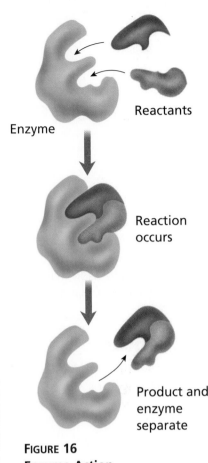

FIGURE 16
Enzyme Action
After a reaction, an enzyme molecule is unchanged.

Section 3 Assessment

Target Reading Skill Relating Cause and Effect Use the information in your graphic organizer about speeding up chemical reactions to help you answer Question 2 below.

Reviewing Key Concepts

1. a. **Defining** What is activation energy?
   b. **Describing** What role does activation energy play in chemical reactions?
   c. **Making Generalizations** Look at the diagram in Figure 13, and make a generalization about activation energy in exothermic and endothermic reactions.
2. a. **Identifying** What are four ways that chemists can control the rates of chemical reactions?
   b. **Applying Concepts** Which would react more quickly in a chemical reaction: a single sugar cube or an equal mass of sugar crystals? Explain.

Lab zone **At-Home Activity**

Comparing Reaction Rates Place an iron nail in a plastic cup. Add enough water to almost cover the nail. Place a small piece of fine steel wool in another cup and add the same amount of water. Ask family members to predict what will happen overnight. The next day, examine the nail and steel wool. Compare the amount of rust on each. Were your family's predictions correct? Explain how surface areas affect reaction rates.

Temperature and Enzyme Activity

Problem

Catalase is an enzyme that speeds up the break-down of hydrogen peroxide into water and oxygen gas. Hydrogen peroxide is a poisonous waste product of reactions in living things. How does temperature affect the action of the enzyme catalase?

Skills Focus

calculating, interpreting data, drawing conclusions

Materials

- forceps
- stopwatch
- test tube with a one-hole stopper
- 0.1% hydrogen peroxide solution
- filter paper disks soaked in liver preparation (catalase enzyme) and kept at four different temperatures (room temperature, 0–4°C, 37°C, and 100°C)
- container to hold water (beaker or bowl)

Procedure

1. Form a hypothesis that predicts how the action of the catalase enzyme will differ at the different temperatures to be tested.

2. Fill a container with water. Then fill a test tube with 0.1% hydrogen peroxide solution until the test tube is overflowing. Do this over a sink or the container of water.

3. Make a data table similar to the one shown.

4. Moisten the small end of a one-hole stopper with water.

5. Using forceps, remove a filter paper disk soaked in liver preparation (catalase enzyme) that has been kept at room temperature. Stick it to the moistened end of the one-hole stopper.

6. Your partner should be ready with the stopwatch for the next step.

7. Place the stopper firmly into the test tube, hold your thumb over the hole, and quickly invert the test tube. Start the stopwatch. Put the inverted end of the test tube into the container of water, as shown in the photograph, and remove your thumb.

Data Table		
Temperature (°C)	Time (sec)	Average Time for Class (sec)

Catalase from blood reacts ▶
with hydrogen peroxide.

8. Observe what happens to the filter paper inside the test tube. Record the time it takes for the disk to rise to the top. If the disk does not rise within 2 minutes, record "no reaction" and go on to Step 9.

9. Rinse the test tube and repeat the procedure with catalase enzyme disks kept at 0°C, 37°C, and 100°C. **CAUTION:** *When you remove the disk kept in the hot water bath, do not use your bare hands. Avoid spilling the hot water.*

Analyze and Conclude

1. **Observing** What makes the disk float to the top of the inverted test tube?

2. **Calculating** Calculate the average time for each temperature based on the results of the entire class. Enter the results in your data table.

3. **Graphing** Make a line graph of the data you collected. Label the horizontal axis (*x*-axis) "Temperature" with a scale from 0°C to 100°C. Label the vertical axis (*y*-axis) "Time" with a scale from 0 to 30 seconds. Plot the class average time for each temperature.

4. **Interpreting Data** What evidence do you have that your hypothesis from Step 1 is either supported or not supported?

5. **Interpreting Data** How is the time it takes the disk to rise to the top of the inverted tube related to the rate of the reaction?

6. **Drawing Conclusions** What can you conclude about the activity of the enzyme at the various temperatures you tested? (*Hint:* Enzyme activity is greater when the rate of reaction is faster.)

7. **Predicting** Make a prediction about how active the enzyme would be at 10°C, 60°C, and 75°C. Give reasons to support your prediction.

8. **Communicating** A buildup of hydrogen peroxide in living things can damage cells. The normal human body temperature is 37°C. Write a paragraph relating your results to the body's temperature and its need to break down hydrogen peroxide.

Design an Experiment

The activity of an enzyme also depends upon the concentration of the enzyme. Design an experiment that explores the relationship between enzyme activity and enzyme concentration. (Your teacher can give you disks soaked with different enzyme concentrations.) *Obtain your teacher's permission before carrying out your investigation.*

Go Online
PHSchool.com
For: Data sharing
Visit: PHSchool.com
Web Code: cgd-2023

Fire and Fire Safety

Reading Preview

Key Concepts
- What are the three things necessary to maintain a fire?
- Why should you know about the causes of fire and how to prevent a fire?

Key Terms
- combustion • fuel

Target Reading Skill
Using Prior Knowledge Before you read, write what you know about fire safety in a graphic organizer like the one below. As you read, continue to write in what you learn.

What You Know
1. A fire needs fuel to burn.
2.

What You Learned
1.
2.

Firefighters battle a blaze. ▼

Discover Activity

How Does Baking Soda Affect a Fire?

1. Put on your safety goggles.
2. Secure a small candle in a holder or a ball of clay. After instructions from your teacher, use a match to light the candle.
3. Place a beaker next to the candle. Measure 1 large spoonful of baking soda into the beaker. Add about 100 mL of water and stir. Add about 100 mL of vinegar.
4. As soon as the mixture stops foaming, tip the beaker as if you are pouring something out of it onto the flame. **CAUTION:** *Do not pour any liquid on the candle.*
5. Observe what happens to the flame.

Think It Over

Developing Hypotheses The gas produced in the beaker was carbon dioxide, CO_2. Based on the results of this experiment, develop a hypothesis to explain what you observed in Step 5.

The call comes in. Fire! A blaze has been spotted in a warehouse near gasoline storage tanks. Firefighters scramble aboard the ladder truck and the hose truck. Lights flash, sirens blare, and traffic swerves to clear a path for the trucks. The firefighters know from their training that fire is a chemical reaction that can be controlled—but only if they reach it in time.

Understanding Fire

Fire is the result of **combustion,** a rapid reaction between oxygen and a substance called a fuel. A **fuel** is a material that releases energy when it burns. Common fuels include oil, wood, gasoline, natural gas, and paper. Combustion of these types of fuel always produces carbon dioxide and water. When fuels don't burn completely, products such as smoke and poisonous gases may be produced.

The Fire Triangle Although a combustion reaction is very exothermic and fast, a fire cannot start unless conditions are right. **The following three things are necessary to start and maintain a fire— fuel, oxygen, and heat.**

You probably know that oxygen is one of the gases in air. About 20 percent of the air around you is composed of oxygen gas. If air can reach the fuel, so can oxygen. A large fire can create a strong draft that pulls air toward it. As the air around the flame is heated, it rises rapidly. Cooler air flows toward the fire, replacing the heated air and bringing a fresh supply of oxygen. If you stand in front of a fire in a fireplace, you can feel the air flow toward the fire.

Heat is a part of the fire triangle. Fuel and oxygen can be together, but they won't react until something provides the activation energy to start combustion. This energy can come from a lighted match, an electric spark, or the heat from a stove. Once combustion starts, the heat released supplies more activation energy to keep the reaction going.

Once started, a fire can continue burning as long as all components of the fire triangle are available. Coal in abandoned mines under the town of Centralia, Pennsylvania, started burning in 1962. The coal is still burning. Many old airshafts lead into the tunnels. Because some airshafts cannot be located and sealed, air continues to flow into the mines, supporting the fire. Heat and poisonous gases coming up from the fire through cracks in the ground made living in Centralia difficult. Everyone eventually moved away. No one knows how long this fire will continue to burn.

Reading Checkpoint What is heat's role in starting a fire?

FIGURE 17
The Fire Triangle
The fire triangle can be controlled in the grill below. If any point of the fire triangle is missing, a fire will not continue.
Applying Concepts *How would closing the lower air vents affect the fire?*

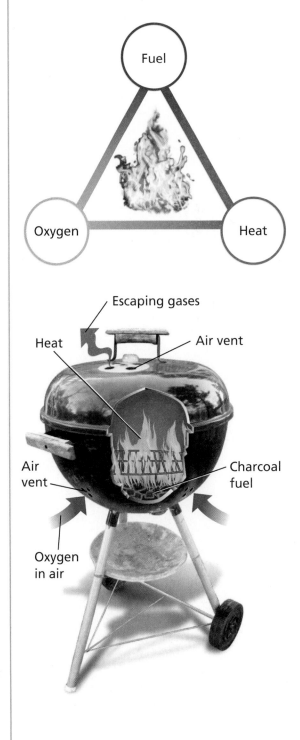

Fuel

Oxygen

Heat

Escaping gases

Heat

Air vent

Air vent

Charcoal fuel

Oxygen in air

Controlling Fire Use your knowledge of chemical reactions to think of ways to control a fire. What if you remove one part of the fire triangle? For example, you can get the fuel away from the flames. You can also keep oxygen from getting to the fuel. Finally, you can cool the combustion reaction.

How do firefighters usually fight fires? They use hoses to spray huge amounts of water on the flames. Water removes two parts of the fire triangle. First, water covers the fuel, which keeps it from coming into contact with oxygen. Second, evaporation of the water uses a large amount of heat, causing the fire to cool. Without heat, there isn't enough energy to continue the combustion. Therefore, the reaction stops.

Home Fire Safety

Every year, fire claims thousands of lives in the United States. **If you know how to prevent fires in your home and what to do if a fire starts, you are better prepared to take action.** You may save your home or even your life! The most common sources of home fires are small heaters, cooking, and faulty electrical wiring. The fires that cause the most deaths start from carelessness with cigarettes.

Fighting Fires You can fight a small fire by using what you know about the fire triangle. For example, carbon dioxide gas can smother a fire by preventing contact between the fuel and oxygen in the air. Therefore, you can put out a small fire on the stove by throwing baking soda on it. Baking soda decomposes when heated and releases carbon dioxide gas. Or, you can use the cover of a saucepan to cut off the flow of oxygen.

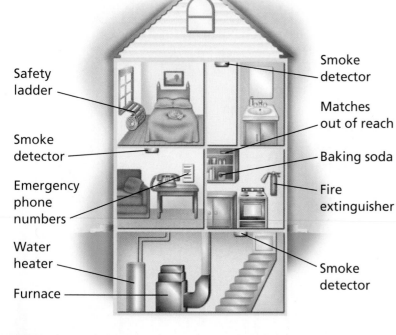

Safety ladder

Smoke detector

Emergency phone numbers

Water heater

Furnace

Smoke detector

Matches out of reach

Baking soda

Fire extinguisher

Smoke detector

FIGURE 18
A Fire-Safe House
This fire-safe house has many fire-prevention and fire safety features. *Inferring Why are smoke detectors located on every floor?*

A small fire is easy to control. You can cool a match enough to stop combustion just by blowing on it. A small fire in a trash can may be doused with a pan of water. If the fire spreads to the curtains, however, even a garden hose might not deliver enough water to put it out.

One of the most effective ways to fight a small fire is with a fire extinguisher. But a fire that is growing as you fight it is out of control. If a fire is out of control, there is only one safe thing to do—get away from the fire and call the fire department.

Preventing Trouble The best form of fire safety is prevention. Figure 18 shows some features of a fire-safe house. You can also check your home to be sure that all flammable items are stored safely away from sources of flames, such as the kitchen stove. Fires can be dangerous and deadly, but many fires can be prevented if you are careful. Understanding the chemistry of fire gives you a way to reduce risk and increase your family's safety.

 How does baking soda put a fire out?

FIGURE 19
Fire-Prevention Devices
Fire extinguishers and baking soda can be used to interrupt the fire triangle. Smoke detectors can help you identify a fire and escape to safety.

Section 4 Assessment

Target Reading Skill Previewing Visuals Review your graphic organizer and revise it based on what you just learned in the section.

Reviewing Key Concepts

1. **a. Listing** What three things are required for combustion?
   b. Explaining How does the fire triangle help you control fire?
   c. Applying Concepts To stop a forest fire, firefighters may remove all the trees in a strip of land that lies in the path of the fire. What part of the fire triangle is affected? Explain.
2. **a. Reviewing** Why is it important to know about the causes of fire and how to prevent fires?
   b. Identifying What are the three most common causes of home fires?
   c. Problem Solving Choose one common cause of home fires. Describe measures that can be taken to prevent fires of this type.

Lab zone At-Home Activity

Family Safety Plan Work with your family to formulate a fire safety plan. How can fires be prevented in your home? How can fires be put out if they occur? Is there a functioning smoke detector on each floor of the home, especially near the bedrooms? How can the fire department be contacted in an emergency? Design a fire escape route. Make sure all family members know the route as well as a meeting place outside.

The BIG Idea   **Chemical Changes in Matter** Chemical reactions are processes in which substances react and form one or more new substances.

1 Observing Chemical Change

Key Concepts

- Matter can be described in terms of two kinds of properties—physical properties and chemical properties. Changes in matter can be described in terms of physical changes and chemical changes.

- Chemical changes occur when bonds break and new bonds form.

- Chemical reactions involve two main kinds of changes that you can observe—formation of new substances and changes in energy.

Key Terms

matter	chemical reaction
chemistry	precipitate
physical property	endothermic reaction
chemical property	exothermic reaction
physical change	

2 Describing Chemical Reactions

Key Concepts

- Chemical equations use chemical formulas and other symbols instead of words to summarize a reaction.

- The principle of conservation of mass states that, in a chemical reaction, the total mass of the reactants must equal the total mass of the products.

- To describe a reaction accurately, a chemical equation must show the same number of each type of atom on both sides of the equation.

- Many chemical reactions can be classified in one of three categories: synthesis, decomposition, or replacement.

Key Terms

chemical equation	open system
reactant	coefficient
product	synthesis
conservation of mass	decomposition
closed system	replacement

3 Controlling Chemical Reactions

Key Concepts

- All chemical reactions need a certain amount of activation energy to get started.

- Chemists can control rates of reactions by changing factors such as surface area, temperature, and concentration, and by using substances called catalysts and inhibitors.

Key Terms

activation energy
concentration
catalyst
enzyme
inhibitor

4 Fire and Fire Safety

Key Concepts

- The following three things are necessary to start and maintain a fire—fuel, oxygen, and heat.

- If you know how to prevent fires in your home and what to do if a fire starts, you are better prepared to take action.

Key Terms

combustion
fuel

Review and Assessment

Go Online
PHSchool.com

For: Self-Assessment
Visit: PHSchool.com
Web Code: cga-2020

Organizing Information

Concept Mapping Copy the chemical reactions concept map onto a separate sheet of paper. Then complete it and add a title. (For more on Concept Mapping, see the Skills Handbook.)

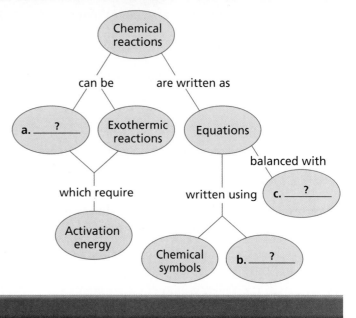

Reviewing Key Terms

Choose the letter of the best answer.

1. Which of the following is *not* a physical property?
   a. flexibility
   b. ability to catch fire
   c. melting point
   d. ability to conduct electricity

2. A chemical reaction that gives off heat is likely to be
   a. endothermic.
   b. a precipitate.
   c. a physical change.
   d. exothermic.

3. You can balance a chemical equation by changing the
   a. subscripts.
   b. coefficients.
   c. reactants.
   d. products.

4. A chemical reaction in which two elements combine to form a compound is called a
   a. synthesis reaction.
   b. replacement reaction.
   c. decomposition reaction.
   d. precipitation reaction.

5. The activation energy of a chemical reaction
   a. is supplied by a catalyst.
   b. is released at the end.
   c. starts the reaction.
   d. changes with time.

6. A chemical reaction in which a fuel combines rapidly with oxygen is a (an)
   a. inhibited reaction.
   b. combustion reaction.
   c. enzyme reaction.
   d. endothermic reaction.

Writing in Science

Explanation You are a writer for a children's book about chemistry. Write a paragraph that young children would understand that explains the concept of "activation energy." Be sure to use examples, such as the burning of wood or gas.

Chemical Reactions

Video Preview
Video Field Trip
▶ Video Assessment

Review and Assessment

Checking Concepts

7. What are the two kinds of changes that occur in matter? Describe how you can tell one from the other.

8. Why can't you balance a chemical equation by changing the subscripts of the reactants or the products?

9. You find the mass of a piece of iron metal, let it rust, and measure the mass again. The mass has increased. Does this violate the principle of conservation of mass? Explain.

10. How do enzymes in your body make chemical reactions occur at safe temperatures?

11. Why does spraying water on a fire help to put the fire out?

12. How are inhibitors useful in controlling chemical reactions?

Thinking Critically

13. **Problem Solving** Steel that is exposed to water and salt rusts quickly. If you were a shipbuilder, how would you protect a new ship? Explain why your solution works.

14. **Classifying** The following are balanced equations for chemical reactions. Classify each of the equations as synthesis, decomposition, or replacement.

    a. $2\,Al + Fe_2O_3 \longrightarrow 2\,Fe + Al_2O_3$
    b. $2\,Ag + S \longrightarrow Ag_2S$
    c. $CaCO_3 \longrightarrow CaO + CO_2$
    d. $2\,NO + O_2 \longrightarrow 2\,NO_2$

15. **Relating Cause and Effect** Firefighters open doors very carefully because sometimes a room will burst violently into flames when the door is opened. Based on your knowledge of the fire triangle, explain why this happens.

16. **Inferring** Some statues are made of materials that can react in acid rain and begin to dissolve. It has been observed that statues with smooth surfaces are dissolved by acid rain much slower than statues with very detailed carvings. Explain this observation.

Math Practice

Balance the chemical equations in Questions 17–20.

17. $MgO + HBr \longrightarrow MgBr_2 + H_2O$

18. $N_2 + O_2 \longrightarrow N_2O_5$

19. $C_2H_4 + O_2 \longrightarrow CO_2 + H_2O$

20. $Fe + HCl \longrightarrow FeCl_2 + H_2$

Applying Skills

Use the energy diagram to answer Questions 21–23.

The two graphs below represent the same chemical reaction under different conditions.

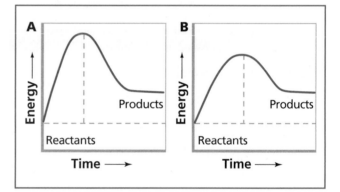

21. **Interpreting Data** How does the energy of the products compare with the energy of the reactants?

22. **Classifying** Tell whether this reaction is exothermic or endothermic.

23. **Applying Concepts** What change in condition might account for the lower "hump" in the second graph? Explain.

Lab zone Chapter **Project**

Performance Assessment Make a poster of your test results. Display your reaction chamber for the class. Discuss how your chamber was built to the specifications agreed upon by the class. Describe its safety features. Based on your results, rate how effectively your chamber works as a closed system.

Standardized Test Prep

Test-Taking Tip

Watching for Qualifiers

Many multiple-choice questions use qualifiers such as the words *best, except for, most,* and *least.* For example, you might be asked what is the *best* method for determining the density of a liquid. When you answer that kind of question, you need to read all the answer choices very carefully. Some of the answers may be correct, but not the best answer. In another question you may be told that a particular condition is satisfied by all the answer choices *except for* one. If you read the question too quickly, you may miss this two-word qualifier. In this type of question, the incorrect statement is actually the correct answer choice.

Sample Question

Each chemical equation below is correctly balanced *except for*

A $NaOH + HCl \longrightarrow NaCl + H_2O$
B $SO_3 + H_2O \longrightarrow H_2SO_4$
C $AgNO_3 + H_2S \longrightarrow Ag_2S + HNO_3$
D $Fe + H_2SO_4 \longrightarrow FeSO_4 + H_2$

Answer

The correct answer is **C.** A balanced chemical equation shows the same number of each type of atom on both sides of the equation. The left side of the equation shows a total of 1 Ag, 1 N, 3 O, 2 H, and 1 S. The right side shows 1 N and 3 O, but 2 Ag and only 1 H, so the equation is not balanced.

Choose the letter of the best answer.

1. Which of the following is the *best* evidence for a chemical reaction?
   A gas bubbles
   B formation of a new substance
   C change of state
   D change in temperature

2. Which shows a balanced chemical equation for the decomposition of aluminum oxide (Al_2O_3)?
   F $Al_2O_3 \longrightarrow 2\,Al + O_2$
   G $Al_2O_3 \longrightarrow 2\,Al + 3\,O_2$
   H $2\,Al_2O_3 \longrightarrow 4\,Al + O_2$
   J $2\,Al_2O_3 \longrightarrow 4\,Al + 3\,O_2$

Base your answers to Questions 3 and 4 on the diagram below. The diagram represents molecules of two different elements that are gases. The elements react chemically to produce a third gas.

3. The diagram represents a(n)
   A endothermic reaction in which energy is released.
   B exothermic reaction in which energy is absorbed.
   C exothermic reaction in which energy is released.
   D reaction in which energy is destroyed.

4. What can be inferred from the diagram?
   F Matter is not created or destroyed in a chemical reaction.
   G The rate of a reaction depends on the surface area of the reactants.
   H A gas molecule always consists of two identical atoms.
   J The product is carbon monoxide gas.

Constructed Response

5. Zinc metal (Zn) reacts with hydrochloric acid (HCl) to produce hydrogen gas (H_2) and zinc chloride ($ZnCl_2$). A scientist has powdered zinc and a chunk of zinc of equal mass. Available in the lab are dilute HCl and concentrated HCl. Which combination of zinc and acid would react most quickly? Explain why the combination you chose would make the reaction occur most quickly.

The BIG Idea
Properties of Matter

Q How may properties of acids and bases be determined?

Solutions containing transition metal ▶
compounds are often very colorful.

Lab zone™ **Chapter Project**

Make Your Own Indicator

As you learn about acids and bases in this chapter, you can make your own solutions that will tell you if something is an acid or a base. Then you can use your solutions to test for acids and bases among substances found in your home.

Your Goal To make acid-base indicators from flowers, fruits, vegetables, or other common plant materials

To complete the project, you must

- make one or more indicators that will turn colors in acids and bases
- use your indicators to test a number of substances
- compare your indicators to a standard pH scale
- rank the tested substances according to their pH
- follow the safety guidelines in Appendix A

Plan It! Brainstorm with your classmates about foods, spices, flowers, or other plant materials that have definite, deep colors. Think about fruits and vegetables you may find in a supermarket. These materials may make good candidates for your indicators.

Understanding Solutions

Reading Preview

Key Concepts
- What are the characteristics of solutions, colloids, and suspensions?
- What happens to the particles of a solute when a solution forms?
- How do solutes affect the freezing point and boiling point of a solvent?

Key Terms
- solution • solvent • solute
- colloid • suspension

Target Reading Skill

Identifying Main Ideas As you read the *What Is a Solution?* section, write the main idea in a graphic organizer like the one below. Then write supporting details that further explain the main idea.

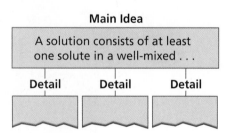

Main Idea

A solution consists of at least one solute in a well-mixed . . .

| Detail | Detail | Detail |

Discover **Activity**

What Makes a Mixture a Solution?

1. Put about 50 or 60 milliliters of water into a plastic cup. Add a spoonful of pepper and stir well.
2. To a similar amount of water in a second cup, add a spoonful of table salt. Stir well.
3. Compare the appearance of the two mixtures.

Think It Over

Observing What is the difference between the two mixtures? What other mixtures have you seen that are similar to pepper and water? That are similar to table salt and water?

Imagine a hot summer day. You've been outdoors and now you're really thirsty. A tall, cool glass of plain tap water would taste great. But exactly what is tap water?

Tap water is more than just water. It's a mixture of pure water (H_2O) and a variety of other substances, such as chloride, fluoride, and metallic ions. Gases, such as oxygen and carbon dioxide, are also dissolved in tap water. The dissolved substances give tap water its taste.

What Is a Solution?

Tap water is one example of a mixture called a solution. A **solution** is a well-mixed mixture that contains a solvent and at least one solute. The **solvent** is the part of a solution present in the largest amount. It dissolves the other substances. The **solute** is the substance that is present in a solution in a smaller amount and is dissolved by the solvent. **A solution has the same properties throughout. It contains solute particles (molecules or ions) that are too small to see.**

Solutions With Water In many common solutions, the solvent is water. Sugar in water, for example, is the starting solution for flavored soft drinks. Adding food coloring gives the drink color. Dissolving carbon dioxide gas in the mixture produces a fizzy soda. Water dissolves so many substances that it is often called the "universal solvent."

Life depends on water solutions. Nutrients used by plants are dissolved in water in the soil. Sap is a solution that carries sugar dissolved in water to tree cells. Water is the solvent in blood, saliva, and tears. Reactions in cells take place in solution. To keep cells working, you must replace the water you lose in sweat and urine—two other water solutions.

Solutions Without Water Many solutions are made with solvents other than water, as you can see in Figure 1. For example, gasoline is a solution of several different liquid fuels. You don't even need a liquid solvent to make solutions. A solution may be made of any combination of gases, liquids, or solids.

Reading Checkpoint **What solvent is essential to living things?**

Examples of Common Solutions		
Solute	**Solvent**	**Solution**
Gas	Gas	Air (oxygen and other gases in nitrogen)
Gas	Liquid	Soda water (carbon dioxide in water)
Liquid	Liquid	Antifreeze (ethylene glycol in water)
Solid	Liquid	Dental filling (silver in mercury)
Solid	Liquid	Ocean water (sodium chloride and other compounds in water)
Solid	Solid	Brass (zinc and copper)

FIGURE 1
Solutions can be made from any combination of solids, liquids, and gases.
Interpreting Photos *What are the solutes and solvent for stainless steel?*

Salt water is a solution of sodium chloride and other compounds in water.

The air in these gas bubbles is a solution of oxygen and other gases in nitrogen.

Stainless steel is a solution of chromium, nickel, and carbon in iron.

FIGURE 2
Comparing Three Mixtures
Solutions are different from colloids and suspensions.
Interpreting Photographs *In which mixture can you see the particles?*

Colloid
Fats and proteins in milk form globular particles that are big enough to scatter light, but are too small to be seen.

Suspension
Suspended particles of "snow" in water are easy to see.

Solution
In a solution of glass cleaner, particles are uniformly distributed and too small to scatter light.

Colloids and Suspensions

Not all mixtures are solutions. Colloids and suspensions are mixtures that have different properties than solutions.

Colloids Have you ever made a gelatin dessert? To do so, you stir powdered gelatin in hot water until the two substances are uniformly mixed. The liquid looks like a solution, but it's not. Gelatin is a colloid. A **colloid** (KAHL oyd) is a mixture containing small, undissolved particles that do not settle out.

Solutions and colloids differ in the size of their particles and how they affect the path of light. **A colloid contains larger particles than a solution. The particles are still too small to be seen easily, but are large enough to scatter a light beam.** For example, fog—a colloid that consists of water droplets in air—scatters the headlight beams of cars. In addition to gelatin and fog, milk, mayonnaise, shaving cream, and whipped cream are examples of colloids.

Suspensions If you did the Discover Activity, you noticed that no matter how much you stir pepper and water, the two never really seem to "mix" completely. When you stop stirring, you can still see pepper flakes floating on the water's surface and collecting at the bottom of the cup. Pepper and water make a suspension. A **suspension** (suh SPEN shun) is a mixture in which particles can be seen and easily separated by settling or filtration. **Unlike a solution, a suspension does not have the same properties throughout. It contains visible particles that are larger than the particles in solutions or colloids.**

Reading Checkpoint Which kind of mixture has the largest particles?

Lab zone Try This Activity

Scattered Light

1. Pour 50 mL of a gelatin-and-water mixture into a small, clean glass beaker.
2. Pour 50 mL of a saltwater solution into another clean beaker that is about the same size.
3. Compare the appearance of the two liquids.
4. In a darkened room, shine a small flashlight through the side of the beaker that contains gelatin. Repeat this procedure with the saltwater solution.
5. Compare the appearance of the light inside the two beakers.

Inferring What evidence tells you that gelatin is a colloid?

Particles in a Solution

Why do solutes seem to disappear when you mix them with a solvent? If you had a microscope powerful enough to look at the mixture's particles, what would you see? **When a solution forms, particles of the solute leave each other and become surrounded by particles of the solvent.**

Ionic and Molecular Solutes Figure 3 shows what happens when an ionic solid mixes with water. The positive and negative ions are attracted to the polar water molecules. Water molecules surround each ion as it leaves the surface of the crystal. As each layer of the solid is exposed, more ions can dissolve.

However, not every substance breaks into ions when it dissolves in water. A molecular solid, such as sugar, breaks up into individual neutral molecules. The polar water molecules attract the slightly polar sugar molecules. This causes the sugar molecules to move away from each other. But covalent bonds within the molecules are not broken.

Solutes and Conductivity You have a water solution, but you don't know if the solute is salt or sugar. How could you find out? Think about what you learned about the electrical conductivity of compounds. A solution of ionic compounds in water conducts electricity, but a water solution of molecular compounds may not. You could test the conductivity of the solution. If no ions are present (as in a sugar solution), electricity will not flow.

Reading Checkpoint Which kind of solution conducts electricity?

Go Online
active art

For: Salt Dissolving in Water activity
Visit: PHSchool.com
Web Code: cgp-2031

FIGURE 3
Salt Dissolving in Water
When an ionic solid—like table salt—dissolves, water molecules surround and separate the positive and negative ions. Notice that the sodium ions attract the oxygen ends of the water molecules.

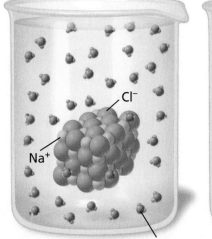

Water

Water

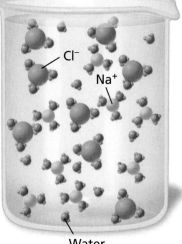

Water

Designing Experiments

How does the mass of a solute affect the boiling temperature of a given volume of water? Design an experiment using a solute, water, a balance, a hot plate, and a thermometer.

What variables should remain constant in your experiment? What is the manipulated variable? What will be the responding variable?

With approval from your teacher, do the experiment.

Effects of Solutes on Solvents

The freezing point of water is 0°C, and the boiling point is 100°C. These statements are true enough for pure water under everyday conditions, but the addition of solutes to water can change these properties. **Solutes lower the freezing point and raise the boiling point of a solvent.**

Lower Freezing Points Solutes lower the freezing point of a solvent. When liquid water freezes, water molecules join together to form crystals of solid ice. Pure water is made only of water molecules that freeze at 0°C. In a salt solution, solute particles are present in the water when it freezes. The solute particles make it harder for the water molecules to form crystals. The temperature must drop lower than 0°C for the solution to freeze. Figure 4 illustrates the particles in pure water and in a saltwater solution.

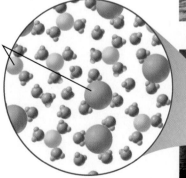

Freshwater lake ▶

Solute particles

Saltwater bay ▶

FIGURE 4
Salt's Effect on Freezing Point
Fresh water on the surface of a lake is frozen. Under similar conditions, salt water is not frozen.

Higher Boiling Points Solutes raise the boiling point of a solvent. To see why, think about the difference between the molecules of a liquid and those of a gas of the same substance. In a liquid, molecules are moving close to each other. In a gas, they are far apart and moving more rapidly. As the temperature of a liquid rises, the molecules gain energy and escape into the air. In pure water, all the molecules are water. But in a solution, some of the particles are water molecules and others are particles of solute. The presence of the solute makes it harder for the water molecules to escape, so more energy is needed. The temperature must go higher than 100°C for the water to boil.

Car manufacturers make use of the effects of solutes to protect engines from heat and cold. The coolant in a car radiator is a solution of water and another liquid called antifreeze. (Often the antifreeze is ethylene glycol.) The mixture of the two liquids has a higher boiling point and lower freezing point than water alone. Because this solution can absorb more of the heat given off by the running engine, risk of damage to the car from overheating is greatly reduced. The risk of damage from freezing in very cold weather is also reduced.

FIGURE 5
Calling Solutes to the Rescue?
This couple might have prevented their car from overheating by using the proper coolant in the radiator. **Relating Cause and Effect** *Explain how coolant works.*

 Reading Checkpoint **Does salt water have a lower or higher freezing point than pure water?**

Section 1 Assessment

Target Reading Skill Identifying Main Ideas Use your graphic organizer to help you answer Question 1 below.

Reviewing Key Concepts

1. a. Defining What is a solution?
   b. Comparing and Contrasting How are solutions different from colloids and suspensions?
   c. Inferring Suppose you mix food coloring in water to make it blue. Have you made a solution or a suspension? Explain.
2. a. Reviewing What happens to the solute particles when a solution forms?
   b. Sequencing Describe as a series of steps how table salt in water makes a solution that can conduct electricity.
3. a. Summarizing What effects do solutes have on a solvent's freezing and boiling points?

   b. Relating Cause and Effect Why is the temperature needed to freeze ocean water lower than the temperature needed to freeze the surface of a freshwater lake?
   c. Applying Concepts Why does salt sprinkled on icy roads cause the ice to melt?

Lab zone **At-Home Activity**

Passing Through With a family member, mix together a spoonful each of sugar and pepper in about 100 mL of warm water in a plastic container. Pour the mixture through a coffee filter into a second container. Ask your family member what happened to the sugar. Let the water evaporate overnight. Describe the difference between a solution and a suspension.

Speedy Solutions

Problem

How can you control the rate at which certain salts dissolve in water?

Skills Focus

controlling variables, drawing conclusions, designing experiments

Materials

- spoon
- solid stoppers, #4
- thermometers
- hot plate
- balance
- stirring rods
- ice
- timer or watch
- test tube rack
- test tubes, 25 × 150 mm
- coarse, rock, and table salt
- graduated cylinders and beakers, various sizes

Design a Plan 🔬 🥽 🧤

1. Make a list of all the variables you can think of that could affect the speed at which sodium chloride dissolves in water.

2. Compare your list with your classmates' lists, and add other variables.

3. Choose one variable from your list to test.

4. Write a hypothesis predicting the effect of your chosen variable on the speed of dissolving.

5. Decide how to work with your choice.
   - If you choose temperature, you might perform tests at 10°C, 20°C, 30°C, 40°C, and 50°C.
   - If you choose stirring, you might stir for various amounts of time.

6. Plan at least three tests for whichever variable you choose. Remember to control all other variables.

7. Write down a series of steps for your procedure and safety guidelines for your experiment. Be quite detailed in your plan.

8. As part of your procedure, prepare a data table in which to record your results. Fill in the headings on your table that identify the manipulated variable and the responding variable. (*Hint:* Remember to include units.)

Data Table			
Manipulated Variable	Dissolving Time		
	Test 1	Test 2	Test 3

9. Have your teacher approve your procedure, safety guidelines, and data table.

10. Perform the experiment.

Analyze and Conclude

1. **Controlling Variables** Which is the manipulated variable in your experiment? Which is the responding variable? How do you know which is which?

2. **Controlling Variables** List three variables you held constant in your procedure. Explain why controlling these variables makes your data more meaningful.

3. **Graphing** Make a line graph of your data. Label the horizontal axis with the manipulated variable. Label the vertical axis with the responding variable. Use an appropriate scale for each axis and label the units.

4. **Drawing Conclusions** Study the shape of your graph. Write a conclusion about the effect of the variable you tested on the speed at which salt dissolves in water.

5. **Drawing Conclusions** Does your conclusion support the hypothesis you wrote in Step 4 of your Plan? Explain.

6. **Designing Experiments** What advantage would there be in running your tests a second or third time?

7. **Predicting** If you switched procedures with another student who tested the same variable as you, do you think you would get the same results? Explain why or why not.

8. **Communicating** Write an e-mail to a friend explaining how your results relate to what you have learned about particles and solubility.

More to Explore

Choose another variable from the list you made in Steps 1 and 2 of your Plan. Repeat the process with that variable. Of the two variables you chose, which was easier to work with? Explain.

2 Concentration and Solubility

Reading Preview

Key Concepts
- How is concentration measured?
- Why is solubility useful in identifying substances?
- What factors affect the solubility of a substance?

Key Terms
- dilute solution
- concentrated solution
- solubility
- saturated solution
- unsaturated solution
- supersaturated solution

Target Reading Skill
Building Vocabulary As you read, carefully note the definition of each Key Term. Also note other details in the paragraph that contains the definition. Use all this information to write a meaningful sentence using the Key Term.

Making Maple Syrup ▼

Collecting sap

Boiling sap

Syrup

Lab zone Discover Activity

Does It Dissolve?

1. Put half a spoonful of soap flakes into a small plastic cup. Add about 50 mL of water and stir. Observe whether the soap flakes dissolve.
2. Clean out the cup. Repeat the test for a few other solids and liquids provided by your teacher.
3. Classify the items you tested into two groups: those that dissolved easily and those that did not.

Think It Over
Drawing Conclusions Based on your observations, does the physical state (solid or liquid) of a substance affect whether or not it dissolves in water? Explain.

Have you ever had syrup on your pancakes? You probably know that it's made from the sap of maple trees. Is something that sweet really made in a tree? Well, not exactly.

Concentration

The sap of a maple tree and pancake syrup differ in their concentrations. That is, they differ in the amount of solute (sugar) dissolved in a certain amount of solvent (water). The sap is a **dilute solution,** a mixture that has only a little solute dissolved in a certain amount of solvent. The syrup, on the other hand, is a **concentrated solution**—one that has a lot of solute dissolved in the solvent.

Changing Concentration You can change the concentration of a solution by adding more solute. You can also change it by adding or removing solvent. For example, fruit juices are sometimes packaged as concentrates, which are concentrated solutions. In making the concentrate, water was removed from the natural juice. When you make juice from the concentrate, you add water, making a dilute solution.

Measuring Concentration You know that maple syrup is more concentrated than maple sap. But you probably do not know the actual concentration of either solution. **To measure concentration, you compare the amount of solute to the amount of solvent or to the total amount of solution.**

Often, the method used to describe concentration depends on the type of solution. For example, you might measure the mass of a solute or solvent in grams. Or you might measure the volume of a solute or solvent in milliliters or liters. You can report concentration as the percent of solute in solution by volume or mass.

 Reading Checkpoint How can you change the concentration of a solution?

 **Math Skills**

Calculating a Concentration

To calculate the concentration of a solution, compare the amount of solute to the amount of solution and multiply by 100 percent.

For example, if a solution contains 10 grams of solute dissolved in 100 grams of solution, then its concentration can be reported as 10 percent.

$$\frac{10 \text{ g}}{100 \text{ g}} \times 100\% = 10\%$$

Practice Problem A solution contains 12 grams of solute dissolved in 36 grams of solution. What is the concentration of the solution?

Solubility

If a substance dissolves in water, a question you might ask is, "How much can dissolve?" Suppose you add sugar to a glass of iced tea. Is there a limit to how "sweet" you can make the tea? The answer is yes. At the temperature of iced tea, several spoonfuls of sugar are about all you can add. At some point, no matter how much you stir the tea, no more sugar will dissolve. **Solubility** is a measure of how much solute can dissolve in a solvent at a given temperature.

When you've added so much solute that no more dissolves, you have a **saturated solution.** If you add more sugar to a saturated solution of iced tea, the extra sugar just settles to the bottom of the glass. On the other hand, if you can continue to dissolve more solute, you still have an **unsaturated solution.**

FIGURE 6
Dissolving Sugar in Tea
At some point, this boy will not be able to dissolve any more sugar in his tea.
Applying Concepts *What term describes how much sugar can dissolve in a solvent?*

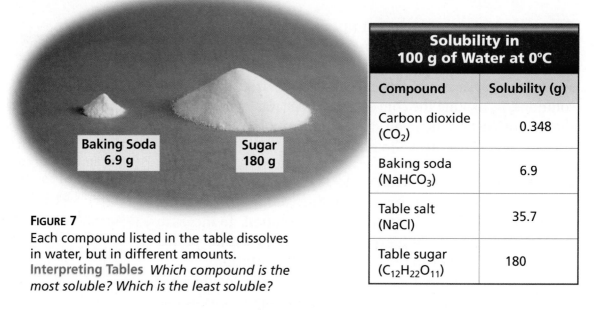

Solubility in 100 g of Water at 0°C	
Compound	Solubility (g)
Carbon dioxide (CO_2)	0.348
Baking soda ($NaHCO_3$)	6.9
Table salt (NaCl)	35.7
Table sugar ($C_{12}H_{22}O_{11}$)	180

Baking Soda 6.9 g

Sugar 180 g

FIGURE 7
Each compound listed in the table dissolves in water, but in different amounts.
Interpreting Tables *Which compound is the most soluble? Which is the least soluble?*

Working With Solubility The solubility of a substance tells you how much solute you can dissolve before a solution becomes saturated. Solubility is given for a specific solvent (such as water) under certain conditions (such as temperature). Look at the table in Figure 7. It compares the solubility of some familiar compounds. In this case, the solvent is water and the temperature is 0°C. From the table, you can see that 6.9 grams of baking soda will dissolve in 100 grams of water at 0°C. But the same mass of water at the same temperature will dissolve 180 grams of table sugar!

Using Solubility Solubility can be used to help identify a substance because it is a characteristic property of matter. Suppose you had a white powder that looked like table salt or sugar. You wouldn't know for sure whether the powder is salt or sugar. And you wouldn't use taste to identify it. Instead, you could measure its solubility in water at 0°C and compare the results to the data in Figure 7.

Reading Checkpoint   **What does the solubility of a substance tell you?**

Factors Affecting Solubility

Which dissolves more sugar: iced tea or hot tea? You have already read that there is a limit to solubility. An iced tea and sugar solution quickly becomes saturated. Yet a hot, steaming cup of the same tea can dissolve much more sugar before the limit is reached. The solubilities of solutes change when conditions change. **Factors that affect the solubility of a substance include pressure, the type of solvent, and temperature.**

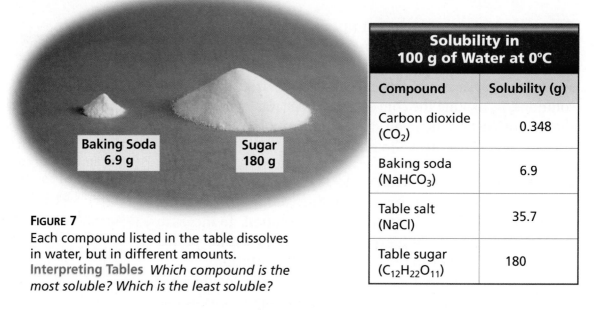

Lab zone Skills **Activity**

Predicting

Make a saturated solution of baking soda in water. Add one small spoonful of baking soda to about 250 mL of cool water. Stir until the baking soda dissolves. Continue adding baking soda until no more dissolves. Keep track of how much baking soda you use. Then predict what would happen if you used warm water instead. Make a plan to test your prediction. With approval from your teacher, carry out your plan. Did your results confirm your prediction? Explain.

Pressure Pressure affects the solubility of gases. The higher the pressure of the gas over the solvent, the more gas can dissolve. To increase the carbon dioxide concentration in soft drinks, the gas is added under high pressure. Opening the bottle or can reduces the pressure. The escaping gas makes the sound you hear.

Scuba divers are aware of the effect of pressure on gases. Air is about 80 percent nitrogen. When divers breathe from tanks of compressed air, nitrogen from the air dissolves in their blood in greater amounts as they descend. This occurs because the pressure underwater increases with depth. If divers return to the surface too quickly, nitrogen bubbles come out of solution and block blood flow. Divers double over in pain, which is why this condition is sometimes called "the bends."

Solvents Sometimes you just can't make a solution because the solute and solvent are not compatible. Have you ever tried to mix oil and vinegar, which is mostly water, to make salad dressing? If you have, you've seen how the dressing quickly separates into layers after you stop shaking it. Oil and water separate because water is a polar compound and oil is nonpolar. Polar compounds and nonpolar compounds do not mix very well.

For liquid solutions, the solvent affects how well a solute dissolves. The expression "like dissolves like" gives you a clue to which solutes are soluble in which solvents. Ionic and polar compounds usually dissolve in polar solvents. Nonpolar compounds do not usually dissolve in polar solvents. If you work with paints, you know that water-based (latex) paints can be cleaned up with just soap and water. But cleaning up oil-based paints may require a nonpolar solvent, such as turpentine.

FIGURE 8
Pressure Changes Solubility
Opening a shaken bottle of soda water may produce quite a spray as dissolved gas comes out of solution.

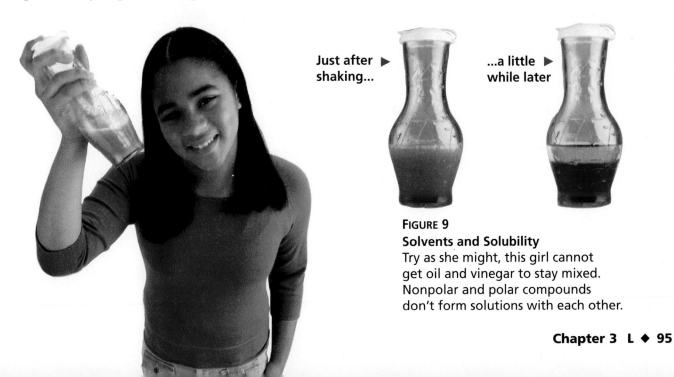

Just after ▶ shaking...

...a little ▶ while later

FIGURE 9
Solvents and Solubility
Try as she might, this girl cannot get oil and vinegar to stay mixed. Nonpolar and polar compounds don't form solutions with each other.

Temperature and Solubility

The solubility of the compound potassium nitrate (KNO_3) varies in water at different temperatures.

1. **Reading Graphs** At which temperature shown in the graph is KNO_3 least soluble in water?

2. **Reading Graphs** Approximately what mass of KNO_3 is needed to saturate a water solution at 40°C?

3. **Calculating** About how much more soluble is KNO_3 at 40°C than at 20°C?

4. **Interpreting Data** Does solubility increase at the same rate with every 20°C increase in temperature? Explain.

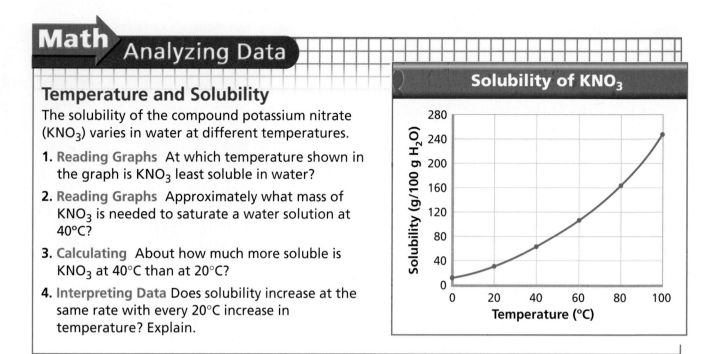

Solubility of KNO₃

y-axis: Solubility (g/100 g H₂O)

x-axis: Temperature (°C)

Temperature For most solids, solubility increases as the temperature increases. That is why the temperature is reported when solubilities are listed. For example, the solubility of table sugar in 100 grams of water changes from 180 grams at 0°C to 231 grams at 25°C to 487 grams at 100°C.

Cooks use this increased solubility of sugar when they make desserts such as rock candy, fudge, or peanut brittle. To make peanut brittle, you start with a mixture of sugar, corn syrup, and water. At room temperature, not enough of the required sugar can dissolve in the water. The mixture must be heated until it begins to boil. Nuts and other ingredients are added before the mixture cools. Some recipes call for temperatures above 100°C. Because the exact temperature can affect the result, cooks use a candy thermometer to check the temperature.

Unlike most solids, gases become less soluble when the temperature goes up. For example, more carbon dioxide will dissolve in cold water than in hot water. Carbon dioxide makes soda water fizzy when you pour it into a glass. If you open a warm bottle of soda water, carbon dioxide escapes the liquid in greater amounts than if the soda water had been chilled. Why does warm soda taste "flat"? It contains less gas. If you like soda water that's very fizzy, open it when it's cold!

FIGURE 10
Temperature Changes Solubility
Some hard candy is made by cooling a sugar water solution. **Interpreting Photographs** *Why does sugar form crystals when the solution is cooled?*

FIGURE 11
A Supersaturated Solution
Dropping a crystal of solute into a supersaturated solution (left) causes the excess solute to rapidly come out of solution (center). Soon, the formation of crystals is complete (right).

When heated, a solution can dissolve more solute than it can at cooler temperatures. If a heated, saturated solution cools slowly, sometimes the extra solute will remain dissolved. A **supersaturated solution** has more dissolved solute than is predicted by its solubility at the given temperature. When you disturb a supersaturated solution by dropping in a crystal of the solute, the extra solute will come out of solution.

For: Links on solubility
Visit: www.SciLinks.org
Web Code: scn-1232

Reading Checkpoint As temperature increases, what happens to the solubility of a gas?

Section 2 Assessment

Target Reading Skill Building Vocabulary
Use your sentences about the Key Terms to help answer the questions.

Reviewing Key Concepts

1. a. Reviewing What is concentration?
  b. Describing What quantities are compared when the concentration of a solution is measured?
  c. Applying Concepts Solution A contains 50 g of sugar. Solution B contains 100 g of sugar. Can you tell which solution has a higher sugar concentration? Explain.
2. a. Defining What is solubility?
  b. Explaining How can solubility help you identify a substance?
  c. Calculating Look back at the table in Figure 7. At 0°C, about how many times more soluble in water is sugar than salt?

3. a. Listing What are three factors that affect solubility?
  b. Summarizing How does temperature affect the solubility of most solids?
  c. Relating Cause and Effect When you heat water and add sugar, all of the sugar dissolves. When you cool the solution, some sugar comes out of solution. Explain.

4. Calculating a Concentration What is the concentration of a solution that contains 45 grams of sugar in 500 grams of solution?
5. Calculating a Concentration How much sugar is dissolved in 500 grams of a solution if the solution is 70 percent sugar by mass?

Describing Acids and Bases

Reading Preview

Key Concepts
- What are the properties of acids and bases?
- Where are acids and bases commonly used?

Key Terms
- acid • corrosive • indicator
- base

Target Reading Skill
Asking Questions Before you read, preview the red headings. In a graphic organizer like the one below, ask a *what* question for each heading. As you read, write the answers to your questions.

Describing Acids and Bases

Question	Answer
What is an acid?	An acid is . . .

Discover **Activity**

What Colors Does Litmus Paper Turn?

1. Use a plastic dropper to put a drop of lemon juice on a clean piece of red litmus paper. Put another drop on a clean piece of blue litmus paper. Observe.
2. Rinse your dropper with water. Then test other substances the same way. You might test orange juice, ammonia cleaner, tap water, vinegar, and solutions of soap, baking soda, and table salt. Record all your observations.
3. Wash your hands when you are finished.

Think It Over
Classifying Group the substances based on how they make the litmus paper change color. What other properties do the items in each group have in common?

Did you have any fruit for breakfast today—perhaps an orange, an apple, or fruit juice? If so, an acid was part of your meal. The last time you washed your hair, did you use shampoo? If your answer is yes, then you may have used a base.

You use many products that contain acids and bases. In addition, the chemical reactions of acids and bases even keep you alive! What are acids and bases—how do they react, and what are their uses?

Properties of Acids

What is an acid, and how do you know when you have one? In order to identify an acid, you can test its properties. **Acids** are compounds whose characteristic properties include the kinds of reactions they undergo. **An acid is a substance that tastes sour, reacts with metals and carbonates, and turns blue litmus paper red.** Some common acids you may have heard of are hydrochloric acid, nitric acid, sulfuric acid, carbonic acid, and acetic acid.

◄ Lemons are acidic.

Sour Taste If you've ever tasted a lemon, you've had first-hand experience with the sour taste of acids. Can you think of other foods that sometimes taste sour, or tart? Citrus fruits—lemons, grapefruits, oranges, and limes—are acidic. They all contain citric acid. Other fruits (cherries, tomatoes, apples) and many other types of foods contain acids, too.

Although sour taste is a characteristic of many acids, it is not one you should use to identify a compound as an acid. Scientists never taste chemicals in order to identify them. Though acids in sour foods may be safe to eat, many other acids are not.

Reactions With Metals Do you notice the bubbles in Figure 12? Acids react with certain metals to produce hydrogen gas. Not all metals react this way, but magnesium, zinc, and iron do. When they react, the metals seem to disappear in the solution. This observation is one reason acids are described as **corrosive,** meaning they "eat away" at other materials.

The metal plate in Figure 12 is being etched with acid. Etching is one method of making printing plates that are then used to print works of art on paper. To make an etching, an artist first coats a metal plate with an acid-resistant material—often beeswax. Then the design is cut into the beeswax with a sharp tool, exposing some of the metal. When the plate is treated with acid, the acid eats away the design in the exposed metal. Later, ink applied to the plate collects in the grooves made by the acid. The ink is transferred to the paper when the etching is printed.

FIGURE 12
Etching With Acid
Metal etching takes advantage of the reaction of an acid with a metal. Lines are cut in a wax coating on a plate. Here, hydrochloric acid eats away at the exposed zinc metal, forming bubbles you can see in the close-up. **Applying Concepts** *What gas forms in this reaction?*

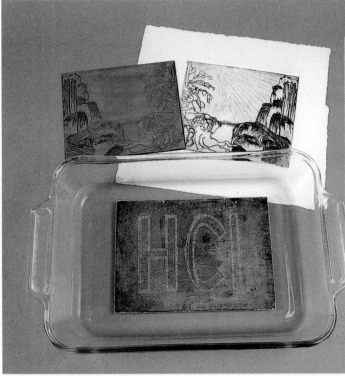

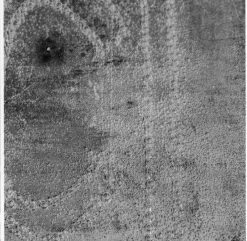

Reactions With Carbonates Acids also react with carbonate ions in a characteristic way. Recall that an ion is an atom or a group of atoms that has an electric charge. Carbonate ions contain carbon and oxygen atoms bonded together. They carry an overall negative charge (CO_3^{2-}). One product of an acid's reaction with carbonates is the gas carbon dioxide.

Geologists, scientists who study Earth, use this property of acids to identify rocks containing certain types of limestone. Limestone is a compound that contains the carbonate ion. If a geologist pours dilute hydrochloric acid on a limestone rock, bubbles of carbon dioxide appear on the rock's surface.

Reactions With Indicators If you did the Discover activity, you used litmus paper to test several substances. Litmus is an example of an **indicator,** a compound that changes color when in contact with an acid or a base. Look at Figure 13 to see what happens to litmus paper as it is dipped in a solution containing acid. Vinegar, lemon juice, and other acids turn blue litmus paper red. Sometimes chemists use other indicators to test for acids, but litmus is one of the easiest to use.

Properties of Bases

Bases are another group of compounds that can be identified by their common properties. **A base is a substance that tastes bitter, feels slippery, and turns red litmus paper blue.** Bases often are described as the "opposite" of acids. Common bases include sodium hydroxide, calcium hydroxide, and ammonia.

FIGURE 13
The Litmus Test
Litmus paper is an easy way to identify quickly whether an unknown compound is an acid or a base. *Inferring What can you infer about a liquid that does not change the color of blue litmus paper?*

Acids turn blue litmus paper red.

Acid

Bases turn red litmus paper blue.

Base

Bitter Taste Have you ever tasted tonic water? The slightly bitter taste is caused by the base quinine. Bases taste bitter. Soaps, some shampoos, and detergents taste bitter too, but you wouldn't want to identify these as bases by a taste test!

Slippery Feel Picture yourself washing a dog. As you massage the soap into the dog's fur, you notice that your hands feel slippery. This slippery feeling is another characteristic of bases. But just as you avoid tasting a substance to identify it, you wouldn't want to touch it. Strong bases can irritate or burn your skin. A safer way to identify bases is by their other properties.

Reactions With Indicators As you might guess, if litmus paper can be used to test acids, it can be used to test bases, too. Look at Figure 13 to see what happens to a litmus paper as it is dipped in a basic solution. Bases turn red litmus paper blue. Like acids, bases react with other indicators. But litmus paper gives a reliable, safe test. An easy way to remember which color litmus turns for acids or bases is to remember the letter *b*. **B**ases turn litmus paper **b**lue.

Other Reactions of Bases Unlike acids, bases don't react with carbonates to produce carbon dioxide. At first, you may think it is useless to know that a base doesn't react with certain chemicals. But if you know what a compound doesn't do, you know something about it. For example, you know it's not an acid. Another important property of bases is how they react with acids. You will learn more about these reactions in Section 4.

For: Links on acids and bases
Visit: www.SciLinks.org
Web Code: scn-1233

 Reading Checkpoint What is one safe way to identify a base?

FIGURE 15
Uses of Acids

Acids play an important role in our nutrition and are also found in valuable products used in homes and industries.

Acids in the Home ▶
People often use dilute solutions of acids to clean brick and other surfaces. Hardware stores sell muriatic (hydrochloric) acid, which is used to clean bricks and metals.

Acids and Food ▼
Many of the vitamins in the foods you eat are acids.

Acids and Industry ▼
Farmers and manufacturers depend on acids for many uses.

Sulfuric acid is used in car batteries, to refine petroleum, and to treat iron and steel.

Tomatoes and oranges contain ascorbic acid, or vitamin C.

Folic acid, needed for healthy cell growth, is found in green leafy vegetables.

Nitric acid and phosphoric acid are used to make fertilizers for crops, lawns, and gardens.

LAWN FERTILIZER
All you need for a thicker, greener lawn
31-3-9

Uses of Acids and Bases

Where can you find acids and bases? Almost anywhere. You already learned that acids are found in many fruits and other foods. In fact, many of them play important roles in the body as vitamins, including ascorbic acid, or vitamin C, and folic acid. Many cell processes also produce acids as waste products. For example, lactic acid builds up in your muscles when you make them work hard.

Manufacturers, farmers, and builders are only some people who depend on acids and bases in their work. **Acids and bases have many uses around the home and in industry.** Look at Figure 15 and Figure 16 to learn about a few of them. Many of the uses of bases take advantage of their ability to react with acids.

Reading Checkpoint What vitamin is an acid?

FIGURE 16
Uses of Bases

The reactions of bases make them valuable raw materials for a range of products.

Bases in the Home ▶
Ammonia solutions are safe to spray with bare hands, but gloves must be worn when working with drain cleaners.

You can't mistake the odor of household cleaning products made with ammonia.

Drain cleaners contain sodium hydroxide (lye).

Bases and Food ▼
Baking soda reacts with acids to produce carbon dioxide gas in baked goods. Without these gas bubbles, this delicious variety of breads, biscuits, cakes, and cookies would not be light and fluffy.

Bases and Industry ▲
Mortar and cement are manufactured using the bases calcium oxide and calcium hydroxide. Gardeners sometimes add calcium oxide to soil to make the soil less acidic for plants.

Section 3 Assessment

Target Reading Skill Asking Questions Work with a partner to check the answers in your graphic organizer.

Reviewing Key Concepts

1. a. Listing What are four properties of acids? Of bases?
  b. Describing How can you use litmus paper to distinguish an acid from a base?
  c. Applying Concepts How might you tell if a food contains an acid as one of its ingredients?
2. a. Reviewing What are three practical uses of an acid? Of a base?
  b. Making Generalizations Where are you most likely to find acids and bases in your own home? Explain.

c. Making Judgments Why is it wise to wear gloves when spreading fertilizer in a garden?

Writing in Science

Wanted Poster A bottle of acid is missing from the chemistry lab shelf! Design a wanted poster describing properties of the missing acid. Also include descriptions of tests a staff member from the chemistry lab could *safely* perform to determine if a bottle that is found actually contains acid. Add a caution on your poster that warns people *not* to touch any bottles they find. Instead, they should notify the chemistry lab.

Acids and Bases in Solution

Reading Preview

Key Concepts
- What kinds of ions do acids and bases form in water?
- What does pH tell you about a solution?
- What happens in a neutralization reaction?

Key Terms
- hydrogen ion (H^+)
- hydroxide ion (OH^-)
- pH scale • neutralization • salt

Target Reading Skill

Previewing Visuals When you preview, you look ahead at the material to be read. Preview Figure 21. Then write two questions that you have about the diagram in a graphic organizer like the one below. As you read, answer your questions.

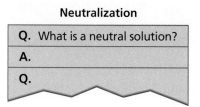

Neutralization

Q. What is a neutral solution?	
A.	
Q.	

For: More on pH scale
Visit: PHSchool.com
Web Code: cgd-2034

Discover Activity

What Can Cabbage Juice Tell You?

1. Using a dropper, put 5 drops of red cabbage juice into each of three separate plastic cups.
2. Add 10 drops of lemon juice (an acid) to one cup. Add 10 drops of ammonia cleaner (a base) to another. Keep the third cup for comparison. Record the colors you see.
3. Now add ammonia, 1 drop at a time, to the cup containing lemon juice. Keep adding ammonia until the color no longer changes. Record all color changes you see.
4. Add lemon juice a drop at a time to the ammonia until the color no longer changes. Record the changes you see.

Think It Over

Forming Operational Definitions Based on your observations, what could you add to your definitions of acids and bases?

A chemist pours hydrochloric acid into a beaker. Then she adds sodium hydroxide to the acid. The mixture looks the same, but the beaker becomes warm. If she tested the solution with litmus paper, what color would the paper turn? Would you be surprised if it did not change color at all? If exactly the right amounts and concentrations of the acid and the base were mixed, the beaker would hold nothing but salt water!

Acids and Bases in Solution

How can two corrosive chemicals, an acid and a base, produce something harmless to the touch? To answer this question, you must know what happens to acids and bases in solution.

Acids What do acids have in common? Notice that each formula in the list of acids in Figure 17 begins with hydrogen. The acids you will learn about in this section produce one or more hydrogen ions and a negative ion in solution with water. A **hydrogen ion** (H^+) is an atom of hydrogen that has lost its electron. The negative ion may be a nonmetal or a polyatomic ion. Hydrogen ions are the key to the reactions of acids.

Important Acids and Bases			
Acid	**Formula**	**Base**	**Formula**
Hydrochloric acid	HCl	Sodium hydroxide	NaOH
Nitric acid	HNO_3	Potassium hydroxide	KOH
Sulfuric acid	H_2SO_4	Calcium hydroxide	$Ca(OH)_2$
Carbonic acid	H_2CO_3	Aluminum hydroxide	$Al(OH)_3$
Acetic acid	$HC_2H_3O_2$	Ammonia	NH_3
Phosphoric acid	H_3PO_4	Calcium oxide	CaO

FIGURE 17
The table lists some commonly encountered acids and bases.
Making Generalizations *What do all of the acid formulas in the table have in common?*

Acids in water solution separate into hydrogen ions (H^+) and negative ions. In the case of hydrochloric acid, for example, hydrogen ions and chloride ions form:

$$HCl \xrightarrow{\text{water}} H^+ + Cl^-$$

Now you can add to the definition of acids you learned in Section 3. **An acid is any substance that produces hydrogen ions (H^+) in water.** These hydrogen ions cause the properties of acids. For instance, when you add certain metals to an acid, hydrogen ions interact with the metal atoms. One product of the reaction is hydrogen gas (H_2). Hydrogen ions also react with blue litmus paper, turning it red. That's why every acid gives the same litmus test result.

Bases The formulas of bases give you clues to what ions they have in common. You can see in the table in Figure 17 that many bases are made of positive ions combined with hydroxide ions. The **hydroxide ion (OH^-)** is a negative ion, made of oxygen and hydrogen. When bases dissolve in water, the positive ions and hydroxide ions separate. Look, for example, at what happens to sodium hydroxide:

$$NaOH \xrightarrow{\text{water}} Na^+ + OH^-$$

Not every base contains hydroxide ions. For example, the gas ammonia (NH_3) does not. But in solution, ammonia is a base that reacts with water to form hydroxide ions.

$$NH_3 + H_2O \longrightarrow NH_4^+ + OH^-$$

Notice that in both reactions, there are negative hydroxide ions. **A base is any substance that produces hydroxide ions (OH^-) in water.** Hydroxide ions are responsible for the bitter taste and slippery feel of bases, and turn red litmus paper blue.

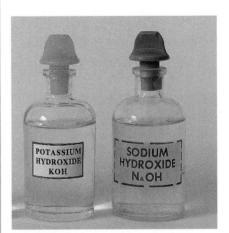

FIGURE 18
Comparing Bases
Many bases are made of positive ions combined with hydroxide ions.

Strong Acid   **Weak Acid**

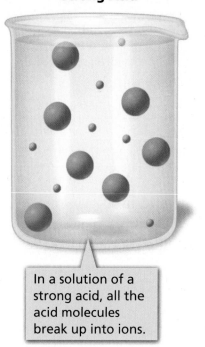

Key

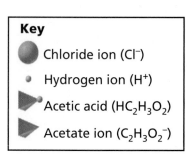

Chloride ion (Cl⁻)

Hydrogen ion (H⁺)

Acetic acid (HC₂H₃O₂)

Acetate ion (C₂H₃O₂⁻)

In a solution of a strong acid, all the acid molecules break up into ions.

In a solution of a weak acid, fewer molecules break up into ions.

FIGURE 19
Acids in Solution
Strong acids and weak acids act differently in water. Hydrochloric acid (left) is a strong acid. Acetic acid (right) is a weak acid.

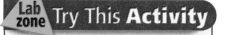

Lab zone Try This **Activity**

pHone Home

1. Select materials such as fruit juices, soda water, coffee, tea, and antacids. If the sample is solid, dissolve some in a cup of water. Use a liquid as is.

2. Predict which materials are most acidic or most basic.

3. Using a plastic dropper, transfer a drop of one sample onto a fresh strip of pH test paper.

4. Compare the color of the strip to the pH test scale on the package.

5. Repeat for all your samples, rinsing the dropper between tests.

Interpreting Data List the samples from lowest to highest pH. Did any results surprise you?

Strength of Acids and Bases

Acids and bases may be strong or weak. Strength refers to how well an acid or a base produces ions in water. As shown in Figure 19, the molecules of a strong acid react to form ions in solution. With a weak acid, very few molecules form ions. At the same concentration, a strong acid produces more hydrogen ions (H⁺) than a weak acid does. Examples of strong acids include hydrochloric acid, sulfuric acid, and nitric acid. Most other acids, such as acetic acid, are weak acids.

Strong bases react in a water solution in a similar way to strong acids. A strong base produces more hydroxide (OH⁻) ions than does an equal concentration of a weak base. Ammonia is a weak base. Lye, or sodium hydroxide, is a strong base.

Measuring pH Knowing the concentration of hydrogen ions is the key to knowing how acidic or basic a solution is. To describe the concentration of ions, chemists use a numeric scale called pH. The **pH scale** is a range of values from 0 to 14. It expresses the concentration of hydrogen ions in a solution.

Figure 20 shows where some familiar substances fit on the pH scale. Notice that the most acidic substances are at the low end of the scale. The most basic substances are at the high end of the scale. You need to remember two important points about pH. **A low pH tells you that the concentration of hydrogen ions is high. In contrast, a high pH tells you that the concentration of hydrogen ions is low.** If you keep these ideas in mind, you can make sense of how the scale works.

You can find the pH of a solution by using indicators. The student in Figure 20 is using indicator paper that turns a different color for each pH value. Matching the color of the paper with the colors on the test scale tells how acidic or basic the solution is. A pH lower than 7 is acidic. A pH higher than 7 is basic. If the pH is 7, the solution is neutral. That means it's neither an acid nor a base. Pure water has a pH of 7.

Using Acids and Bases Safely Strength determines, in part, how safe acids and bases are to use. People often say that a solution is weak when they mean it is dilute. This could be a dangerous mistake! Even a dilute solution of hydrochloric acid can eat a hole in your clothing. An equal concentration of acetic acid, however, will not. In order to handle acids and bases safely, you need to know both their pH and their concentration.

 Reading Checkpoint How would a weak base differ from an equal concentration of a strong base?

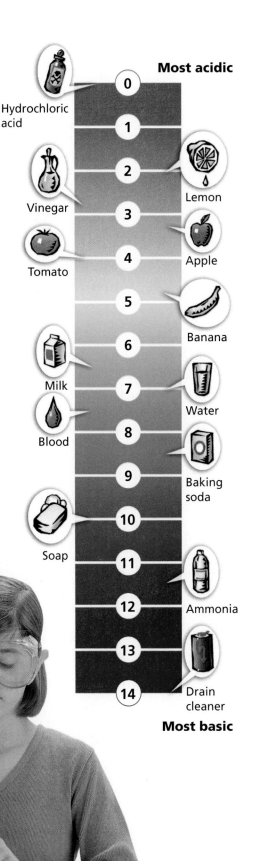

FIGURE 20
The pH Scale
The pH scale classifies solutions as acidic or basic. Indicator paper turns a different color for each pH value. Interpreting Diagrams *If a solution has a pH of 9, is it acidic or basic?*

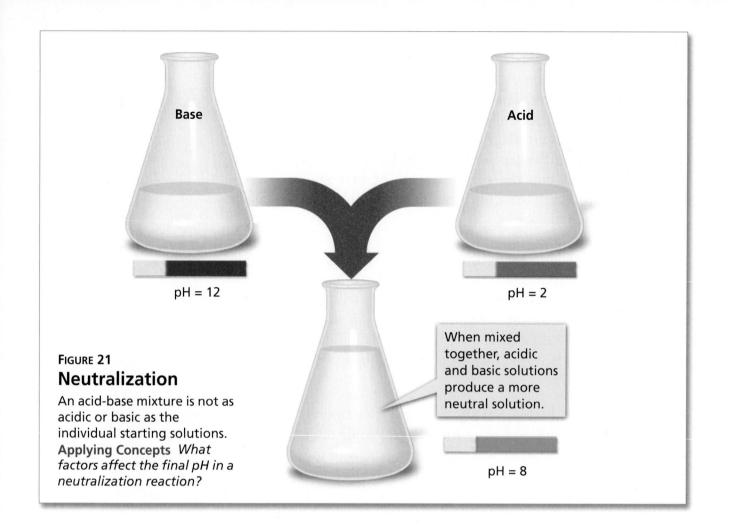

Base

pH = 12

Acid

pH = 2

When mixed together, acidic and basic solutions produce a more neutral solution.

pH = 8

Neutralization
An acid-base mixture is not as acidic or basic as the individual starting solutions.
Applying Concepts *What factors affect the final pH in a neutralization reaction?*

Acid-Base Reactions

The story at the start of this section describes a chemist who mixed hydrochloric acid with sodium hydroxide. She got a solution of table salt (sodium chloride) and water.

$$HCl + NaOH \longrightarrow H_2O + Na^+ + Cl^-$$

If you tested the pH of the mixture, it would be close to 7, or neutral. In fact, a reaction between an acid and a base is called **neutralization** (noo truh lih ZAY shun).

Reactants After neutralization, an acid-base mixture is not as acidic or basic as the individual starting solutions were. Sometimes an acid-base reaction even results in a neutral solution. The final pH depends on such factors as the volumes, concentrations, and identities of the reactants. For example, some acids and bases react to form products that are not neutral. Also, common sense tells you that if only a small amount of strong base is reacted with a much larger amount of strong acid, the solution will remain acidic.

Products "Salt" may be the familiar name of the stuff you sprinkle on food. But to a chemist, the word refers to a specific group of compounds. A **salt** is any ionic compound that can be made from the neutralization of an acid with a base. A salt is made from the positive ion of a base and the negative ion of an acid.

Look at the equation for the reaction of nitric acid with potassium hydroxide:

$$HNO_3 + KOH \longrightarrow H_2O \; 1 \; K^+ + NO_3^-$$

One product of the reaction is water. The other product is potassium nitrate (KNO_3), a salt. **In a neutralization reaction, an acid reacts with a base to produce a salt and water.** Potassium nitrate is written in the equation as separate K^+ and NO_3^- ions because it is soluble in water. Some salts, such as potassium nitrate, are soluble. Others form precipitates because they are insoluble. Look at the table in Figure 22 to see a list of some common salts and their formulas.

Common Salts	
Salt	**Uses**
Sodium chloride NaCl	Food flavoring; food preservative
Potassium iodide KI	Additive in "iodized" salt that prevents iodine deficiency
Calcium chloride $CaCl_2$	De-icer for roads and walkways
Potassium chloride KCl	Salt substitute in foods
Calcium carbonate $CaCO_3$	Found in limestone and seashells
Ammonium nitrate NH_4NO_3	Fertilizer; active ingredient in cold packs

FIGURE 22
Each salt listed in this table can be formed by the reaction between an acid and a base.

Reading Checkpoint What is a salt?

Section 4 Assessment

Target Reading Skill Previewing Visuals Refer to your questions and answers about Figure 21 to help you answer Question 3 below.

Reviewing Key Concepts

1. a. **Identifying** Which element is found in all the acids described in this section?
   b. **Describing** What kinds of ions do acids and bases form in water?
   c. **Predicting** What ions will the acid HNO_3 form when dissolved in water?

2. a. **Reviewing** What does a substance's pH tell you?
   b. **Comparing and Contrasting** If a solution has a pH of 6, would the solution contain more or fewer hydrogen ions (H^+) than an equal volume of solution with a pH of 3?
   c. **Making Generalizations** Would a dilute solution of HCl also be weak? Explain.

3. a. **Reviewing** What are the reactants of a neutralization reaction?
   b. **Explaining** What happens in a neutralization reaction?
   c. **Problem Solving** What acid reacts with KOH to produce the salt KCl?

Lab zone At-Home **Activity**

pH Lineup With a family member, search your house and refrigerator for the items found on the pH scale shown in Figure 20. Line up what you are able to find in order of increasing pH. Then ask your family member to guess why you ordered the substances in this way. Use the lineup to explain what pH means and how it is measured.

The Antacid Test

Problem

Which antacid neutralizes stomach acid with the smallest number of drops?

Skills Focus

designing experiments, interpreting data, measuring

Materials
- 3 plastic droppers
- small plastic cups
- dilute hydrochloric acid (HCl), 50 mL
- methyl orange solution, 1 mL
- liquid antacid, 30 mL of each brand tested

Procedure 🥽 🥼 ✂️ 🗑️

PART 1

1. Using a plastic dropper, put 10 drops of hydrochloric acid (HCl) into one cup.
   CAUTION: *HCl is corrosive. Rinse spills and splashes immediately with water.*

2. Use another plastic dropper to put 10 drops of liquid antacid into another cup.

3. In your notebook, make a data table like the one below. Record the colors of the HCl and the antacid.

Data Table		
Substance	Original Color	Color With Indicator
Hydrochloric Acid		
Antacid Brand A		
Antacid Brand B		

4. Add 2 drops of methyl orange solution to each cup. Record the colors you see.

5. Test each of the other antacids. Discard all the solutions and cups as directed by your teacher.

PART 2

6. Methyl orange changes color at a pH of about 4. Predict the color of the solution you expect to see when an antacid is added to a mixture of methyl orange and HCl.

7. Design a procedure for testing the reaction of each antacid with HCl. Decide how many drops of acid and methyl orange you need to use each time.

8. Devise a plan for adding the antacid so that you can detect when a change occurs. Decide how much antacid to add each time and how to mix the solutions to be sure the indicator is giving accurate results.

9. Make a second data table to record your observations.

10. Carry out your procedure and record your results.

11. Discard the solutions and cups as directed by your teacher. Rinse the plastic droppers thoroughly.

12. Wash your hands thoroughly when done.

Analyze and Conclude

1. **Designing Experiments** What is the function of the methyl orange solution?

2. **Interpreting Data** Do your observations support your predictions from Step 6? Explain why or why not.

3. **Inferring** Why do you think antacids reduce stomach acid? Explain your answer, using the observations you made.

4. **Controlling Variables** Explain why it is important to use the same number of drops of HCl in each trial.

5. **Measuring** Which antacid neutralized the HCl with the smallest number of drops? Give a possible explanation for the difference.

6. **Calculating** If you have the same volume (number of drops) of each antacid, which one can neutralize the most acid?

7. **Drawing Conclusions** Did your procedure give results from which you could draw conclusions about which brand of antacid was most effective? Explain why or why not.

8. **Communicating** Write a brochure that explains to consumers what information they need to know in order to decide which brand of antacid is the best buy.

Design an Experiment

A company that sells a liquid antacid claims that its product works faster than tablets to neutralize stomach acid. Design an experiment to compare how quickly liquid antacids and chewable antacid tablets neutralize hydrochloric acid. *Obtain your teacher's permission before carrying out your investigation.*

Digestion and pH

Reading Preview

Key Concepts
- Why must your body digest food?
- How does pH affect digestion?

Key Terms
- digestion
- mechanical digestion
- chemical digestion

Target Reading Skill

Sequencing A sequence is the order in which a series of events occurs. As you read, make a flowchart that shows the sequence of changes in pH as food moves through the digestive system.

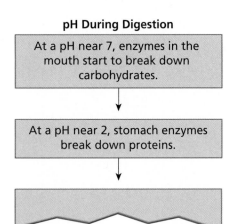

pH During Digestion

At a pH near 7, enzymes in the mouth start to break down carbohydrates.

↓

At a pH near 2, stomach enzymes break down proteins.

↓

Lab zone — Discover **Activity**

Where Does Digestion Begin?

1. Obtain a bite-sized piece of crusty bread.
2. Chew the bread for about one minute. Do not swallow until after you notice a change in taste.

Think It Over
Inferring How did the bread taste before and after you chewed it? How can you explain the change in taste?

You may have seen commercials like the following: A man has a stomachache after eating spicy food. A voice announces that the problem is excess stomach acid. The remedy is an antacid tablet.

Ads like this one highlight the role of chemistry in digestion. You need to have acid in your stomach. But too much acid is a problem. Other parts of your digestive system need to be basic. What roles do acids and bases play in the digestion of food?

What Is Digestion?

Foods are made mostly of water and three groups of compounds: carbohydrates, proteins, and fats. Except for water, your body can't use foods in the form they are in when you eat them. **Foods must be broken down into simpler substances that your body can use for raw materials and energy.**

FIGURE 23
Digestion
This sandwich is about to begin a journey that includes changes in pH.

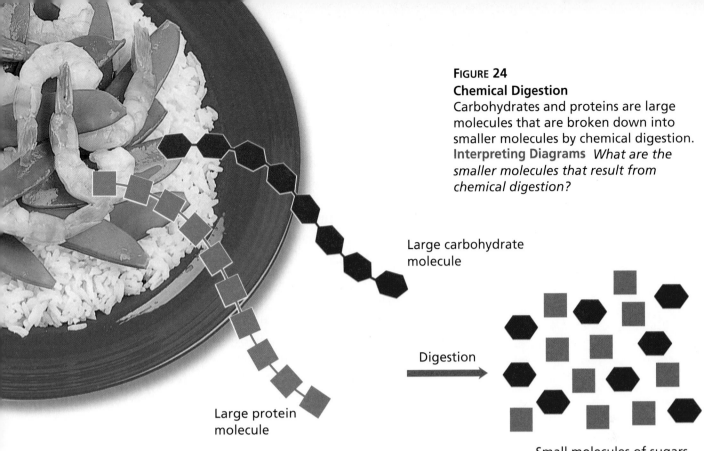

FIGURE 24
Chemical Digestion
Carbohydrates and proteins are large molecules that are broken down into smaller molecules by chemical digestion.
Interpreting Diagrams *What are the smaller molecules that result from chemical digestion?*

Large carbohydrate molecule

Digestion

Large protein molecule

Small molecules of sugars and amino acids

The process of **digestion** breaks down the complex molecules of foods into smaller molecules. Digestion has two parts—mechanical and chemical.

Mechanical Digestion **Mechanical digestion** is a physical process in which large pieces of food are torn and ground into smaller pieces. The result is similar to what happens when a sugar cube is hit with a hammer. The size of the food is reduced, but the food isn't changed into other compounds.

Chemical Digestion **Chemical digestion** breaks large molecules into smaller ones. Look at Figure 24 to see what happens to large carbohydrate and protein molecules during chemical digestion. They are broken down into much smaller molecules. Some molecules are used by the body to get energy. Others become building blocks for muscle, bone, skin, and other organs.

Chemical digestion takes place with the help of enzymes. You may recall that enzymes are catalysts that speed up reactions in living things. Enzymes require just the right conditions to work, including temperature and pH. **Some digestive enzymes work at a low pH. For others, the pH must be high or neutral.**

Reading Checkpoint What happens to foods during chemical digestion?

pH in the Digestive System

A bite of sandwich is about to take a journey through your digestive system. Figure 25 shows the main parts of the human digestive system. As you read, trace the food's pathway through the body. Keep track of the pH changes that affect the food molecules along the way.

Your Mouth The first stop in the journey is your mouth. Your teeth chew and mash the food. The food also is mixed with a watery fluid called saliva. Have you ever felt your mouth water at the smell of something delicious? The odor of food can trigger production of saliva.

What would you expect the usual pH of saliva to be? Remember that saliva tastes neither sour nor bitter. So you're correct if you think your mouth has a pH near 7, the neutral point.

Saliva contains amylase (AM uh lays), an enzyme that helps break down the carbohydrate starch into smaller sugar molecules. Amylase works best when the pH is near 7. You can sense the action of this enzyme if you chew a piece of bread. After about two minutes in your mouth, the starch is broken down into sugars. The sugars make the bread taste sweet.

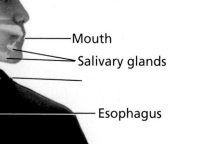

Mouth

Salivary glands

Esophagus

Stomach

Large intestine

Small intestine

FIGURE 25
Foods are exposed to several changes in pH as they move through the digestive system.
Relating Cause and Effect *Why do certain digestive enzymes work only in certain parts of the digestive system?*

pH Changes During Digestion	
Organ	**pH**
Mouth	7
Stomach	2
Small intestine	8

Your Stomach Next, the food is swallowed and arrives in your stomach, where mechanical digestion continues. Also, chemical digestion begins for foods that contain protein, such as meat, fish, and beans. Cells in the lining of your stomach release enzymes and hydrochloric acid. In contrast to the near-neutral pH of your mouth, the pH here drops to a very acidic level of about 2.

The low pH in your stomach helps digestion take place. Pepsin is one enzyme that works in your stomach. Pepsin helps break down proteins into small molecules called amino acids. Most enzymes work best in a solution that is nearly neutral. But pepsin is different. It works most effectively in acids.

Your Small Intestine Your stomach empties its contents into the small intestine. Here, digestive fluid containing bicarbonate ions (HCO_3^-) surrounds the food. This ion creates a slightly basic solution, with a pH of about 8. At this slightly basic pH, enzymes of the small intestine work best. These enzymes complete the breakdown of carbohydrates, fats, and proteins.

By now, the large food molecules from the sandwich have been split up into smaller ones. These smaller molecules pass through the walls of the small intestine into your bloodstream and are carried to the cells that will use them.

Go Online
SciLINKS

For: Links on digestion and pH
Visit: www.SciLinks.org
Web Code: scn-1235

Reading Checkpoint What acid do the cells in the lining of your stomach release?

Section 5 Assessment

Target Reading Skill Sequencing Refer to your flowchart about the digestive system as you answer Question 2.

Reviewing Key Concepts

1. **a. Reviewing** What are the two parts of digestion?
   b. Comparing and Contrasting How do these two processes differ?
   c. Inferring People who have lost most of their teeth may have trouble chewing their food. How does this affect their digestive process?
2. **a. Listing** What is the pH in your mouth? Stomach? Small intestine?
   b. Sequencing Arrange the three body locations in part (a) from least acidic to most acidic.
   c. Applying Concepts Why are pH variations in different parts of the digestive system important to the process of digestion?

Writing in Science

News Report Suppose you are a news reporter who can shrink down in size and be protected from changes in the environment with a special suit. You are assigned to accompany a bite of food as it travels through the digestive system. Report your findings in a dramatic but accurate way. Include a catchy headline.

The BIG Idea **Properties of Matter** When acids and bases form solutions in water, their properties may be tested with indicators and observed in chemical reactions.

1 Understanding Solutions

Key Concepts

- A solution has the same properties throughout. It contains solute particles that are too small to see.

- A colloid contains larger particles than a solution. The particles are still too small to be seen easily, but are large enough to scatter a light beam.

- Unlike a solution, a suspension does not have the same properties throughout. It contains visible particles that are larger than the particles in solutions or colloids.

- When a solution forms, particles of the solute leave each other and become surrounded by particles of the solvent.

- Solutes lower the freezing point and raise the boiling point of a solvent.

Key Terms

solution	solute	suspension
solvent	colloid	

2 Concentration and Solubility

Key Concepts

- To measure concentration, you compare the amount of solute to the amount of solvent or to the total amount of solution.

- Solubility can be used to help identify a substance because it is a characteristic property of matter.

- Factors that affect the solubility of a substance include pressure, the type of solvent, and temperature.

Key Terms

dilute solution
concentrated solution
solubility
saturated solution
unsaturated solution
supersaturated solution

3 Describing Acids and Bases

Key Concepts

- An acid is a substance that tastes sour, reacts with metals and carbonates, and turns blue litmus paper red.

- A base is a substance that tastes bitter, feels slippery, and turns red litmus paper blue.

- Acids and bases have many uses around the home and in industry.

Key Terms

• acid • corrosive • indicator • base

4 Acids and Bases in Solution

Key Concepts

- An acid is any substance that produces hydrogen ions (H^+) in water.

- A base is any substance that produces hydroxide ions (OH^-) in water.

- A low pH tells you that the concentration of hydrogen ions is high. In contrast, a high pH tells you that the concentration of hydrogen ions is low.

- In a neutralization reaction, an acid reacts with a base to produce a salt and water.

Key Terms

• hydrogen ion (H^+) • hydroxide ion (OH^-)
• pH scale • neutralization • salt

5 Digestion and pH

Key Concepts

- Foods must be broken down into simpler substances that your body can use for raw materials and energy.

- Some digestive enzymes work at a low pH. For others, the pH must be high or neutral.

Key Terms

digestion	chemical digestion
mechanical digestion	

Review and Assessment

Go Online
PHSchool.com

For: Self-Assessment
Visit: PHSchool.com
Web Code: cga-2030

Organizing Information

Concept Mapping Copy the concept map about solutions onto a sheet of paper. Then complete it and add a title. (For more on Concept Mapping, see the Skills Handbook.)

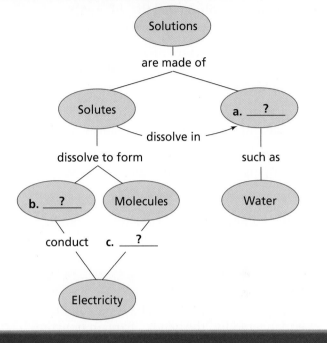

Reviewing Key Terms

Choose the letter of the best answer.

1. Sugar water is an example of a
   a. suspension.
   b. solution.
   c. solute.
   d. colloid.

2. A solution in which more solute may be dissolved at a given temperature is a(n)
   a. neutral solution.
   b. unsaturated solution.
   c. supersaturated solution.
   d. saturated solution.

3. A compound that changes color when it contacts an acid or a base is called a(n)
   a. solute.
   b. solvent.
   c. indicator.
   d. salt.

4. A polyatomic ion made of hydrogen and oxygen is called a
   a. hydroxide ion.
   b. hydrogen ion.
   c. salt.
   d. base.

5. Ammonia is an example of a(n)
   a. acid.   **b.** salt.
   c. base.   **d.** antacid.

6. The physical part of digestion is called
   a. digestion.
   b. mechanical digestion.
   c. chemical digestion.
   d. solubility.

Writing in Science

Product Label Suppose you are a marketing executive for a maple syrup company. Write a description of the main ingredients of maple syrup that can be pasted on the syrup's container. Use what you've learned about concentration to explain how dilute tree sap becomes sweet, thick syrup.

Acids, Bases, and Solutions
Video Preview
Video Field Trip
▶ Video Assessment

Review and Assessment

Checking Concepts

7. Explain how you can tell the difference between a solution and a clear colloid.

8. Describe at least two differences between a dilute solution and a concentrated solution of sugar water.

9. Tomatoes are acidic. Predict two properties of tomato juice that you would be able to observe.

10. Explain how an indicator helps you distinguish between an acid and a base.

11. Give an example of a very acidic pH value.

12. What combination of acid and base can be used to make the salt sodium chloride?

Thinking Critically

13. **Applying Concepts** A scuba diver can be endangered by "the bends." Explain how the effects of pressure on the solubility of gases is related to this condition.

14. **Relating Cause and Effect** If you leave a glass of cold tap water on a table, sometime later you may see tiny bubbles of gas form in the water. Explain what causes these bubbles to appear.

15. **Drawing Conclusions** You have two clear liquids. One turns blue litmus paper red and one turns red litmus paper blue. If you mix them and retest with both litmus papers, no color changes occur. Describe the reaction that took place when the liquids were mixed.

16. **Comparing and Contrasting** Compare the types of particles formed in a water solution of an acid with those formed in a water solution of a base.

17. **Problem Solving** Fill in the missing salt product in the reaction below.

$$HCl + KOH \longrightarrow H_2O + \underline{\ ?\ }$$

18. **Predicting** Suppose a person took a dose of antacid greater than what is recommended. Predict how this action might affect the digestion of certain foods.

Math Practice

19. **Calculating a Concentration** If you have 1,000 grams of a 10-percent solution of sugar water, how much sugar is dissolved in the solution?

20. **Calculating a Concentration** The concentration of an alcohol and water solution is 25 percent alcohol by volume. What is the volume of alcohol in 200 mL of the solution?

Applying Skills

Use the diagram to answer Questions 21–24.

The diagram below shows the particles of an unknown acid in a water solution.

Water

Acid

21. **Interpreting Diagrams** How can you tell that the solution contains a weak acid?

22. **Inferring** Which shapes in the diagram represent ions?

23. **Making Models** Suppose another unknown acid is a strong acid. Make a diagram to show the particles of this acid dissolved in water.

24. **Drawing Conclusions** Explain how the pH of a strong acid compares with the pH of a weak acid of the same concentration.

Lab zone Chapter **Project**

Performance Assessment Demonstrate the indicators you prepared. For each indicator, list the substances you tested in order from most acidic to least acidic. Would you use the same materials if you did this project again? Explain.

Standardized Test Prep

Choose the letter of the best answer.

1. Which of the following pH values indicates a solution with the highest concentration of hydrogen ions?
   A pH = 1
   B pH = 2
   C pH = 7
   D pH = 14

2. A small beaker contains 50 milliliters of water at 20°C. If three sugar cubes are placed in the beaker, they will eventually dissolve. Which action would speed up the rate at which the sugar cubes dissolve?
   F Use less water initially.
   G Transfer the contents to a larger beaker.
   H Cool the water and sugar cubes to 5°C.
   J Heat and stir the contents of the beaker.

Use the graph below and your knowledge of science to answer Question 3.

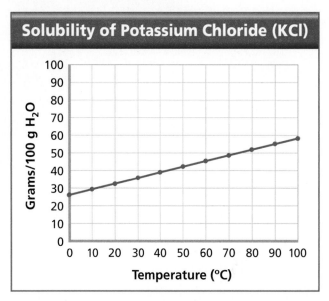

Solubility of Potassium Chloride (KCl)

3. If 30 grams of KCl are dissolved in 100 grams of water at 50°C, the solution can be best described as
   A saturated.
   B supersaturated.
   C unsaturated.
   D soluble.

4. Which safety procedures should be followed when using acids and bases in the laboratory?
   F Wear an apron and safety goggles.
   G Dispose of chemical wastes properly.
   H Wash your hands before leaving the lab.
   J all of the above

Constructed Response

5. Salt water is a solution of table salt (the solute) and water (the solvent). Describe a laboratory procedure that could be used to determine the concentration of salt in a sample of salt water. Indicate all measurements that must be made. (*Hint:* Remember that the concentration of a solution can be expressed as a ratio of the mass of the solute to the mass of the solution.)

Carbon Chemistry

The BIG Idea
Structure and Function

Q **Why does carbon have a central role in the chemistry of living things?**

Butterflies, flowers, and all other living ▶ things contain carbon compounds.

Lab zone™ Chapter **Project**

Check Out the Fine Print

All the foods you eat and drink contain carbon compounds. In this project, you will look closely at the labels on food packages to find carbon compounds.

Your Goal To identify carbon compounds found in different foods

To complete the project you must

- collect at least a dozen labels with lists of ingredients and nutrition facts
- identify the carbon compounds listed, as well as substances that do not contain carbon
- interpret the nutrition facts on labels to compare amounts of substances in each food
- classify compounds in foods into the categories of polymers found in living things

Plan It! Brainstorm with your classmates about what kinds of packaged foods you want to examine. After your teacher approves your plan, start collecting and studying food labels.

Properties of Carbon

Reading Preview

Key Concepts
- How is carbon able to form such a huge variety of compounds?
- What are four forms of pure carbon?

Key Terms
- diamond • graphite
- fullerene • nanotube

Target Reading Skill

Using Prior Knowledge Before you read, look at the section headings and visuals to see what this section is about. Then, write what you know about carbon in a graphic organizer like the one below. As you read, continue to write in what you learn.

What You Know
1. Carbon atoms have 6 electrons.
2.

What You Learned
1.
2.

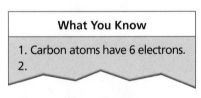

Lab zone Discover **Activity**

Why Do Pencils Write?

1. Tear paper into two pieces about 5 cm by 5 cm. Rub the two pieces back and forth between your fingers.
2. Now rub pencil lead (graphite) on one side of each piece of paper. Try to get as much graphite as possible on the paper.
3. Rub together the two sides covered with graphite.
4. When you are finished, wash your hands.

Think It Over

Observing Did you notice a difference between what you observed in Step 3 and what you observed in Step 1? How could the property of graphite that you observed be useful for purposes other than writing?

Open your mouth and say "aah." Uh-oh, you have a small cavity. Do you know what happens next? Your tooth needs a filling. But first the dentist's drill clears away the decayed part of your tooth.

Why is a dentist's drill hard enough and sharp enough to cut through teeth? The answer has to do with the element carbon. The tip of the drill is covered with diamond chips. Diamond is a form of carbon and the hardest substance on Earth. Because the drill tip is made of diamonds, a dentist's drill stays sharp and useful. To understand why diamond is such a hard substance, you need to take a close look at the carbon atom and the bonds it forms.

FIGURE 1
Uses of Carbon
This colorized photo shows the tip of a dentist's drill (yellow). The tip is made of diamond and is strong enough to bore into a tooth (blue).

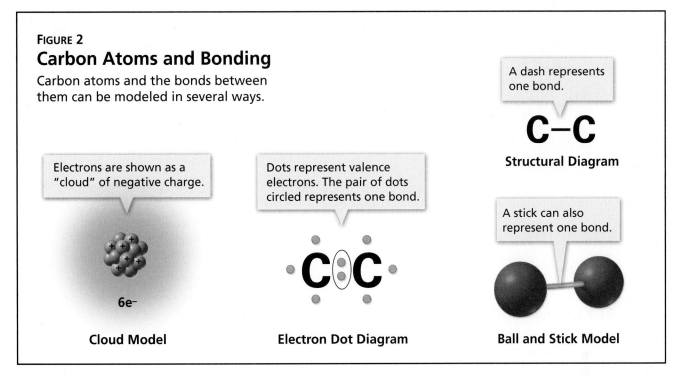

FIGURE 2
Carbon Atoms and Bonding
Carbon atoms and the bonds between them can be modeled in several ways.

Electrons are shown as a "cloud" of negative charge.

6e-

Cloud Model

Dots represent valence electrons. The pair of dots circled represents one bond.

Electron Dot Diagram

A dash represents one bond.

C–C

Structural Diagram

A stick can also represent one bond.

Ball and Stick Model

Carbon Atoms and Bonding

Recall that the atomic number of carbon is 6, which means that the nucleus of a carbon atom contains 6 protons. Surrounding the nucleus are 6 electrons. Of these electrons, four are valence electrons—the electrons available for bonding.

As you have learned, a chemical bond is the force that holds two atoms together. A bond between two atoms results from changes involving the atoms' valence electrons. Atoms gain, lose, or share valence electrons in a way that makes the atoms most stable. A carbon atom can share its valence electrons with other atoms, forming covalent bonds. Figure 2 shows ways that covalent bonds may be represented.

Atoms of most elements form chemical bonds. Carbon, however, is unique. **Few elements have the ability of carbon to bond with both itself and other elements in so many different ways. With four valence electrons, each carbon atom is able to form four bonds.** Therefore, it is possible to form molecules made of thousands of carbon atoms. By comparison, hydrogen, oxygen, and nitrogen can form only one, two, or three bonds, respectively, and cannot form such long chains.

As you can see in Figure 3, it is possible to arrange the same number of carbon atoms in different ways. Carbon atoms can form straight chains, branched chains, and rings. Sometimes, two or more carbon rings can even join together.

Straight chain

Branched chain

Ring

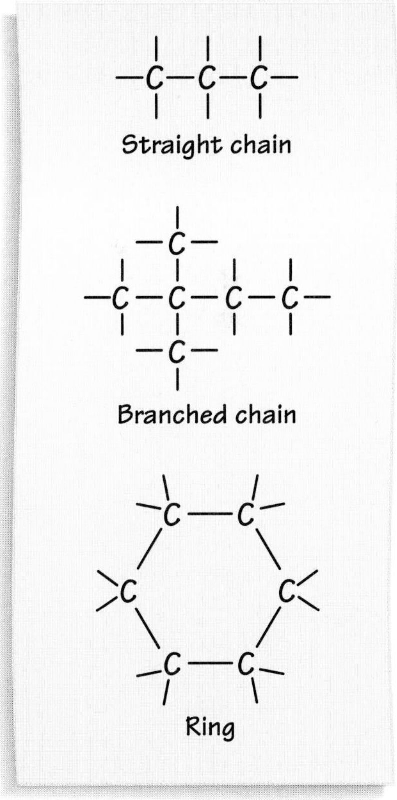

FIGURE 3
Arrangements of Carbon Atoms
Carbon chains and rings form the backbones for molecules that may contain other atoms.

✔ **Reading Checkpoint** What happens to a carbon atom's valence electrons when it bonds with another atom?

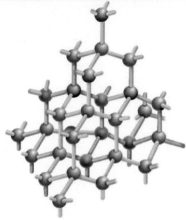

Crystal Structure of Diamond
The carbon atoms in a diamond are arranged in a crystal structure.

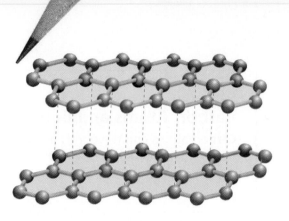

Layered Structure of Graphite
The carbon atoms in graphite are arranged in layers. The dashed lines show the weak bonds between the layers.

FIGURE 4
Forms of Pure Carbon

Pure carbon exists in the form of diamond, graphite, fullerenes, and nanotubes. The properties of each form result from the unique repeating pattern of its carbon atoms. **Interpreting Diagrams** *Which form of carbon has a crystal structure?*

Forms of Pure Carbon

Because of the ways that carbon forms bonds, the pure element can exist in different forms. **Diamond, graphite, fullerenes, and nanotubes are four forms of the element carbon.**

Diamond The hardest mineral, **diamond,** forms deep within Earth. At very high temperatures and pressures, carbon atoms form diamond crystals. Each carbon atom is bonded strongly to four other carbon atoms. The result is a solid that is extremely hard and nonreactive. The melting point of diamond is more than 3,500°C—as hot as the surface temperatures of some stars.

Diamonds are prized for their brilliance and clarity when cut as gems. Industrial chemists are able to make diamonds artificially, but these diamonds are not considered beautiful enough to use as gems. Both natural and artificial diamonds are used in industry. Diamonds work well in cutting tools, such as drills.

Graphite Every time you write with a pencil, you leave a layer of carbon on the paper. The "lead" in a lead pencil is actually mostly **graphite,** another form of the element carbon. In graphite, each carbon atom is bonded tightly to three other carbon atoms in flat layers. However, the bonds between atoms in different layers are very weak, so the layers slide past one another easily.

If you run your fingers over pencil marks, you can feel how slippery graphite is. Because it is so slippery, graphite makes an excellent lubricant in machines. Graphite reduces friction between the moving parts. In your home, you might use a graphite spray to help a key work better in a sticky lock.

✓ **Reading Checkpoint** Why is diamond such a hard and nonreactive substance?

Spherical Structure of a Fullerene
The carbon atoms in a fullerene form a sphere that resembles a geodesic dome.

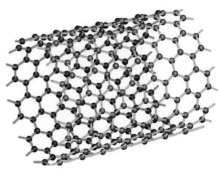

Cylindrical Structure of a Nanotube
The carbon atoms in a nanotube are arranged in a cylinder.

Fullerenes and Nanotubes In 1985, scientists made a new form of carbon. It consists of carbon atoms arranged in the shape of a hollow sphere. This form of carbon was named a **fullerene** (FUL ur een), for the architect Buckminster Fuller, who designed dome-shaped buildings called geodesic domes. One type of fullerene has been nicknamed "buckyballs."

In 1991, yet another form of carbon was made—the nanotube. In a **nanotube,** carbon atoms are arranged in the shape of a long, hollow cylinder, or tube. You can think of a nanotube as a sheet of graphite rolled into a cylinder. Only a few nanometers wide in diameter, nanotubes are tiny, light, flexible, and extremely strong. Nanotubes are also good conductors of electricity and heat.

Scientists are looking for ways to use the unique properties of fullerenes and nanotubes. For example, chemists are studying how fullerenes and nanotubes may be used to deliver medicine molecules into cells. Nanotubes may also be used as conductors in electronic devices and as super-strong cables.

Go **O**nline
active art

For: Carbon Bonding activity
Visit: PHSchool.com
Web Code: cgp-2041

Section 1 Assessment

Target Reading Skill **Using Prior Knowledge** Review your graphic organizer and revise it based on what you learned in this section.

Reviewing Key Concepts

1. a. Identifying How many bonds can a carbon atom form?
   b. Explaining What bonding properties of carbon allow it to form so many different compounds?
2. a. Listing List the four forms of pure carbon.

   b. Describing Describe the carbon bonds in graphite.
   c. Relating Cause and Effect How do the differences in carbon bonds explain why graphite and diamonds have different properties?

Writing in Science

Explanation Draw electron dot diagrams for a straight carbon chain and a branched chain. Then, write an explanation of what you did to show how the carbons are bonded.

Carbon Compounds

Reading Preview

Key Concepts
- What are some properties of organic compounds?
- What are some properties of hydrocarbons?
- What kind of structures and bonding do hydrocarbons have?
- What are some characteristics of substituted hydrocarbons, esters, and polymers?

Key Terms
- organic compound
- hydrocarbon
- structural formula • isomer
- saturated hydrocarbon
- unsaturated hydrocarbon
- substituted hydrocarbon
- hydroxyl group • alcohol
- organic acid • carboxyl group
- ester • polymer • monomer

Target Reading Skill

Outlining As you read, make an outline about carbon compounds. Use the red headings for the main ideas and the blue headings for supporting ideas.

Lab zone

Discover **Activity**

What Do You Smell?

1. Your teacher will provide you with some containers. Wave your hand toward your nose over the top of each container.
2. Try to identify each of the odors.
3. After you record what you think is in each container, compare your guesses to the actual substance.

Think It Over

Developing Hypotheses Develop a hypothesis to explain the differences between the smell of one substance and another.

Imagine that you are heading out for a day of shopping. Your first purchase is a cotton shirt. Then you go to the drug store, where you buy a bottle of shampoo and a pad of writing paper. Your next stop is a hardware store. There, you buy propane fuel for your camping stove. Your final stop is the grocery store, where you buy olive oil, cereal, meat, and vegetables.

What do all of these purchases have in common? They all are made of carbon compounds. Carbon atoms act as the backbone or skeleton for the molecules of these compounds. Carbon compounds include gases (such as propane), liquids (such as olive oil), and solids (such as cotton). Mixtures of carbon compounds are found in foods, paper, and shampoo. In fact, more than 90 percent of all known compounds contain carbon.

FIGURE 5
Carbon Everywhere
Carbon is a part of your daily life. Even during a simple shopping trip, you'll likely encounter many carbon compounds.

"Carbon Compounds" to Buy

cotton shirt
fleece hat
fishing line
writing paper
propane refills
cereal
ground beef
tuna
vegetables
cooking oil
sugar

FIGURE 6
Where Organic Compounds Are Found
These three lists represent only a few of the places where organic compounds can be found. Organic compounds are in all living things, in products from living things, and in human-made materials.

Part of Living Things

Muscle
Blood
Seeds
Leaves
Feathers
Skin

From Living Things

Wool
Cotton
Wood
Silk
Paper
Natural gas

Produced Artificially

Gasoline
Fleece
Plastics
Shampoo
Detergent
Cosmetics

Organic Compounds

Carbon compounds are so numerous that they are given a specific name. With some exceptions, compounds that contain carbon are called **organic compounds.** This term is used because scientists once thought that organic compounds could be produced only by living things. (The word *organic* means "of living things.") Today, however, scientists know that organic compounds also can be found in products made from living things and in materials produced artificially in laboratories and factories. Organic compounds are part of the solid matter of every organism on Earth. They are part of products that are made from organisms, such as paper made from the wood of trees. Plastics, fuels, cleaning solutions, and many other such products also contain organic compounds. The raw materials for most manufactured organic compounds come from petroleum, or crude oil.

Many organic compounds have similar properties in terms of melting points, boiling points, odor, electrical conductivity, and solubility. Many organic compounds have low melting points and low boiling points. As a result, they are liquids or gases at room temperature. Organic liquids generally have strong odors. They also do not conduct electricity. Many organic compounds do not dissolve well in water. You may have seen vegetable oil, which is a mixture of organic compounds, form a separate layer in a bottle of salad dressing.

Reading Checkpoint What is an organic compound?

aspirin
hand cream

Hydrocarbons

Scientists classify organic compounds into different categories. The simplest organic compounds are the hydrocarbons. A **hydrocarbon** (HY droh KAHR bun) is a compound that contains only the elements carbon and hydrogen.

You might already recognize several common hydrocarbons. Methane, the main gas in natural gas, is used to heat homes. Propane is used in portable stoves and gas grills and to provide heat for hot-air balloons. Butane is the fuel in most lighters. Gasoline is a mixture of several different hydrocarbons.

Properties of Hydrocarbons Have you ever been at a gas station after a rainstorm? If so, you may have noticed a thin rainbow-colored film of gasoline or oil floating on a puddle, like the one in Figure 7. **Like many other organic compounds, hydrocarbons mix poorly with water. Also, all hydrocarbons are flammable.** Being flammable means that they burn easily. When hydrocarbons burn, they release a great deal of energy. For this reason, they are used as fuel for stoves, heaters, cars, buses, and airplanes.

Chemical Formulas of Hydrocarbons Hydrocarbon compounds differ in the number of carbon and hydrogen atoms in each molecule. You can write a chemical formula to show how many atoms of each element make up a molecule of a specific hydrocarbon. Recall that a chemical formula includes the chemical symbols of the elements in a compound. For molecular compounds, a chemical formula also shows the number of atoms of each element in a molecule.

The simplest hydrocarbon is methane. Its chemical formula is CH_4. The number 4 indicates the number of hydrogen atoms (H). Notice that the 4 is a subscript. Subscripts are written lower and smaller than the letter symbols of the elements. The symbol for carbon (C) in the formula is written without a subscript. This means that there is one carbon atom in the molecule.

FIGURE 7
Hydrocarbons
Hydrocarbons contain only the elements carbon and hydrogen. From the fuel that heats the air in hot-air balloons (above) to multicolored oil slicks (below right), hydrocarbons are all around you.
Making Generalizations *What properties of hydrocarbons do the hot-air balloon and oil slick demonstrate?*

A hydrocarbon with two carbon atoms is ethane. The formula for ethane is C_2H_6. The subscripts in this formula show that an ethane molecule is made of two carbon atoms and six hydrogen atoms.

A hydrocarbon with three carbon atoms is propane (C_3H_8). How many hydrogen atoms does the subscript indicate? If you answered eight, you are right.

 **Reading Checkpoint** What is a hydrocarbon?

Structure and Bonding in Hydrocarbons

The properties of hydrocarbon compounds are related to the compound's structure. **The carbon chains in a hydrocarbon may be straight, branched, or ring-shaped.** If a hydrocarbon has two or more carbon atoms, the atoms can form a single line, or a straight chain. In hydrocarbons with four or more carbon atoms, it is possible to have branched arrangements of the carbon atoms as well as straight chains.

Structural Formulas To show how atoms are arranged in the molecules of a compound, chemists use a structural formula. A **structural formula** shows the kind, number, and arrangement of atoms in a molecule.

Figure 8 shows the structural formulas for molecules of methane, ethane, and propane. Each dash (—) represents a bond. In methane, each carbon atom is bonded to four hydrogen atoms. In ethane and propane, each carbon atom is bonded to at least one carbon atom as well as to hydrogen atoms. As you look at structural formulas, notice that every carbon atom forms four bonds. Every hydrogen atom forms one bond. There are never any dangling bonds. In other words, both ends of a dash are always connected to something.

FIGURE 8
Structural Formulas
Each carbon atom in these structural formulas is surrounded by four dashes representing four bonds. **Interpreting Diagrams** *In propane, how many hydrogen atoms is each carbon bonded to?*

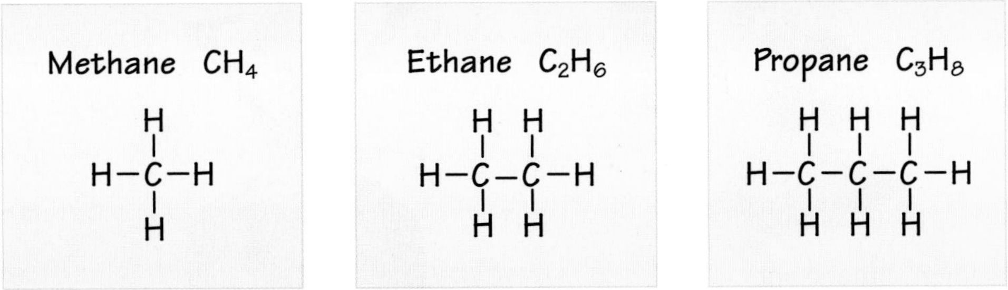

Methane CH_4

$$H-\overset{\displaystyle H}{\underset{\displaystyle H}{C}}-H$$

Ethane C_2H_6

$$H-\overset{\displaystyle H}{\underset{\displaystyle H}{C}}-\overset{\displaystyle H}{\underset{\displaystyle H}{C}}-H$$

Propane C_3H_8

$$H-\overset{\displaystyle H}{\underset{\displaystyle H}{C}}-\overset{\displaystyle H}{\underset{\displaystyle H}{C}}-\overset{\displaystyle H}{\underset{\displaystyle H}{C}}-H$$

Boiling Points of Hydrocarbons

The graph shows the boiling points of several hydrocarbons. *(Note: Some points on the y-axis are negative.)*

Use the graph to answer the following questions.

1. **Reading Graphs** Where is 0°C on the graph?

2. **Interpreting Data** What is the approximate boiling point of C_3H_8? C_5H_{12}? C_6H_{14}?

3. **Calculating** What is the temperature difference between the boiling points of C_3H_8 and C_5H_{12}?

4. **Drawing Conclusions** At room temperature (about 22°C), which of the hydrocarbons are gases? How can you tell?

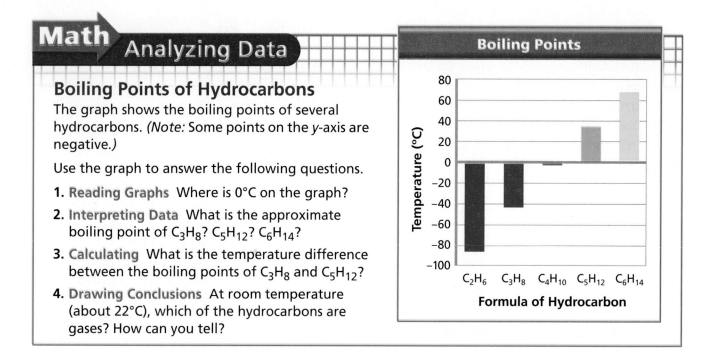

Boiling Points

Temperature (°C) / Formula of Hydrocarbon

C_2H_6 C_3H_8 C_4H_{10} C_5H_{12} C_6H_{14}

Isomers Consider the chemical formula of butane: C_4H_{10}. This formula does not indicate how the atoms are arranged in the molecule. In fact, there are two different ways to arrange the carbon atoms in C_4H_{10}. These two arrangements are shown in Figure 9. Compounds that have the same chemical formula but different structural formulas are called **isomers** (EYE soh murz). Each isomer is a different substance with its own characteristic properties.

Notice in Figure 9 that a molecule of one isomer, butane, is a straight chain. A molecule of the other isomer, isobutane, is a branched chain. Both molecules have 4 carbon atoms and 10 hydrogen atoms, but their atoms are arranged differently. And these two compounds have different properties. For example, butane and isobutane have different melting points and boiling points.

Butane C_4H_{10}

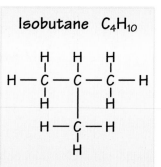

Isobutane C_4H_{10}

FIGURE 9
Isomers
C_4H_{10} has two isomers, butane and isobutane. **Applying Concepts** *Which isomer is a branched chain?*

Double Bonds and Triple Bonds So far in this section, structural formulas have shown only single bonds between any two carbon atoms (C—C). A single dash means a single bond. **In addition to forming a single bond, two carbon atoms can form a double bond or a triple bond.** A carbon atom can also form a single or double bond with an oxygen atom. Structural formulas represent a double bond with a double dash (C=C). A triple bond is indicated by a triple dash (C≡C).

Saturated and Unsaturated Hydrocarbons A hydrocarbon can be classified according to the types of bonds between its carbon atoms. If there are only single bonds, it has the maximum number of hydrogen atoms possible on its carbon chain. These hydrocarbons are called **saturated hydrocarbons.** You can think of each carbon atom as being "saturated," or filled up, with hydrogens. Hydrocarbons with double or triple bonds have fewer hydrogen atoms for each carbon atom than a saturated hydrocarbon does. They are called **unsaturated hydrocarbons.**

Notice that the names of methane, ethane, propane, and butane all end with the suffix *-ane.* In general, a chain hydrocarbon with a name ending in *-ane* is saturated, while a hydrocarbon with a name ending in *-ene* or *-yne* is unsaturated.

The simplest unsaturated hydrocarbon with one double bond is ethene (C₂H₄). Many fruits produce ethene gas. Ethene gas helps the fruit to ripen. The simplest hydrocarbon with one triple bond is ethyne (C₂H₂), which is commonly known as acetylene. Acetylene torches are used in welding.

 Reading Checkpoint What is the difference between saturated and unsaturated hydrocarbons?

FIGURE 10
Unsaturated Hydrocarbons
Ethene gas (C_2H_4), which causes fruits such as apples to ripen, has one double bond. Acetylene (C_2H_2), the fuel in welding torches, has one triple bond.

Ethene C_2H_4

$$H-\overset{\overset{\displaystyle H}{|}}{C}=\overset{\overset{\displaystyle H}{|}}{C}-H$$

Acetylene (Ethyne)
C_2H_2

$$H-C\equiv C-H$$

Substituted Hydrocarbons

Hydrocarbons contain only carbon and hydrogen. But carbon can form stable bonds with several other elements, including oxygen, nitrogen, sulfur, and members of the halogen family. **If just one atom of another element is substituted for a hydrogen atom in a hydrocarbon, a different compound is created.** In a **substituted hydrocarbon,** atoms of other elements replace one or more hydrogen atoms in a hydrocarbon. Substituted hydrocarbons include halogen-containing compounds, alcohols, and organic acids.

Compounds Containing Halogens In some substituted hydrocarbons, one or more halogen atoms replace hydrogen atoms. Recall that the halogen family includes fluorine, chlorine, bromine, and iodine.

One compound, Freon (CCl_2F_2), was widely used as a cooling liquid in refrigerators and air conditioners. When Freon was found to damage the environment, its use was banned in the United States. However, a very hazardous compound that contains halogens, trichloroethane ($C_2H_3Cl_3$), is still used in dry-cleaning solutions. It can cause severe health problems.

Alcohols The group —OH can also substitute for hydrogen atoms in a hydrocarbon. Each —OH, made of an oxygen atom and a hydrogen atom, is called a **hydroxyl group** (hy DRAHKS il). An **alcohol** is a substituted hydrocarbon that contains one or more hydroxyl groups.

Most alcohols dissolve well in water. They also have higher boiling points than hydrocarbons with a similar number of carbons. Therefore, the alcohol methanol (CH_3OH) is a liquid at room temperature, while the hydrocarbon methane (CH_4) is a gas. Methanol, which is extremely toxic, is used to make plastics and synthetic fibers. It is also used in solutions that remove ice from airplanes.

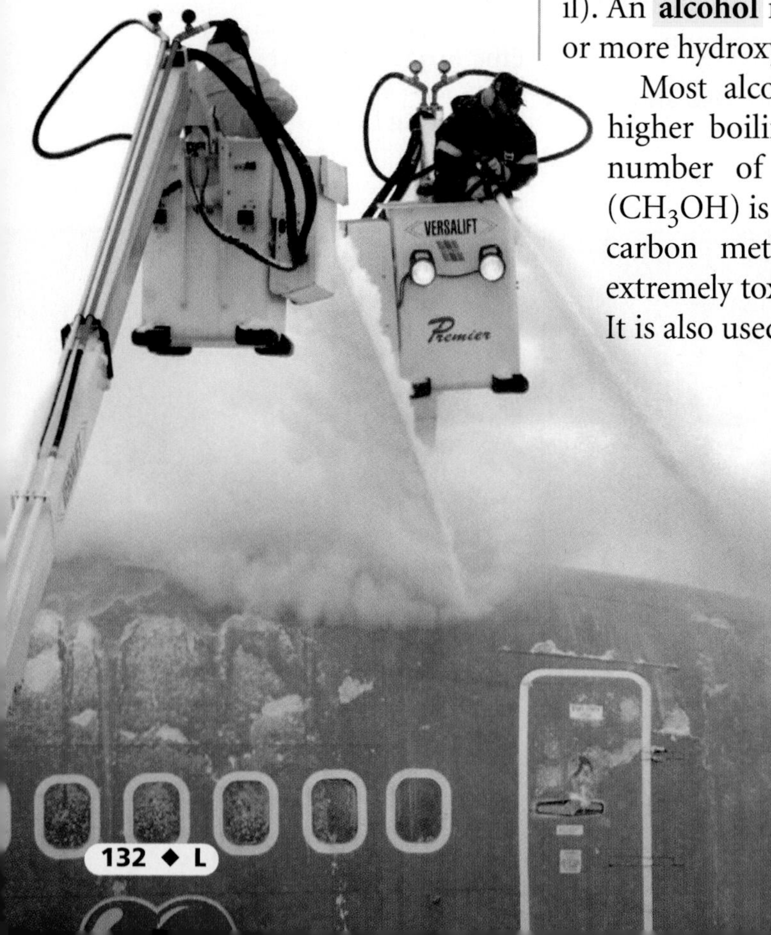

FIGURE 11
Alcohol
Methanol is used for de-icing an airplane in cold weather.
Classifying *What makes methanol a substituted hydrocarbon?*

Methanol CH_3OH

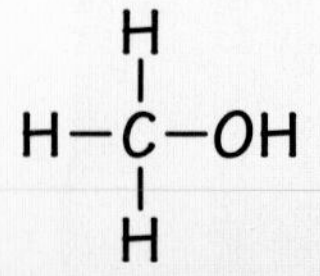

$$H-\overset{\displaystyle H}{\underset{\displaystyle H}{C}}-OH$$

FIGURE 12
Organic Acid
Formic acid is the simplest organic acid. It is the acid produced by ants and is responsible for the pain caused by an ant bite.

When a hydroxyl group is substituted for one hydrogen atom in ethane, the resulting alcohol is ethanol (C_2H_5OH). Ethanol is produced naturally by the action of yeast or bacteria on the sugar stored in corn, wheat, and barley. Ethanol is a good solvent for many organic compounds that do not dissolve in water. It is also added to gasoline to make a fuel for car engines called "gasohol." Ethanol is used in medicines and is found in alcoholic beverages. The ethanol used for industrial purposes is unsafe to drink. Poisonous compounds such as methanol have been added. The resulting poisonous mixture is called denatured alcohol.

Organic Acids Lemons, oranges, and grapefruits taste a little tart or sour, don't they? The sour taste of many fruits comes from citric acid, an organic acid. An **organic acid** is a substituted hydrocarbon that contains one or more carboxyl groups. A **carboxyl group** (kahr BAHKS il) is written as —COOH.

You can find organic acids in many foods. Acetic acid (CH_3COOH) is the main ingredient of vinegar. Malic acid is found in apples. Butyric acid makes butter smell rancid when it goes bad. Stinging nettle plants make formic acid (HCOOH), a compound that causes the stinging feeling. The pain from ant bites also comes from formic acid.

Esters

If you have eaten wintergreen candy, then you are familiar with the smell of an ester. An **ester** is a compound made by chemically combining an alcohol and an organic acid. **Many esters have pleasant, fruity smells.** Esters are responsible for the smells of pineapples, bananas, strawberries, and apples. If you did the Discover activity, you smelled different esters. Other esters are ingredients in medications, including aspirin and the local anesthetic used by dentists.

FIGURE 13
Esters
Strawberries contain esters, which give them a pleasant aroma and flavor.

FIGURE 14
Monomers and Polymers
This chain of plastic beads is somewhat like a polymer molecule. The individual beads are like the monomers that link together to build a polymer.
Comparing and Contrasting *How do polymers differ from monomers?*

Polymers

A very large molecule made of a chain of many smaller molecules bonded together is called a **polymer** (PAHL ih mur). The smaller molecules are called **monomers** (MAHN uh murz). The prefix *poly-* means "many," and the prefix *mono-* means "one." **Organic compounds, such as alcohols, esters, and others, can be linked together to build polymers with thousands or even millions of atoms.**

Some polymers are made naturally by living things. For example, sheep grow coats of wool. Cotton fibers come from the seed pods of cotton plants. And silk comes from the cocoons of silkworms. Other polymers, called synthetic polymers, are made in factories. If you are wearing clothing made from polyester or nylon, you are wearing a synthetic polymer right now! All plastics are synthetic polymers, too.

✔ **Reading Checkpoint** What is a monomer?

Section 2 Assessment

🎯 **Target Reading Skill** Outlining Work with a partner to check the answers in your graphic organizer.

Reviewing Key Concepts

1. **a.** Listing List properties common to many organic compounds.
   b. Applying Concepts You are given two solid materials, one that is organic and one that is not organic. Describe three tests you could perform to help you decide which is which.
2. **a.** Identifying What are some properties of hydrocarbons?
   b. Comparing and Contrasting How are hydrocarbons similar? How are they different?
3. **a.** Reviewing What are three kinds of carbon chains found in hydrocarbons?
   b. Describing Compare the chemical and structural formulas of butane and isobutane.

   c. Problem Solving Draw a structural formula for a compound called butene. In terms of bonding, how does butene differ from butane?
4. **a.** Defining What is a substituted hydrocarbon?
   b. Classifying What kinds of substituted hydrocarbons react to form an ester?
   c. Drawing Conclusions What do you think the term *polyester fabric* refers to?

Lab zone At-Home **Activity**

Mix It Up You can make a simple salad dressing to demonstrate one property of organic compounds. In a transparent container, thoroughly mix equal amounts of a vegetable oil and a fruit juice. Stop mixing, and observe the oil and juice mixture for several minutes. Explain your observations to your family.

How Many Molecules?

Problem

In this lab you will use gumdrops to represent atoms and toothpicks to represent bonds. How many different ways can you put the same number of carbon atoms together?

Skills Focus

making models

Materials

• toothpicks   • multicolored gumdrops
• other materials supplied by your teacher

Procedure

1. You will need gumdrops of one color to represent carbon atoms and gumdrops of another color to represent hydrogen atoms. When building your models, always follow these rules:
   • Each carbon atom forms four bonds.
   • Each hydrogen atom forms one bond.
   CAUTION: *Do not eat any of the food substances in this experiment.*

2. Make a model of CH_4 (methane).

3. Now make a model of C_2H_6 (ethane).

4. Make a model of C_3H_8 (propane). Is there more than one way to arrange the atoms in propane? (*Hint:* Are there any branches in the carbon chain or are all the carbon atoms in one line?)

5. Now make a model of C_4H_{10} (butane) in which all the carbon atoms are in one line.

6. Make a second model of butane with a branched chain.

7. Compare the branched-chain model with the straight-chain model of butane. Are there other ways to arrange the atoms?

8. Predict how many different structures can be formed from C_5H_{12} (pentane).

9. Test your prediction by building as many different models of pentane as you can.

Analyze and Conclude

1. **Making Models** Did any of your models have a hydrogen atom between two carbon atoms? Why or why not?

2. **Observing** How does a branched chain differ from a straight chain?

3. **Drawing Conclusions** How many different structures have the formula C_3H_8? C_4H_{10}? C_5H_{12}? Use diagrams to explain your answers.

4. **Predicting** If you bend a straight chain of carbons, do you make a different structure? Why or why not?

5. **Communicating** Compare the information you can get from models to the information you can get from formulas like C_6H_{14}. How does using models help you understand the structure of a molecule?

More to Explore

Use a third color of gumdrops to model an oxygen atom. An oxygen atom forms two bonds. Use the rules in this lab to model as many different structures for the formula $C_4H_{10}O$ as possible.

Life With Carbon

Reading Preview

Key Concepts
- What are the four main classes of organic compounds in living things?
- How are the organic compounds in living things different from one another?

Key Terms
- carbohydrate • glucose
- complex carbohydrate
- starch • cellulose • protein
- amino acid • lipid
- fatty acid • cholesterol
- nucleic acid • DNA • RNA
- nucleotide

Target Reading Skill

Asking Questions Before you read, preview the red headings. In a graphic organizer like the one below, ask a *what* question for each heading. As you read, write the answers to your questions.

Life With Carbon

Question	Answer
What is a carbohydrate?	A carbohydrate is . . .

Discover Activity

What Is in Milk?

1. Pour 30 mL of milk into a plastic cup.
2. Pour another 30 mL of milk into a second plastic cup. Rinse the graduated cylinder. Measure 15 mL of vinegar and add it to the second cup. Swirl the two liquids together and let the mixture sit for a minute.
3. Set up two funnels with filter paper, each supported in a narrow plastic cup.
4. Filter the milk through the first funnel. Filter the milk and vinegar through the second funnel.
5. What is left in each filter paper? Examine the liquid that passed through each filter paper.

Think It Over

Observing Where did you see evidence of solids? What do you think was the source of these solids?

Have you ever been told to eat all the organic compounds on your plate? Have you heard how eating a variety of polymers and monomers contributes to good health? What? No one has ever said those things to you? Well, maybe what you really heard was something about eating all the vegetables on your plate, or eating a variety of foods to give you a healthy balance of carbohydrates, proteins, fats, and other nutrients. All these nutrients are organic compounds, which are the building blocks of all living things.

A bowl of soup contains a variety of nutrients. ▼

Foods provide organic compounds, which the cells of living things use, change, or store. **The four classes of organic compounds required by living things are carbohydrates, proteins, lipids, and nucleic acids.** Carbohydrates, proteins, and lipids are nutrients. Nutrients (NOO tree unts) are substances that provide the energy and raw materials the body needs to grow, repair worn parts, and function properly.

Carbohydrates

A **carbohydrate** (kahr boh HY drayt) is an energy-rich organic compound made of the elements carbon, hydrogen, and oxygen. The word *carbohydrate* is made of two parts: *carbo-* and *-hydrate*. *Carbo-* means "carbon" and *-hydrate* means "combined with water." If you remember that water is made up of the elements hydrogen and oxygen, then you should be able to remember the three elements in carbohydrates.

Simple Carbohydrates The simplest carbohydrates are sugars. You may be surprised to learn that there are many different kinds of sugars. The sugar listed in baking recipes, which you can buy in bags or boxes at the grocery store, is only one kind. Other sugars are found naturally in fruits, milk, and some vegetables.

One of the most important sugars in your body is **glucose.** Its chemical formula is $C_6H_{12}O_6$. Glucose is sometimes called "blood sugar" because the body circulates glucose to all body parts through blood. The structural formula for a glucose molecule is shown in Figure 15.

The white sugar that sweetens cookies, candies, and many soft drinks is called sucrose. Sucrose is a more complex molecule than glucose and has a chemical formula of $C_{12}H_{22}O_{11}$.

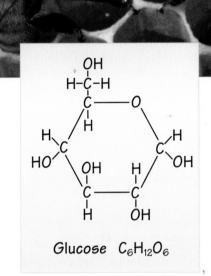

Glucose $C_6H_{12}O_6$

FIGURE 15
Carbohydrates
The honey made by honeybees contains glucose, a simple carbohydrate. **Applying Concepts** *What are some other examples of foods that contain carbohydrates?*

Discovery
CHANNEL
SCHOOL™

Carbon Chemistry

Video Preview
▶ Video Field Trip
Video Assessment

Complex Carbohydrates When you eat plants or food products made from plants, you are often eating complex carbohydrates. Each molecule of a simple carbohydrate, or sugar, is relatively small compared to a molecule of a complex carbohydrate. A **complex carbohydrate** is a polymer—a large, chainlike molecule made of smaller molecules linked together. In this case, the smaller molecules are simple carbohydrates bonded to one another. As a result, just one molecule of a complex carbohydrate may have hundreds of carbon atoms.

Two of the complex carbohydrates assembled from glucose molecules are starch and cellulose. **Starch and cellulose are both polymers built from glucose, but the glucose molecules are arranged differently in each case.** Having different arrangements means that starch and cellulose are different compounds. They serve different functions in the plants that make them. Your body also uses starch very differently from the way it uses cellulose.

• Tech & Design in History •

Advances in Organic Chemistry

Since the first organic compound was synthesized, biologists and chemists have synthesized many useful compounds, both biological and non-biological.

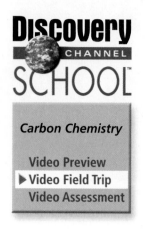

1828 Urea
The first organic compound is synthesized outside a living thing when Friedrich Wohler converts an inorganic compound into urea. Urea is an organic compound found in the urine of mammals and some other land animals.

1897 Aspirin
Felix Hoffman synthesizes aspirin, a safe and effective pain reliever that has also become one of the most widely used.

1955 Diamond
The first artificial diamonds are synthesized for industrial use.

1840   ⚡   1900   1930

Starch Plants store energy in the form of the complex carbohydrate **starch.** You can find starches in food products made from wheat grains, such as bread, cereal, and pasta. Starches are also found in rice, potatoes, and other vegetables.

The process of breaking large molecules, such as starch, into smaller ones involves chemical reactions that occur during digestion. The body digests the large starch molecules from these foods into individual glucose molecules. The body then breaks apart the glucose molecules, releasing energy in the process. This energy allows the body to carry out its life functions.

 Reading Checkpoint **What happens to starch molecules during digestion?**

Writing in Science

Research and Write
Research the development of another synthetic organic compound. Examples include insulin, human growth hormone, or vitamin B_{12}. Write a paragraph telling how the discovery happened and how it changed people's lives.

1998 Fat Substitute
A synthetic food additive replaces fat in snack foods such as potato chips. This food additive is "less fattening" than biological fat because it is not digested or absorbed by the body.

1980 Artificial Skin
Scientists patent an artificial skin made from cow protein and a carbohydrate that comes from shark cartilage. When placed on burn patients, the artificial skin speeds the healing process and produces less scarring than previously used methods.

2001 Cancer Drug
Leukemia is a blood cancer in which white blood cells divide uncontrollably. In 2001, scientists synthesized a cancer drug that directly attacks the protein that triggers the abnormal cell division.

1967 DNA
The first test-tube DNA is synthesized.

1960   1990   2020

Alphabet Soup

Here's how you can model the rearrangement of amino acids in your body.

1. Rearrange the letters of the word *proteins* to make a new word or words. (Don't worry if the new words don't make sense together.)
2. Choose three other words with ten or more letters. Repeat the activity.

Making Models What words did you make from *proteins*? What new words did you make from the words you chose? How does this activity model the way your body uses proteins in food to make new proteins?

FIGURE 16
Cellulose and Proteins
Cellulose, found in celery and other vegetables, is a carbohydrate your body needs. Your body also needs proteins, which are available in fish and meat.

Cellulose Plants build strong stems and roots with the complex carbohydrate **cellulose** and other polymers. If you imagine yourself crunching on a stick of celery, you will be able to imagine what cellulose is like. Most fruits and vegetables are high in cellulose. So are foods made from whole grains. Even though the body can break down starch, it cannot break down cellulose into individual glucose molecules. Therefore the body cannot use cellulose as an energy source. In fact, when you eat foods with cellulose, the molecules pass through you undigested. However, this undigested cellulose helps keep your digestive tract active and healthy. Cellulose is sometimes called fiber.

Proteins

If the proteins in your body suddenly disappeared, you would not have much of a body left! Your muscles, hair, skin, and fingernails are all made of proteins. A bird's feathers, a spider's web, a fish's scales, and the horns of a rhinoceros are also made of proteins.

Chains of Amino Acids What are proteins made of? **Proteins** are polymers formed from smaller molecules called amino acids. An **amino acid,** then, is a monomer and a building block of proteins. There are 20 kinds of amino acids found in living things. **Different proteins are made when different sequences of amino acids are linked into long chains.** Since proteins can be made of combinations of amino acids in any order and number, a huge variety of proteins is possible.

The structure of an amino acid is shown in Figure 17. Each amino acid molecule has a carboxyl group (—COOH). The *acid* in the term *amino acid* comes from this part of the molecule. An amino group, with the structure —NH₂, is the source of the *amino* half of the name. The remaining part of the molecule differs for each kind of amino acid.

Food Proteins Become Your Proteins Some of the best sources of protein include meat, fish, eggs, and milk or milk products. If you did the Discover activity, you used vinegar to separate proteins from milk. Some plant products, such as beans, are good sources of protein as well.

The body uses proteins from food to build and repair body parts and to regulate cell activities. But first the proteins must be digested. Just as starch is broken down into glucose molecules, proteins are broken down into amino acids. Then the body reassembles those amino acids into thousands of different proteins that can be used by cells.

Reading Checkpoint What are good sources of dietary protein?

Lipids

The third class of organic compounds in living things is lipids. Like carbohydrates, **lipids** are energy-rich compounds made of carbon, oxygen, and hydrogen. Lipids include fats, oils, waxes, and cholesterol. **Gram for gram, lipids release twice as much energy in your body as do carbohydrates.** Lipids behave somewhat like hydrocarbons, the compounds made of only carbon and hydrogen. They mix poorly with water.

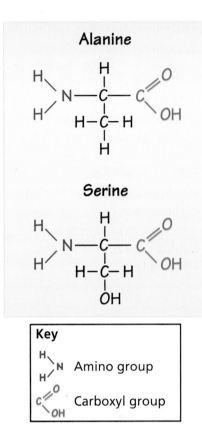

FIGURE 17
Amino Acids
Alanine and serine are two of the 20 amino acids in living things. Each amino acid has a carboxyl group (—COOH) and an amino group (—NH₂).

Alanine

Serine

Key

$\begin{smallmatrix}H\\H\end{smallmatrix}$N   Amino group

C$\begin{smallmatrix}O\\OH\end{smallmatrix}$ Carboxyl group

FIGURE 18
Fats and Oils
Foods that contain fats and oils include peanut butter, butter, cheese, corn, and olives. Classifying *Which class of organic compounds do fats and oils belong to?*

Like Oil or Water?

Oils mix poorly with water. They also do not evaporate very quickly when exposed to air.

1. Obtain a piece of brown paper and some samples of liquids provided by your teacher.
2. Using a dropper, place one drop of liquid from each sample on the paper.
3. Wait 5 minutes.
4. Note which of the liquids leaves a spot.

Inferring Which of the liquids is a fat or oil? How can you tell?

Fats and Oils Have you ever gotten grease on your clothes from foods that contain fats or oils? Fats are found in foods such as meat, butter, and cheese. Oils are found in foods such as corn, sunflower seeds, peanuts, and olives.

Fats and oils have the same basic structure. Each fat or oil is made from three **fatty acids** and one alcohol named glycerol. There is one main difference between fats and oils, however. Fats are usually solid at room temperature, whereas oils are liquid. The temperature at which a fat or an oil becomes a liquid depends on the chemical structure of its fatty acid molecules.

You may hear fats and oils described as "saturated" or "unsaturated." Like saturated hydrocarbons, the fatty acids of saturated fats have no double bonds between carbon atoms. Unsaturated fatty acids are found in oils. Monounsaturated oils have fatty acids with one double bond. Polyunsaturated oils have fatty acids with many double bonds. (Remember that *mono* means "one" and *poly* means "many.") Saturated fats tend to have higher melting points than unsaturated oils have.

Cholesterol Another important lipid is **cholesterol** (kuh LES tuh rawl), a waxy substance found in all animal cells. The body needs cholesterol to build cell structures and to form compounds that serve as chemical messengers. Unlike other lipids, cholesterol is not a source of energy. The body produces the cholesterol it needs from other nutrients. Foods that come from animals—cheese, eggs, and meat—also provide cholesterol. Because plants do not produce cholesterol, foods from plant sources, such as vegetable oils, never contain cholesterol.

Although cholesterol is often found in the same foods as saturated fats, they are different compounds. An excess level of cholesterol in the blood can contribute to heart disease. So can saturated fats. And saturated fats can affect the level of cholesterol in the blood. For this reason it is wise to limit your intake of both nutrients.

Reading Checkpoint What are sources of cholesterol in the diet?

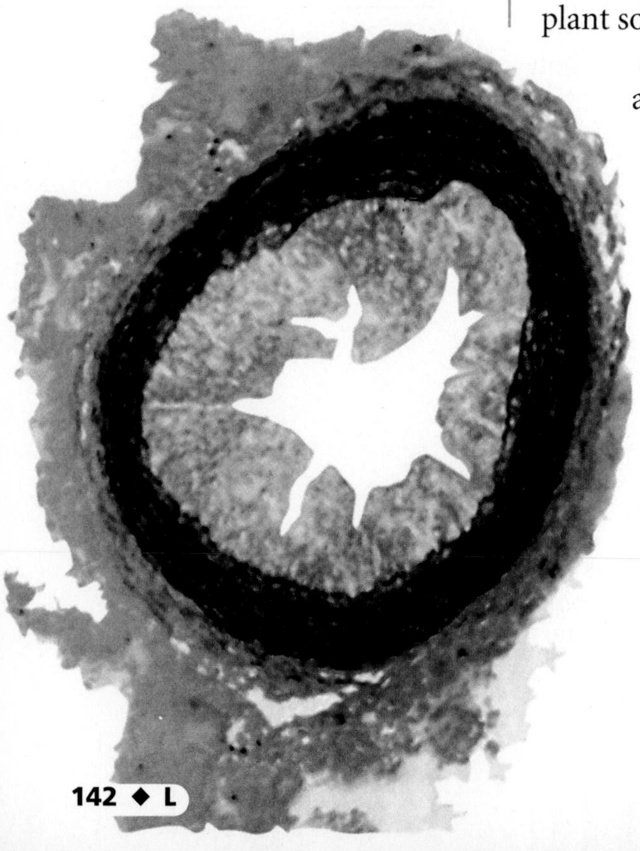

FIGURE 19
Cholesterol
Cholesterol deposits in this artery (shown in cross section) have narrowed the space available for blood to flow through.

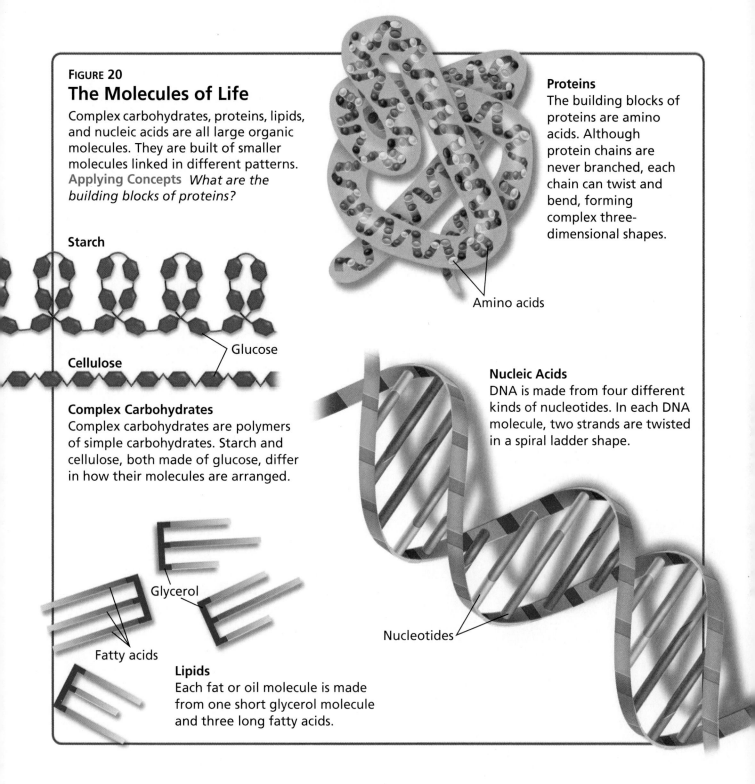

FIGURE 20
The Molecules of Life

Complex carbohydrates, proteins, lipids, and nucleic acids are all large organic molecules. They are built of smaller molecules linked in different patterns. Applying Concepts *What are the building blocks of proteins?*

Starch

Cellulose

Glucose

Complex Carbohydrates
Complex carbohydrates are polymers of simple carbohydrates. Starch and cellulose, both made of glucose, differ in how their molecules are arranged.

Glycerol

Fatty acids

Lipids
Each fat or oil molecule is made from one short glycerol molecule and three long fatty acids.

Proteins
The building blocks of proteins are amino acids. Although protein chains are never branched, each chain can twist and bend, forming complex three-dimensional shapes.

Amino acids

Nucleic Acids
DNA is made from four different kinds of nucleotides. In each DNA molecule, two strands are twisted in a spiral ladder shape.

Nucleotides

Nucleic Acids

The fourth class of organic compounds in living things is nucleic acids. **Nucleic acids** (noo KLEE ik) are very large organic molecules made up of carbon, oxygen, hydrogen, nitrogen, and phosphorus. You have probably heard of one type of nucleic acid—**DNA,** deoxyribonucleic acid (dee ahk see ry boh noo KLEE ik). The other type of nucleic acid, ribonucleic acid (ry boh noo KLEE ik), is called **RNA.**

Nucleotides DNA and RNA are made of different kinds of small molecules connected in a pattern. The building blocks of nucleic acids are called **nucleotides** (NOO klee oh tydz). In even the simplest living things, the DNA contains billions of nucleotides! There are only four kinds of nucleotides in DNA. RNA is also built of only four kinds of nucleotides, but the nucleotides in RNA differ from those in DNA.

DNA and Proteins **The differences among living things depend on the order of nucleotides in their DNA.** The order of DNA nucleotides determines a related order in RNA. The order of RNA nucleotides, in turn, determines the sequence of amino acids in proteins made by a living cell.

Remember that proteins regulate cell activities. Living things differ from one another because their DNA, and therefore their proteins, differ. The cells in a hummingbird grow and function differently from the cells in a flower or in you. When living things reproduce, they pass DNA and the information it carries to the next generation.

 Reading Checkpoint What are the building blocks of nucleic acids?

Other Compounds in Foods

Carbohydrates, proteins, and lipids are not the only compounds your body needs. Your body also needs vitamins, minerals, water, and salts. **Unlike the nutrients discussed so far, vitamins and minerals are needed only in small amounts.** They do not directly provide you with energy or raw materials.

Vitamins Vitamins are organic compounds that serve as helper molecules in a variety of chemical reactions in your body. For example, vitamin C, or ascorbic acid, is important for keeping your skin and gums healthy. Vitamin D helps your bones and teeth develop and keeps them strong.

Minerals Minerals are elements in the form of ions needed by your body. Unlike the other nutrients discussed in this chapter, minerals are not organic compounds. Minerals include calcium, iron, iodine, sodium, and potassium. They are important in many body processes.

FIGURE 21
Vitamins and Minerals
Sources of vitamins and minerals include fruits, vegetables, nuts, meats, and dairy products.
Observing *Which of these foods can you identify in the painting?*

If you eat a variety of foods, you will probably get the vitamins and minerals you need. Food manufacturers add some vitamins and minerals to packaged foods to replace vitamins and minerals that are lost in food processing. Such foods say "enriched" on their labels.

Sometimes manufacturers add extra vitamins and minerals to foods to "fortify," or strengthen, the nutritional value of the food. For example, milk is usually fortified with vitamin A and vitamin D.

Water Although water, H_2O, is not an organic compound, it is a compound that your body needs to survive. In fact, you would be able to survive only a few days without fresh water. Water makes up most of your body's fluids, including about 90 percent of the liquid part of your blood.

Nutrients and other important substances are dissolved in the watery part of the blood and carried throughout the body. Many chemical reactions, such as the breakdown of nutrients, take place in water. Wastes from cells dissolve in the blood and are carried away.

 Reading Checkpoint What is a vitamin?

Go Online
SciLINKS. NSTA

For: Links on organic compounds
Visit: www.SciLinks.org
Web Code: scn-1243

Section 3 Assessment

Target Reading Skill Asking Questions Review your graphic organizer and revise it based on what you just learned in the section.

Reviewing Key Concepts

1. **a. Naming** What are the four main classes of organic compounds required by living things?
   b. Classifying To what class of organic compounds does each of the following belong: glucose, RNA, cholesterol, cellulose, and oil?
   c. Making Generalizations How is each class of organic compounds used by the body?
2. **a. Identifying** What are the building blocks of complex carbohydrates?
   b. Comparing and Contrasting Compare the building blocks found in complex carbohydrates with those found in proteins.
   c. Making Judgments Would it matter if you ate foods that provided only carbohydrates but not proteins? Explain your reasoning.

Writing in Science

Advertisement Collect several food advertisements from magazines and watch some TV commercials. What do the ads say about nutrients? What do they emphasize? What do they downplay? Choose one ad and rewrite it to reflect the nutritional value of the product.

A Sweet Dilemma

Do you have a sweet tooth? Many people do. But there is a price to be paid for sweetness. Excess energy from sugars is easily stored by the body in the form of fat. The bacteria that cause tooth decay use sugars in the mouth as food. And for people who have the disease diabetes, sugary foods can raise blood sugar to a life-threatening level.

▲ Foods made with natural sugar

Food scientists have developed organic compounds that taste sweet but provide few calories per serving. These compounds include saccharin, cyclamate, and aspartame. Aspartame, for example, is 200 times as sweet as the sugar sucrose. Unfortunately, saccharin, cyclamate, and aspartame all have health risks associated with their use.

The Issues

Why Use Artificial Sweeteners?

Artificial sweeteners allow people with diabetes to enjoy sweet foods and beverages safely without raising their blood sugar level. But most people consume artificial sweeteners to lose weight. Advertising has glamorized being thin. In addition, being overweight can lead to serious health conditions, such as heart disease and high blood pressure.

What Are Possible Dangers?

Studies of saccharin and cyclamate have shown that large doses can lead to cancer and birth defects in lab animals. The U.S. Food and Drug Administration (FDA) has banned cyclamate, but many products still contain saccharin. The FDA, therefore, requires all products containing saccharin to have labels warning of possible health risks.

Early tests on aspartame showed it to be safe. For about 1 in every 10,000 people, however, the use of aspartame can be very dangerous. If a person has the genetic disorder called phenylketonuria (PKU), then one of the amino acids in aspartame can interfere with normal development. These people must avoid aspartame, especially as infants.

▲ **Foods made with sugar substitutes**

How Much Is Too Much?

Different people have different health concerns. Thus, the question of how much sugar or artificial sweetener is too much depends on the individual. For some people, no artificial sweetener is the answer. For others, moderate amounts, such as one or two servings a day, may be safe. But more scientific evidence must be collected to answer how much is too much.

You Decide

1. Identify the Problem
In your own words, explain the issues about the use of artificial sweeteners.

2. Analyze the Options
List the pros and cons for using artificial sweeteners as well as the pros and cons for using sugar.

3. Find a Solution
You are planning refreshments for a school event. Should you provide artificially sweetened soft drinks? Write a brief statement supporting your opinion.

Go Online
PHSchool.com

For: More on natural and artificial sweeteners
Visit: PHSchool.com
Web Code: cgh-2040

Consumer **Lab**

Are You Getting Your Vitamins?

Problem

Fruit juices contain vitamin C, an important nutrient. Which juice should you drink to obtain the most vitamin C?

Skills Focus

controlling variables, interpreting data, inferring

Materials

- 6 small cups • 6 plastic droppers • starch solution • iodine solution • vitamin C solution • samples of beverages to be tested (orange juice, apple juice, sports drink, fruit-flavored drink)

Procedure 🔬 🦺 🧤

PART 1 Vitamin C Test

1. Using a plastic dropper, place 25 drops of tap water into one of the small cups. Add 2 drops of starch solution.

2. Add 1 drop of iodine solution to the cup. **CAUTION:** *Iodine solution can stain skin or clothing.* Observe the color of the mixture. Save this cup to use for comparison in Step 4.

3. Using a fresh dropper, place 25 drops of vitamin C solution into another cup. Add 2 drops of starch solution.

4. Add 1 drop of iodine solution to the cup and swirl. Continue adding iodine a drop at a time, swirling after each drop, until you get a dark blue color similar to the color obtained in Step 2. Record the number of iodine drops.

5. Save the cup from Step 4 and use it for comparison during Part 2.

PART 2 Comparison Test

6. Make a data table in your notebook similar to the one on the next page.

7. Which beverage sample do you think has the most vitamin C? Which do you think has the least? Rank your beverage samples according to your predictions.

Data Table			
Test Sample	Drops of Iodine	Predicted Rank	Actual Rank
Vitamin C			
Orange juice			
Apple juice			
Sports drink			
Fruit-flavored drink			

8. Adapt the procedure from Part 1 so you can compare the amount of vitamin C in your beverage samples to the vitamin C solution.

9. Carry out your procedure after your teacher approves.

Analyze and Conclude

1. **Controlling Variables** What was the purpose for the test of the mixture of starch and water in Step 2?

2. **Controlling Variables** What was the purpose for the test of the starch, water, and vitamin C in Step 4?

3. **Drawing Conclusions** What do you think caused differences between your data from Step 2 and Step 4?

4. **Controlling Variables** Why did you have to add the same amount of starch to each of the beverages?

5. **Predicting** What would happen if someone forgot to add the starch to the beverage before they began adding iodine?

6. **Measuring** Of the four drinks you tested, which took the most drops of iodine before changing color? Which took the fewest?

7. **Interpreting Data** Which beverage had the most vitamin C? Which had the least? How do you know?

8. **Inferring** When you tested orange juice, the color of the first few drops of the iodine faded away. What do you think happened to the iodine?

9. **Communicating** If a beverage scored low in your test for vitamin C, does that mean it isn't good for you? Write a paragraph in which you explain what other factors might make a beverage nutritious or take away from its nutrient value.

Design an Experiment

Foods are often labeled with expiration dates. Labels often also say to "refrigerate after opening." Design an experiment to find out if the vitamin C content of orange juice changes over time at different temperatures. *Obtain your teacher's permission before carrying out your investigation.*

The BIG Idea **Structure and Function** Carbon has the ability to combine in many ways with itself and other elements. Carbon molecules serve many different functions in living things.

① Properties of Carbon

Key Concepts

- Few elements have the ability of carbon to bond with both itself and other elements in so many different ways. With four valence electrons, each carbon atom is able to form four bonds.

- Diamond, graphite, fullerenes, and nanotubes are four forms of the element carbon.

Key Terms

diamond	fullerene
graphite	nanotube

② Carbon Compounds

Key Concepts

- Many organic compounds have similar properties, in terms of melting points, boiling points, odor, electrical conductivity, and solubility.

- Hydrocarbons mix poorly with water. Also, all hydrocarbons are flammable.

- The carbon chains in a hydrocarbon may be straight, branched, or ring-shaped. In addition to forming a single bond, two carbon atoms can form a double bond or a triple bond.

- If just one atom of another element is substituted for a hydrogen atom in a hydrocarbon, a different compound is created.

- Many esters have pleasant fruity smells.

- Organic compounds, such as alcohols, esters, and others, can be linked together to build polymers with thousands or even millions of atoms.

Key Terms

- organic compound • hydrocarbon
- structural formula • isomer
- saturated hydrocarbon
- unsaturated hydrocarbon
- substituted hydrocarbon
- hydroxyl group • alcohol • organic acid
- carboxyl group • ester • polymer
- monomer

③ Life With Carbon

Key Concepts

- The four classes of organic compounds required by living things are carbohydrates, proteins, lipids, and nucleic acids.

- Starch and cellulose are both polymers built from glucose, but the glucose molecules are arranged differently in each case.

- Different proteins are made when different sequences of amino acids are linked into long chains.

- Gram for gram, lipids release twice as much energy in your body as do carbohydrates.

- Vitamins and minerals are needed only in small amounts.

- The differences among living things depend on the order of nucleotides in their DNA.

Key Terms

- carbohydrate • glucose
- complex carbohydrate • starch • cellulose
- protein • amino acid • lipid • fatty acid
- cholesterol • nucleic acid • DNA • RNA
- nucleotide

Review and Assessment

Organizing Information

Comparing and Contrasting Copy the Venn Diagram comparing proteins and nucleic acids onto a separate sheet of paper. Then complete it and add a title. (For more on Comparing and Contrasting, See the Skills Handbook.)

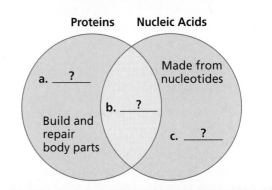

Proteins   Nucleic Acids

a. ___?___

Made from nucleotides

b. ___?___

Build and repair body parts

c. ___?___

Reviewing Key Terms

Choose the letter of the best answer.

1. A form of carbon in which the carbon bonds are arranged in a repeating pattern similar to a geodesic dome is
   a. a fullerene.
   b. graphite.
   c. diamond.
   d. a nanotube.

2. A compound that contains only hydrogen and carbon is defined as
   a. a monomer.
   b. an isomer.
   c. a hydrocarbon.
   d. a polymer.

3. The group $-COOH$ is characteristic of
   a. an organic acid.
   b. an alcohol.
   c. a hydroxyl group.
   d. a hydrocarbon.

4. The smaller molecules from which cellulose is made are
   a. glucose.
   b. amino acids.
   c. nucleotides.
   d. fatty acids.

5. Cholesterol is a type of
   a. nucleic acid.
   b. carbohydrate.
   c. lipid.
   d. cellulose.

If the statement is true, write *true*. If it is false, change the underlined word or words to make the statement true.

6. Because the bonds between layers of carbon atoms are weak, layers of <u>fullerenes</u> slide easily past one another.

7. Hydrocarbons that contain only single bonds are said to be <u>unsaturated hydrocarbons.</u>

8. An <u>organic acid</u> is characterized by one or more hydroxyl groups.

9. <u>Polymers</u> are compounds that have the same chemical formula but different structures.

10. Proteins are made up of long chains of <u>amino acids.</u>

Writing in Science

Web Site You are writing a feature article on carbon for a chemistry Web site. In your article, describe four forms of the element carbon. Include in your descriptions how the carbon atoms are arranged and how the bonds between the carbon atoms affect the properties of the substance. Include any helpful illustration.

DISCOVERY CHANNEL SCHOOL™

Carbon Chemistry

Video Preview
Video Field Trip
▶ Video Assessment

Review and Assessment

Checking Concepts

11. What does a dash written between two carbon symbols in a structural diagram represent?

12. What do diamonds, graphite, fullerenes, and nanotubes have in common?

13. How would you notice the presence of esters in a fruit such as a pineapple?

14. Starches and cellulose are both complex carbohydrates. How does your body treat these compounds differently?

15. Compare and contrast the fatty acids in fats that are solid at room temperature with fatty acids in oils that are liquids.

16. Why is the order of nucleotides in DNA important?

Thinking Critically

17. **Relating Cause and Effect** What features of the element carbon allow it to form the "backbone" of such a varied array of different compounds?

18. **Applying Concepts** Which of the diagrams below represents a saturated hydrocarbon? Which represents an unsaturated hydrocarbon? Explain your answer.

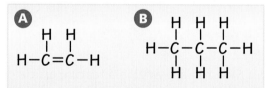

19. **Classifying** Classify each of the following compounds as a hydrocarbon, an alcohol, an organic acid, or a halogen-containing compound:

$C_{12}H_{25}COOH$ C_2H_5Cl
C_7H_{16} C_4H_9OH

20. **Posing Questions** Glucose and fructose are both simple carbohydrates with the formula $C_6H_{12}O_6$. What else do you need to know about glucose and fructose to decide if they should be considered different compounds?

Applying Skills

Use the following structural formulas to answer Questions 21–25.

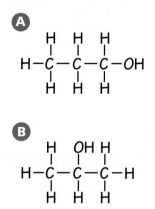

21. **Classifying** Which type of substituted hydrocarbons are compounds A and B? What information in the structural formulas did you use to decide your answer?

22. **Observing** What is the correct subscript for the carbon atoms (C) in the chemical formula that corresponds to each structural formula?

23. **Inferring** Are compounds A and B isomers? How can you tell?

24. **Predicting** Would you expect these two compounds to have identical properties or different properties? Explain.

25. **Problem Solving** What kind of compound would result if an organic acid were chemically combined with compound A? What properties would you expect the new compound to have?

Performance Assessment Display your data table classifying compounds in foods, along with the labels from which you collected your data. Point out the nutrients that are found in almost all foods and the nutrients found in only a few.

Standardized Test Prep

Choose the letter of the best answer.

1. The formula $C_5H_{11}OH$ represents an
   A amino acid.
   B organic acid.
   C alcohol.
   D ester.

2. Material X is a synthetic polymer that is strong and flexible and can be made into thread. Of the following choices, material X is most likely
   F cellulose.
   G fiberglass.
   H silk.
   J nylon.

Use the structural diagrams below and your knowledge of science to answer Questions 3–5.

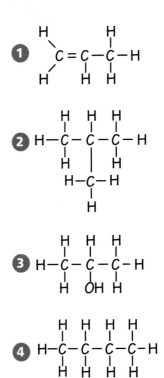

3. Isomers are organic compounds having the same chemical formula but different structural formulas. Which pair of compounds are isomers?
   A 1 and 2   **B** 1 and 3
   C 2 and 3   **D** 2 and 4

4. Which structural diagram represents an unsaturated hydrocarbon?
   F 1   **G** 2
   H 3   **J** 4

5. What is the ratio of carbon atoms to hydrogen atoms in the compound represented by 1?
   A 1 to 9
   B 9 to 1
   C 3 to 6
   D 6 to 3

Constructed Response

6. Explain why carbohydrates, lipids, and proteins are important parts of a well-balanced diet.

Soap—The Dirt Chaser

What slippery substance

- **makes things cleaner, fresher, brighter?**
- **can you put on your head and on your floors?**
- **rids your hands of germs?**

It's soap, which is a cleaner made from materials that are found in nature. People figured out how to make soap by heating natural fats or oils, alkali (a chemical they got from wood ashes), and water. Detergent is also a cleaner. It's similar to soap, but made from manufactured materials.

In a year, the average American uses about 11 kilograms of soap just to keep clean! Some of that soap is used for baths and showers. Soap is also used by medical experts to clean wounds and prevent infection.

In your home you use soaps and detergents to clean dishes, laundry, windows, floors, and much more. Even factories use soaps in the process of making products such as rubber, jewelry, aluminum, antifreeze, leather, and glossy paper.

So, if you lived without soap, you and your surroundings would be a lot dirtier! You would look and feel quite different. You may just owe your way of life to soap!

Car Wash
Young workers apply soap to this windshield.

Soap Molecule

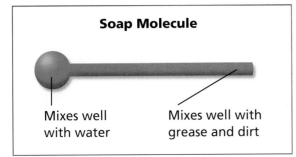

Mixes well with water

Mixes well with grease and dirt

Soap Molecules
These molecules help loosen dirt. Water washes away the dirt.

How Soap Works

1 You rub shampoo and water into your hair.

Wash the Dirt Away

Soap manufacturers claim that their products can wash away the dirt from the dirtiest clothes. How does that work? First, you need to wet the clothes with water that contains soap. The soap then spreads out and soaks into the material.

Each molecule of soap is shaped like a tiny tadpole. The tail-like end is similar to a hydrocarbon molecule. It mixes poorly with water, but it mixes well with dirt and grease. The large end, on the other hand, mixes well with water. When you wash, the soap molecules surround the dirt and break it up into tiny pieces that water can wash away.

Some dirt is difficult to dissolve. It takes longer for the soap molecules to loosen it. In these cases, rubbing, scrubbing, and squeezing may help to lift the dirt.

Some water, called hard water, has minerals dissolved in it—calcium, magnesium, and iron. In hard water, soap forms deposits, called scum. Scum doesn't dissolve and is difficult to wash away. It keeps clean hair from being shiny and leaves a "bathtub ring."

The invention of detergents helped solve the problem of scum and stubborn stains. For many cleaning tasks, detergent is more effective than soap. Detergent also dissolves in cold water more easily than soap.

2 Soap molecules in shampoo loosen the grease and dirt on your hair.

3 Soap molecules break the dirt into tiny pieces.

4 Water carries away the dirt surrounded by soap molecules.

Chemistry of Soap

How is soap made? It's the product of heating two types of compounds—an acid and a base. Acids and bases are compounds that have physical and chemical properties opposite to each other. An acid tastes sour. Grapefruits, pickles, and vinegar have acids in them. A base has properties that make it taste bitter and feel slippery. Bases and acids combine to neutralize each other.

Natural fats and oils are the source of the acids in soapmaking. Fats and oils are polymers, made of three fatty acid monomers and an alcohol called glycerol.

In soapmaking, the fatty acids combine with an alkali solution (made of bases). The mixture is processed using water and heat. The resulting chemical reaction is called *saponification*. Saponification produces the main material of soaps, called "neat" soap. The glycerol left over, also called glycerin, is pumped away.

The difference between solid and liquid soaps depends on the alkali that's added. In a solid soap, the alkali solution is the base sodium hydroxide. In liquid soaps, the alkali solution is the base potassium hydroxide.

Making Soap Using the Continuous Process

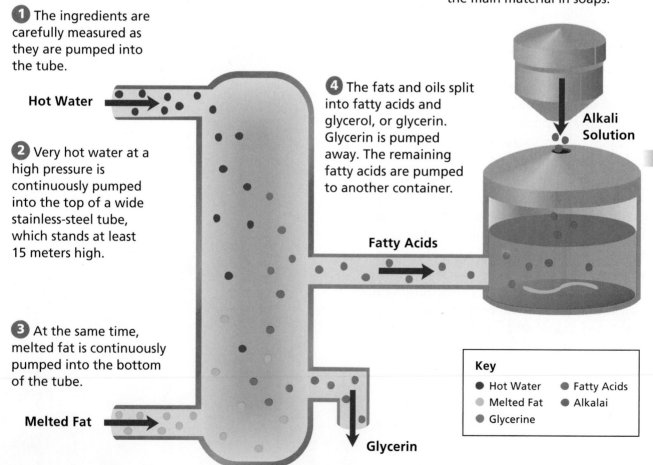

5 In the next container, the fatty acids combine with an alkali solution. Saponification occurs, resulting in neat soap—the main material in soaps.

1 The ingredients are carefully measured as they are pumped into the tube.

Hot Water

2 Very hot water at a high pressure is continuously pumped into the top of a wide stainless-steel tube, which stands at least 15 meters high.

4 The fats and oils split into fatty acids and glycerol, or glycerin. Glycerin is pumped away. The remaining fatty acids are pumped to another container.

Alkali Solution

Fatty Acids

3 At the same time, melted fat is continuously pumped into the bottom of the tube.

Melted Fat

Glycerin

Key
- Hot Water
- Melted Fat
- Glycerine
- Fatty Acids
- Alkalai

Soapmaking

After saponification occurs, neat soap is poured into molds. Other ingredients are sometimes added at this stage. Then the bars are stamped with a brand name or design and wrapped for shipment.

To make cosmetic soaps, an additional process called milling is needed. The neat soap is poured into large slabs instead of into molds. When the slab cools, several sets of rollers press and crush it. This process makes finer, gentler soaps that people can use on their face and hands.

At this stage, a variety of other ingredients can be added, such as scents, colors, or germicides (to kill bacteria). Air can be whipped into soap to make it float. Soapmakers compete to find the combination of ingredients that will be most attractive and smell pleasant to customers.

6 Neat soap is poured into molds and allowed to harden. Before neat soap is made into bars, flakes, or powdered soap, other optional ingredients such as abrasives (scrubbing agents) can be added.

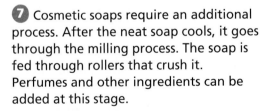

7 Cosmetic soaps require an additional process. After the neat soap cools, it goes through the milling process. The soap is fed through rollers that crush it. Perfumes and other ingredients can be added at this stage.

8 The finished soap is pressed, cut, stamped, and wrapped for shipment.

The Development of Soap

People have made soap for at least 2,300 years. The ancient Babylonians, Arabs, Greeks, Romans, and Celts made soap and sometimes traded it. The English word comes from "saipo," the Celts' name for soap. But these early cultures used soap primarily as a hair dye or a medicine, not as a cleaner! Only in the period from A.D. 100–199 did soap become known as a cleaning agent.

Soapmaking in Western Europe began about A.D. 100. First France was a leading producer, then Italy by 700, and Spain by 800. England didn't begin making soap until about 1200. But even then, most people didn't use soap for bathing.

Around 1790, Nicolas Leblanc, a French scientist, discovered that alkali could be made from common table salt and water. After that, soap could be made more easily and sold for profit.

Cutting Soap
This illustration shows that cutting soap required strength and precision.

In North America beginning around 1650, colonists made their own soap. Families would make up to a year's supply for their own use. Then around 1800, some people started collecting waste fats and ashes from their neighbors and making soap in large quantities. Soon bars of soap were sold from door to door.

In 1806, William Colgate, a soap and candle maker, started a business called Colgate and Company. His company produced soap and another cleaner, toothpaste. Today, nearly all soap is made in factories using large machinery.

The first detergent was produced in Germany around 1916, during World War I. Because fats were in short supply, detergent was meant to be a substitute for fat-based soap. However, people found that detergent was a better cleaner than soap for many purposes. The first household detergents appeared in the United States in 1933.

Soap Ad
This Lenox Soap advertisement is from 1898.

LENOX SOAP
LATHERS FREELY IN HARD WATER

LENOX SOAP
CINCINNATI
PROCTER & GAMBLE

"JUST FITS THE HAND"

Social Studies Activity

Create a time line of important events in the history of soapmaking. Find photos or make illustrations for the time line. Include the following events:

- early uses and users of soap
- beginning of the soapmaking industry
- early North American soapmaking
- first detergent

Before they discovered soap, what do you think people in earlier times used as a cleaner?

Colonial Soapmaking

Making soap in North America in the 1600s was an exhausting, unpleasant process. For months, colonists saved barrels of ashes from their wood fires. Then they poured hot water over the ashes. An alkali solution, called lye, dripped out of a spigot in the bottom of the barrel.

In a large kettle over a roaring outdoor fire, they boiled the alkali solution with fat, such as greases, which they had also saved. They had to keep the fire high and hot and stir the mixture for hours. When it was thick, they ladled the liquid soap into shallow boxes. Families made soap in the spring and sometimes again in the fall.

The following passage is from the novel *The Iron Peacock* by Mary Stetson Clarke. The story takes place in 1650 in Massachusetts Bay Colony. In the passage, two large supports hold a crossbar where the pot is hung over the fire. The women stir the pot with a homemade tool.

Colonial Soapmaking
Soapmaking was an all-day process done at home.

The next morning was fair, the air washed sparkling clear. Duncan built a fire under the framework. Maura measured the grease, adding a quantity of lye. Ross and Duncan placed the crossbar under the handle of the pot and raised it until it rested on the supports. Maura took up a long wooden bar with a shorter one set at right angles to it, and began stirring the contents of the pot.

"We'll be back at noon to lend you a hand," said Duncan.

Maura and Joanna took turns stirring the soap. When Maura judged it to be of the right consistency, they let the fire die down.

After the men had lifted the pot off the fire, Joanna and Maura ladled the thick brown liquid into boxes lined with old pieces of cloth.

It cooled quickly into thick cream-colored slabs. Maura would cut it into cakes in a few days, when it was solid enough to handle. Then she would stack the bars in a dry place where the air could circulate around them until the soap had seasoned enough for use.

Language Arts Activity

Reread the passage and list the steps for making soap. Think of a process or activity that you know well. It can be packing for a trip or preparing for a party. Jot down the steps and number them. Then, write a description of the process. Include steps and details so that a reader unfamiliar with your activity would know how to do it.

A Year's Supply of Soap

What would you do if you had to make a year's supply of your own soap, using modern ingredients? You probably buy the soap you use from a store. But it is still possible to make soap yourself by using the right ingredients and following specific instructions.

Soap recipes are as varied and numerous as food recipes. You can make soap using the oil from avocados, hazelnuts, or sunflower seeds. To add natural scents, you might include rose, cinnamon, cloves, lavender, lemon, mint, grapefruit, pine, rose, vanilla, or something else.

Colors might come from beetroot, cocoa, goldenrod, licorice, paprika, or even seaweed. You can even include "scrubbers" such as cornmeal, oatmeal, or poppy seeds!

Math Activity

Here is the ingredient list for one bar of soap with a mass of 141.8 grams.

List of Ingredients

16.8 grams alkali

45.4 grams water

42.2 grams olive oil

36.2 grams coconut oil

42.2 grams palm oil

Use the list to find the answers to these questions:

• What is the ratio of alkali to oil in this recipe? Round to the nearest tenth.

• If you made a large batch with a total mass of 1.7 kg, about how many bars of soap would you get in that batch?

• How much of each ingredient would you need to make this batch?

• If your family used two bars of soap per month, how many batches of soap would you make to provide one year's supply?

• How many batches would you make if your family used four bars of soap per month through the summer (June, July, and August), two bars per month through the winter (December, January, and February), and three bars per month during the rest of the year?

Soap Study

Organize a class project to survey and test soaps and soap products that are on the market today. Work in small groups. Choose one kind of cleaner to study, such as bar soaps, dishwashing detergents, laundry detergents, or another cleaner.

As your group investigates one kind of product, answer these questions:

- Look at the labels. What kinds of oils and other ingredients are listed?
- What do the makers claim these ingredients do? What language do they use to make these claims?
- How many kinds of surfaces can you clean with this product?

Next, collect several brands. Design an experiment to help you decide which brand works best.

- Decide what you will test for, such as how well the brand cleans grease.
- Develop a grading scale for rating the products.
- Before you begin, predict what your results will be.
- Keep all variables the same except for the brand.
- Perform the tests, collect data, and take careful notes.

Decide how to present your results to the class. You might include photographs of the test results, create a graph, or write a report describing and summarizing the results.

Think Like a Scientist

Scientists have a particular way of looking at the world, or scientific habits of mind. Whenever you ask a question and explore possible answers, you use many of the same skills that scientists do. Some of these skills are described on this page.

Observing

When you use one or more of your five senses to gather information about the world, you are **observing.** Hearing a dog bark, counting twelve green seeds, and smelling smoke are all observations. To increase the power of their senses, scientists sometimes use microscopes, telescopes, or other instruments that help them make more detailed observations.

An observation must be an accurate report of what your senses detect. It is important to keep careful records of your observations in science class by writing or drawing in a notebook. The information collected through observations is called evidence, or data.

Inferring

When you interpret an observation, you are **inferring,** or making an inference. For example, if you hear your dog barking, you may infer that someone is at your front door. To make this inference, you combine the evidence—the barking dog—and your experience or knowledge—you know that your dog barks when strangers approach—to reach a logical conclusion.

Notice that an inference is not a fact; it is only one of many possible interpretations for an observation. For example, your dog may be barking because it wants to go for a walk. An inference may turn out to be incorrect even if it is based on accurate observations and logical reasoning. The only way to find out if an inference is correct is to investigate further.

Predicting

When you listen to the weather forecast, you hear many predictions about the next day's weather—what the temperature will be, whether it will rain, and how windy it will be. Weather forecasters use observations and knowledge of weather patterns to predict the weather. The skill of **predicting** involves making an inference about a future event based on current evidence or past experience.

Because a prediction is an inference, it may prove to be false. In science class, you can test some of your predictions by doing experiments. For example, suppose you predict that larger paper airplanes can fly farther than smaller airplanes. How could you test your prediction?

Activity

Use the photograph to answer the questions below.

Observing Look closely at the photograph. List at least three observations.

Inferring Use your observations to make an inference about what has happened. What experience or knowledge did you use to make the inference?

Predicting Predict what will happen next. On what evidence or experience do you base your prediction?

Classifying

Could you imagine searching for a book in the library if the books were shelved in no particular order? Your trip to the library would be an all-day event! Luckily, librarians group together books on similar topics or by the same author. Grouping together items that are alike in some way is called **classifying.** You can classify items in many ways: by size, by shape, by use, and by other important characteristics.

Like librarians, scientists use the skill of classifying to organize information and objects. When things are sorted into groups, the relationships among them become easier to understand.

Activity

Classify the objects in the photograph into two groups based on any characteristic you choose. Then use another characteristic to classify the objects into three groups.

Making Models

Have you ever drawn a picture to help someone understand what you were saying? Such a drawing is one type of model. A model is a picture, diagram, computer image, or other representation of a complex object or process. **Making models** helps people understand things that they cannot observe directly.

Scientists often use models to represent things that are either very large or very small, such as the planets in the solar system, or the parts of a cell. Such models are physical models—drawings or three-dimensional structures that look like the real thing. Other models are mental models—mathematical equations or words that describe how something works.

Activity

This student is using a model to demonstrate what causes day and night on Earth. What do the flashlight and the tennis ball in the model represent?

Communicating

Whenever you talk on the phone, write a report, or listen to your teacher at school, you are communicating. **Communicating** is the process of sharing ideas and information with other people. Communicating effectively requires many skills, including writing, reading, speaking, listening, and making models.

Scientists communicate to share results, information, and opinions. Scientists often communicate about their work in journals, over the telephone, in letters, and on the Internet.

They also attend scientific meetings where they share their ideas with one another in person.

Activity

On a sheet of paper, write out clear, detailed directions for tying your shoe. Then exchange directions with a partner. Follow your partner's directions exactly. How successful were you at tying your shoe? How could your partner have communicated more clearly?

Making Measurements

By measuring, scientists can express their observations more precisely and communicate more information about what they observe.

Measuring in SI

The standard system of measurement used by scientists around the world is known as the International System of Units, which is abbreviated as SI (**Système International d'Unités,** in French). SI units are easy to use because they are based on powers of 10. Each unit is ten times larger than the next smallest unit and one tenth the size of the next largest unit. The table lists the prefixes used to name the most common SI units.

Length To measure length, or the distance between two points, the unit of measure is the **meter (m).** The distance from the floor to a doorknob is approximately one meter. Long distances, such as the distance between two cities, are measured in kilometers (km). Small lengths are measured in centimeters (cm) or millimeters (mm). Scientists use metric rulers and meter sticks to measure length.

Common SI Prefixes

Prefix	Symbol	Meaning
kilo-	k	1,000
hecto-	h	100
deka-	da	10
deci-	d	0.1 (one tenth)
centi-	c	0.01 (one hundredth)
milli-	m	0.001 (one thousandth)

Liquid Volume To measure the volume of a liquid, or the amount of space it takes up, you will use a unit of measure known as the **liter (L).** One liter is the approximate volume of a medium-size carton of milk. Smaller volumes are measured in milliliters (mL). Scientists use graduated cylinders to measure liquid volume.

Common Conversions

1 km	=	1,000 m
1 m	=	100 cm
1 m	=	1,000 mm
1 cm	=	10 mm

Activity

The larger lines on the metric ruler in the picture show centimeter divisions, while the smaller, unnumbered lines show millimeter divisions. How many centimeters long is the shell? How many millimeters long is it?

Activity

The graduated cylinder in the picture is marked in milliliter divisions. Notice that the water in the cylinder has a curved surface. This curved surface is called the *meniscus.* To measure the volume, you must read the level at the lowest point of the meniscus. What is the volume of water in this graduated cylinder?

Common Conversion

1 L	=	1,000 mL

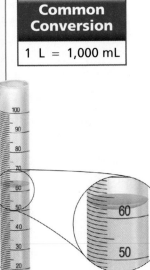

Mass To measure mass, or the amount of matter in an object, you will use a unit of measure known as the **gram (g).** One gram is approximately the mass of a paper clip. Larger masses are measured in kilograms (kg). Scientists use a balance to find the mass of an object.

Common Conversion
1 kg = 1,000 g

Activity

The mass of the potato in the picture is measured in kilograms. What is the mass of the potato? Suppose a recipe for potato salad called for one kilogram of potatoes. About how many potatoes would you need?

0.25 KG

Temperature To measure the temperature of a substance, you will use the **Celsius scale.** Temperature is measured in degrees Celsius (°C) using a Celsius thermometer. Water freezes at 0°C and boils at 100°C.

Time The unit scientists use to measure time is the **second (s).**

Activity

What is the temperature of the liquid in degrees Celsius?

Converting SI Units

To use the SI system, you must know how to convert between units. Converting from one unit to another involves the skill of **calculating,** or using mathematical operations. Converting between SI units is similar to converting between dollars and dimes because both systems are based on powers of ten.

Suppose you want to convert a length of 80 centimeters to meters. Follow these steps to convert between units.

1. Begin by writing down the measurement you want to convert—in this example, 80 centimeters.

2. Write a conversion factor that represents the relationship between the two units you are converting. In this example, the relationship is 1 meter = 100 centimeters. Write this conversion factor as a fraction, making sure to place the units you are converting from (centimeters, in this example) in the denominator.

3. Multiply the measurement you want to convert by the fraction. When you do this, the units in the first measurement will cancel out with the units in the denominator. Your answer will be in the units you are converting to (meters, in this example).

Example

80 centimeters = ▦ meters

$$80 \text{ centimeters} \times \frac{1 \text{ meter}}{100 \text{ centimeters}} = \frac{80 \text{ meters}}{100}$$

$$= 0.8 \text{ meters}$$

Activity

Convert between the following units.
1. 600 millimeters = ▦ meters
2. 0.35 liters = ▦ milliliters
3. 1,050 grams = ▦ kilograms

Conducting a Scientific Investigation

In some ways, scientists are like detectives, piecing together clues to learn about a process or event. One way that scientists gather clues is by carrying out experiments. An experiment tests an idea in a careful, orderly manner. Although experiments do not all follow the same steps in the same order, many follow a pattern similar to the one described here.

Posing Questions

Experiments begin by asking a scientific question. A scientific question is one that can be answered by gathering evidence. For example, the question "Which freezes faster—fresh water or salt water?" is a scientific question because you can carry out an investigation and gather information to answer the question.

Developing a Hypothesis

The next step is to form a hypothesis. A **hypothesis** is a possible explanation for a set of observations or answer to a scientific question. In science, a hypothesis must be something that can be tested. A hypothesis can be worded as an *If . . . then . . .* statement. For example, a hypothesis might be *"If I add table salt to fresh water, then the water will freeze at a lower temperature."* A hypothesis worded this way serves as a rough outline of the experiment you should perform.

Designing an Experiment

Next you need to plan a way to test your hypothesis. Your plan should be written out as a step-by-step procedure and should describe the observations or measurements you will make.

Two important steps involved in designing an experiment are controlling variables and forming operational definitions.

Controlling Variables In a well-designed experiment, you need to keep all variables the same except for one. A **variable** is any factor that can change in an experiment. The factor that you change is called the **manipulated variable**. In this experiment, the manipulated variable is the amount of table salt added to the water. Other factors, such as the amount of water or the starting temperature, are kept constant.

The factor that changes as a result of the manipulated variable is called the **responding variable.** The responding variable is what you measure or observe to obtain your results. In this experiment, the responding variable is the temperature at which the water freezes.

An experiment in which all factors except one are kept constant is called a **controlled experiment.** Most controlled experiments include a test called the control. In this experiment, Container 3 is the control. Because no salt is added to Container 3, you can compare the results from the other containers to it. Any difference in results must be due to the addition of salt alone.

Forming Operational Definitions Another important aspect of a well-designed experiment is having clear operational definitions. An **operational definition** is a statement that describes how a particular variable is to be measured or how a term is to be defined. For example, in this experiment, how will you determine if the water has frozen? You might decide to insert a stick in each container at the start of the experiment. Your operational definition of "frozen" would be the time at which the stick can no longer move.

Experimental Procedure
1. Fill 3 containers with 300 milliliters of cold tap water.
2. Add 10 grams of salt to Container 1; stir. Add 20 grams of salt to Container 2; stir. Add no salt to Container 3.
3. Place the 3 containers in a freezer.
4. Check the containers every 15 minutes. Record your observations.

Interpreting Data

The observations and measurements you make in an experiment are called **data.** At the end of an experiment, you need to analyze the data to look for any patterns or trends. Patterns often become clear if you organize your data in a data table or graph. Then think through what the data reveal. Do they support your hypothesis? Do they point out a flaw in your experiment? Do you need to collect more data?

Drawing Conclusions

A **conclusion** is a statement that sums up what you have learned from an experiment. When you draw a conclusion, you need to decide whether the data you collected support your hypothesis or not. You may need to repeat an experiment several times before you can draw any conclusions from it. Conclusions often lead you to pose new questions and plan new experiments to answer them.

Activity

Is a ball's bounce affected by the height from which it is dropped? Using the steps just described, plan a controlled experiment to investigate this problem.

Technology Design Skills

Engineers are people who use scientific and technological knowledge to solve practical problems. To design new products, engineers usually follow the process described here, even though they may not follow these steps in the exact order. As you read the steps, think about how you might apply them in technology labs.

Identify a Need

Before engineers begin designing a new product, they must first identify the need they are trying to meet. For example, suppose you are a member of a design team in a company that makes toys. Your team has identified a need: a toy boat that is inexpensive and easy to assemble.

Research the Problem

Engineers often begin by gathering information that will help them with their new design. This research may include finding articles in books, magazines, or on the Internet. It may also include talking to other engineers who have solved similar problems. Engineers often perform experiments related to the product they want to design.

For your toy boat, you could look at toys that are similar to the one you want to design. You might do research on the Internet. You could also test some materials to see whether they will work well in a toy boat.

Drawing for a boat design ▼

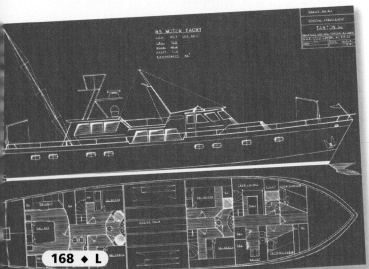

Design a Solution

Research gives engineers information that helps them design a product. When engineers design new products, they usually work in teams.

Generating Ideas Often design teams hold brainstorming meetings in which any team member can contribute ideas. **Brainstorming** is a creative process in which one team member's suggestions often spark ideas in other group members. Brainstorming can lead to new approaches to solving a design problem.

Evaluating Constraints During brainstorming, a design team will often come up with several possible designs. The team must then evaluate each one.

As part of their evaluation, engineers consider constraints. **Constraints** are factors that limit or restrict a product design. Physical characteristics, such as the properties of materials used to make your toy boat, are constraints. Money and time are also constraints. If the materials in a product cost a lot, or if the product takes a long time to make, the design may be impractical.

Making Trade-offs Design teams usually need to make trade-offs. In a **trade-off,** engineers give up one benefit of a proposed design in order to obtain another. In designing your toy boat, you will have to make trade-offs. For example, suppose one material is sturdy but not fully waterproof. Another material is more waterproof, but breakable. You may decide to give up the benefit of sturdiness in order to obtain the benefit of waterproofing.

Build and Evaluate a Prototype

Once the team has chosen a design plan, the engineers build a prototype of the product. A **prototype** is a working model used to test a design. Engineers evaluate the prototype to see whether it works well, is easy to operate, is safe to use, and holds up to repeated use.

Think of your toy boat. What would the prototype be like? Of what materials would it be made? How would you test it?

Troubleshoot and Redesign

Few prototypes work perfectly, which is why they need to be tested. Once a design team has tested a prototype, the members analyze the results and identify any problems. The team then tries to **troubleshoot,** or fix the design problems. For example, if your toy boat leaks or wobbles, the boat should be redesigned to eliminate those problems.

Communicate the Solution

A team needs to communicate the final design to the people who will manufacture and use the product. To do this, teams may use sketches, detailed drawings, computer simulations, and word descriptions.

Activity

You can use the technology design process to design and build a toy boat.

Research and Investigate

1. Visit the library or go online to research toy boats.

2. Investigate how a toy boat can be powered, including wind, rubber bands, or baking soda and vinegar.

3. Brainstorm materials, shapes, and steering for your boat.

Design and Build

4. Based on your research, design a toy boat that
   • is made of readily available materials
   • is no larger than 15 cm long and 10 cm wide

   • includes a power system, a rudder, and an area for cargo
   • travels 2 meters in a straight line carrying a load of 20 pennies

5. Sketch your design and write a step-by-step plan for building your boat. After your teacher approves your plan, build your boat.

Evaluate and Redesign

6. Test your boat, evaluate the results, and troubleshoot any problems.

7. Based on your evaluation, redesign your toy boat so it performs better.

Creating Data Tables and Graphs

How can you make sense of the data in a science experiment?
The first step is to organize the data to help you understand them.
Data tables and graphs are helpful tools for organizing data.

Data Tables

You have gathered your materials and set up your experiment. But before you start, you need to plan a way to record what happens during the experiment. By creating a data table, you can record your observations and measurements in an orderly way.

Suppose, for example, that a scientist conducted an experiment to find out how many Calories people of different body masses burn while doing various activities. The data table shows the results.

Notice in this data table that the manipulated variable (body mass) is the heading of one column. The responding variable (for

Calories Burned in 30 Minutes			
Body Mass	Experiment 1: Bicycling	Experiment 2: Playing Basketball	Experiment 3: Watching Television
30 kg	60 Calories	120 Calories	21 Calories
40 kg	77 Calories	164 Calories	27 Calories
50 kg	95 Calories	206 Calories	33 Calories
60 kg	114 Calories	248 Calories	38 Calories

Experiment 1, the number of Calories burned while bicycling) is the heading of the next column. Additional columns were added for related experiments.

Bar Graphs

To compare how many Calories a person burns doing various activities, you could create a bar graph. A bar graph is used to display data in a number of separate, or distinct, categories. In this example, bicycling, playing basketball, and watching television are the three categories.

To create a bar graph, follow these steps.

1. On graph paper, draw a horizontal, or *x*-, axis and a vertical, or *y*-, axis.

2. Write the names of the categories to be graphed along the horizontal axis. Include an overall label for the axis as well.

3. Label the vertical axis with the name of the responding variable. Include units of measurement. Then create a scale along the axis by marking off equally spaced numbers that cover the range of the data collected.

4. For each category, draw a solid bar using the scale on the vertical axis to determine the height. Make all the bars the same width.

5. Add a title that describes the graph.

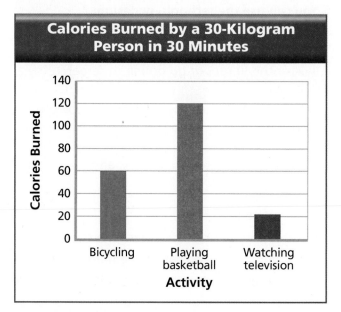

Line Graphs

To see whether a relationship exists between body mass and the number of Calories burned while bicycling, you could create a line graph. A line graph is used to display data that show how one variable (the responding variable) changes in response to another variable (the manipulated variable). You can use a line graph when your manipulated variable is **continuous,** that is, when there are other points between the ones that you tested. In this example, body mass is a continuous variable because there are other body masses between 30 and 40 kilograms (for example, 31 kilograms). Time is another example of a continuous variable.

Line graphs are powerful tools because they allow you to estimate values for conditions that you did not test in the experiment. For example, you can use the line graph to estimate that a 35-kilogram person would burn 68 Calories while bicycling.

To create a line graph, follow these steps.

1. On graph paper, draw a horizontal, or *x*-, axis and a vertical, or *y*-, axis.

2. Label the horizontal axis with the name of the manipulated variable. Label the vertical axis with the name of the responding variable. Include units of measurement.

3. Create a scale on each axis by marking off equally spaced numbers that cover the range of the data collected.

4. Plot a point on the graph for each piece of data. In the line graph above, the dotted lines show how to plot the first data point (30 kilograms and 60 Calories). Follow an imaginary vertical line extending up from the horizontal axis at the 30-kilogram mark. Then follow an imaginary horizontal line extending across from the vertical axis at the 60-Calorie mark. Plot the point where the two lines intersect.

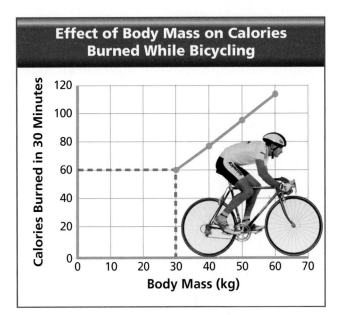

Effect of Body Mass on Calories Burned While Bicycling

5. Connect the plotted points with a solid line. (In some cases, it may be more appropriate to draw a line that shows the general trend of the plotted points. In those cases, some of the points may fall above or below the line. Also, not all graphs are linear. It may be more appropriate to draw a curve to connect the points.)

6. Add a title that identifies the variables or relationship in the graph.

Activity

Create line graphs to display the data from Experiment 2 and Experiment 3 in the data table.

Activity

You read in the newspaper that a total of 4 centimeters of rain fell in your area in June, 2.5 centimeters fell in July, and 1.5 centimeters fell in August. What type of graph would you use to display these data? Use graph paper to create the graph.

Circle Graphs

Like bar graphs, circle graphs can be used to display data in a number of separate categories. Unlike bar graphs, however, circle graphs can only be used when you have data for *all* the categories that make up a given topic. A circle graph is sometimes called a pie chart. The pie represents the entire topic, while the slices represent the individual categories. The size of a slice indicates what percentage of the whole a particular category makes up.

The data table below shows the results of a survey in which 24 teenagers were asked to identify their favorite sport. The data were then used to create the circle graph at the right.

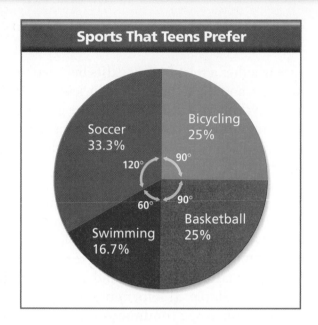

Sports That Teens Prefer

Favorite Sports	
Sport	**Students**
Soccer	8
Basketball	6
Bicycling	6
Swimming	4

To create a circle graph, follow these steps.

1. Use a compass to draw a circle. Mark the center with a point. Then draw a line from the center point to the top of the circle.

2. Determine the size of each "slice" by setting up a proportion where x equals the number of degrees in a slice. (*Note:* A circle contains 360 degrees.) For example, to find the number of degrees in the "soccer" slice, set up the following proportion:

$$\frac{\text{Students who prefer soccer}}{\text{Total number of students}} = \frac{x}{\text{Total number of degrees in a circle}}$$

$$\frac{8}{24} = \frac{x}{360}$$

Cross-multiply and solve for x.

$$24x = 8 \times 360$$
$$x = 120$$

The "soccer" slice should contain 120 degrees.

3. Use a protractor to measure the angle of the first slice, using the line you drew to the top of the circle as the 0° line. Draw a line from the center of the circle to the edge for the angle you measured.

4. Continue around the circle by measuring the size of each slice with the protractor. Start measuring from the edge of the previous slice so the wedges do not overlap. When you are done, the entire circle should be filled in.

5. Determine the percentage of the whole circle that each slice represents. To do this, divide the number of degrees in a slice by the total number of degrees in a circle (360), and multiply by 100%. For the "soccer" slice, you can find the percentage as follows:

$$\frac{120}{360} \times 100\% = 33.3\%$$

6. Use a different color for each slice. Label each slice with the category and with the percentage of the whole it represents.

7. Add a title to the circle graph.

Activity

In a class of 28 students, 12 students take the bus to school, 10 students walk, and 6 students ride their bicycles. Create a circle graph to display these data.

Math Review

Scientists use math to organize, analyze, and present data.
This appendix will help you review some basic math skills.

Mean, Median, and Mode

The **mean** is the average, or the sum of the data divided by the number of data items. The middle number in a set of ordered data is called the **median.** The **mode** is the number that appears most often in a set of data.

> **Example**
>
> A scientist counted the number of distinct songs sung by seven different male birds and collected the data shown below.
>
> | Male Bird Songs | | | | | | | |
> |---|---|---|---|---|---|---|---|
> | **Bird** | A | B | C | D | E | F | G |
> | **Number of Songs** | 36 | 29 | 40 | 35 | 28 | 36 | 27 |
>
> To determine the mean number of songs, add the total number of songs and divide by the number of data items—in this case, the number of male birds.
>
> **Mean = $\frac{231}{7}$ = 33 songs**
>
> To find the median number of songs, arrange the data in numerical order and find the number in the middle of the series.
>
> **27 28 29 35 36 36 40**
>
> The number in the middle is 35, so the median number of songs is 35.
> The mode is the value that appears most frequently. In the data, 36 appears twice, while each other item appears only once. Therefore, 36 songs is the mode.

> **Practice**
>
> Find out how many minutes it takes each student in your class to get to school. Then find the mean, median, and mode for the data.

Probability

Probability is the chance that an event will occur. Probability can be expressed as a ratio, a fraction, or a percentage. For example, when you flip a coin, the probability that the coin will land heads up is 1 in 2, or $\frac{1}{2}$, or 50 percent.

The probability that an event will happen can be expressed in the following formula.

$$P(\text{event}) = \frac{\text{Number of times the event can occur}}{\text{Total number of possible events}}$$

> **Example**
>
> A paper bag contains 25 blue marbles, 5 green marbles, 5 orange marbles, and 15 yellow marbles. If you close your eyes and pick a marble from the bag, what is the probability that it will be yellow?
>
> $$P(\text{yellow marbles}) = \frac{15 \text{ yellow marbles}}{50 \text{ marbles total}}$$
>
> $$P = \frac{15}{50}, \text{ or } \frac{3}{10}, \text{ or } 30\%$$

> **Practice**
>
> Each side of a cube has a letter on it. Two sides have *A*, three sides have *B*, and one side has *C*. If you roll the cube, what is the probability that *A* will land on top?

Area

The **area** of a surface is the number of square units that cover it. The front cover of your textbook has an area of about 600 cm^2.

Area of a Rectangle and a Square To find the area of a rectangle, multiply its length times its width. The formula for the area of a rectangle is

$$A = \ell \times w, \text{ or } A = \ell w$$

Since all four sides of a square have the same length, the area of a square is the length of one side multiplied by itself, or squared.

$$A = s \times s, \text{ or } A = s^2$$

Example

A scientist is studying the plants in a field that measures 75 m × 45 m. What is the area of the field?

$$A = \ell \times w$$
$$A = 75 \text{ m} \times 45 \text{ m}$$
$$A = 3{,}375 \text{ m}^2$$

Area of a Circle The formula for the area of a circle is

$$A = \pi \times r \times r, \text{ or } A = \pi r^2$$

The length of the radius is represented by r, and the value of π is approximately $\frac{22}{7}$.

Example

Find the area of a circle with a radius of 14 cm.

$$A = \pi r^2$$
$$A = 14 \times 14 \times \frac{22}{7}$$
$$A = 616 \text{ cm}^2$$

Practice

Find the area of a circle that has a radius of 21 m.

Circumference

The distance around a circle is called the circumference. The formula for finding the circumference of a circle is

$$C = 2 \times \pi \times r, \text{ or } C = 2\pi r$$

Example

The radius of a circle is 35 cm. What is its circumference?

$$C = 2\pi r$$
$$C = 2 \times 35 \times \frac{22}{7}$$
$$C = 220 \text{ cm}$$

Practice

What is the circumference of a circle with a radius of 28 m?

Volume

The volume of an object is the number of cubic units it contains. The volume of a wastebasket, for example, might be about 26,000 cm^3.

Volume of a Rectangular Object To find the volume of a rectangular object, multiply the object's length times its width times its height.

$$V = \ell \times w \times h, \text{ or } V = \ell w h$$

Example

Find the volume of a box with length 24 cm, width 12 cm, and height 9 cm.

$$V = \ell w h$$
$$V = 24 \text{ cm} \times 12 \text{ cm} \times 9 \text{ cm}$$
$$V = 2{,}592 \text{ cm}^3$$

Practice

What is the volume of a rectangular object with length 17 cm, width 11 cm, and height 6 cm?

Fractions

A **fraction** is a way to express a part of a whole. In the fraction $\frac{4}{7}$, 4 is the numerator and 7 is the denominator.

Adding and Subtracting Fractions To add or subtract two or more fractions that have a common denominator, first add or subtract the numerators. Then write the sum or difference over the common denominator.

To find the sum or difference of fractions with different denominators, first find the least common multiple of the denominators. This is known as the least common denominator. Then convert each fraction to equivalent fractions with the least common denominator. Add or subtract the numerators. Then write the sum or difference over the common denominator.

> **Example**
>
> $$\frac{5}{6} - \frac{3}{4} = \frac{10}{12} - \frac{9}{12} = \frac{10-9}{12} = \frac{1}{12}$$

Multiplying Fractions To multiply two fractions, first multiply the two numerators, then multiply the two denominators.

> **Example**
>
> $$\frac{5}{6} \times \frac{2}{3} = \frac{5 \times 2}{6 \times 3} = \frac{10}{18} = \frac{5}{9}$$

Dividing Fractions Dividing by a fraction is the same as multiplying by its reciprocal. Reciprocals are numbers whose numerators and denominators have been switched. To divide one fraction by another, first invert the fraction you are dividing by—in other words, turn it upside down. Then multiply the two fractions.

> **Example**
>
> $$\frac{2}{5} \div \frac{7}{8} = \frac{2}{5} \times \frac{8}{7} = \frac{2 \times 8}{5 \times 7} = \frac{16}{35}$$

> **Practice**
>
> Solve the following: $\frac{3}{7} \div \frac{4}{5}$.

Decimals

Fractions whose denominators are 10, 100, or some other power of 10 are often expressed as decimals. For example, the fraction $\frac{9}{10}$ can be expressed as the decimal 0.9, and the fraction $\frac{7}{100}$ can be written as 0.07.

Adding and Subtracting With Decimals To add or subtract decimals, line up the decimal points before you carry out the operation.

> **Example**
>
> | 27.4 | 278.635 |
> |---|---|
> | + 6.19 | − 191.4 |
> | 33.59 | 87.235 |

Multiplying With Decimals When you multiply two numbers with decimals, the number of decimal places in the product is equal to the total number of decimal places in each number being multiplied.

> **Example**
>
> 46.2 (one decimal place)
> × 2.37 (two decimal places)
> 109.494 (three decimal places)

Dividing With Decimals To divide a decimal by a whole number, put the decimal point in the quotient above the decimal point in the dividend.

> **Example**
>
> $15.5 \div 5$
>
>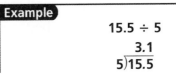

To divide a decimal by a decimal, you need to rewrite the divisor as a whole number. Do this by multiplying both the divisor and dividend by the same multiple of 10.

> **Example**
>
> $1.68 \div 4.2 = 16.8 \div 42$
>
> $$\frac{0.4}{42)16.8}$$

> **Practice**
>
> Multiply 6.21 by 8.5.

Ratio and Proportion

A **ratio** compares two numbers by division. For example, suppose a scientist counts 800 wolves and 1,200 moose on an island. The ratio of wolves to moose can be written as a fraction, $\frac{800}{1,200}$, which can be reduced to $\frac{2}{3}$. The same ratio can also be expressed as 2 to 3 or 2 : 3.

A **proportion** is a mathematical sentence saying that two ratios are equivalent. For example, a proportion could state that $\frac{800 \text{ wolves}}{1,200 \text{ moose}} = \frac{2 \text{ wolves}}{3 \text{ moose}}$. You can sometimes set up a proportion to determine or estimate an unknown quantity. For example, suppose a scientist counts 25 beetles in an area of 10 square meters. The scientist wants to estimate the number of beetles in 100 square meters.

> **Example**
>
> 1. Express the relationship between beetles and area as a ratio: $\frac{25}{10}$, simplified to $\frac{5}{2}$.
> 2. Set up a proportion, with x representing the number of beetles. The proportion can be stated as $\frac{5}{2} = \frac{x}{100}$.
> 3. Begin by cross-multiplying. In other words, multiply each fraction's numerator by the other fraction's denominator.
>
> $5 \times 100 = 2 \times x$, or $500 = 2x$
>
> 4. To find the value of x, divide both sides by 2. The result is 250, or 250 beetles in 100 square meters.

> **Practice**
>
> Find the value of x in the following proportion: $\frac{6}{7} = \frac{x}{49}$.

Percentage

A **percentage** is a ratio that compares a number to 100. For example, there are 37 granite rocks in a collection that consists of 100 rocks. The ratio $\frac{37}{100}$ can be written as 37%. Granite rocks make up 37% of the rock collection.

You can calculate percentages of numbers other than 100 by setting up a proportion.

> **Example**
>
> Rain falls on 9 days out of 30 in June. What percentage of the days in June were rainy?
>
> $$\frac{9 \text{ days}}{30 \text{ days}} = \frac{d\%}{100\%}$$
>
> To find the value of d, begin by cross-multiplying, as for any proportion:
>
> $9 \times 100 = 30 \times d \qquad d = \frac{900}{30} \qquad d = 30$

> **Practice**
>
> There are 300 marbles in a jar, and 42 of those marbles are blue. What percentage of the marbles are blue?

Significant Figures

The **precision** of a measurement depends on the instrument you use to take the measurement. For example, if the smallest unit on the ruler is millimeters, then the most precise measurement you can make will be in millimeters.

The sum or difference of measurements can only be as precise as the least precise measurement being added or subtracted. Round your answer so that it has the same number of digits after the decimal as the least precise measurement. Round up if the last digit is 5 or more, and round down if the last digit is 4 or less.

Example

Subtract a temperature of 5.2°C from the temperature 75.46°C.

75.46 − 5.2 = 70.26

5.2 has the fewest digits after the decimal, so it is the least precise measurement. Since the last digit of the answer is 6, round up to 3. The most precise difference between the measurements is 70.3°C.

Practice

Add 26.4 m to 8.37 m. Round your answer according to the precision of the measurements.

Significant figures are the number of nonzero digits in a measurement. Zeroes between nonzero digits are also significant. For example, the measurements 12,500 L, 0.125 cm, and 2.05 kg all have three significant figures. When you multiply and divide measurements, the one with the fewest significant figures determines the number of significant figures in your answer.

Example

Multiply 110 g by 5.75 g.

110 × 5.75 = 632.5

Because 110 has only two significant figures, round the answer to 630 g.

Scientific Notation

A **factor** is a number that divides into another number with no remainder. In the example, the number 3 is used as a factor four times.

An **exponent** tells how many times a number is used as a factor. For example, $3 \times 3 \times 3 \times 3$ can be written as 3^4. The exponent 4 indicates that the number 3 is used as a factor four times. Another way of expressing this is to say that 81 is equal to 3 to the fourth power.

Example

$$3^4 = 3 \times 3 \times 3 \times 3 = 81$$

Scientific notation uses exponents and powers of ten to write very large or very small numbers in shorter form. When you write a number in scientific notation, you write the number as two factors. The first factor is any number between 1 and 10. The second factor is a power of 10, such as 10^3 or 10^6.

Example

The average distance between the planet Mercury and the sun is 58,000,000 km. To write the first factor in scientific notation, insert a decimal point in the original number so that you have a number between 1 and 10. In the case of 58,000,000, the number is 5.8.

To determine the power of 10, count the number of places that the decimal point moved. In this case, it moved 7 places.

$$58,000,000 \text{ km} = 5.8 \times 10^7 \text{ km}$$

Practice

Express 6,590,000 in scientific notation.

Reading Comprehension Skills

Each section in your textbook introduces a Target Reading Skill. You will improve your reading comprehension by using the Target Reading Skills described below.

Using Prior Knowledge

Your prior knowledge is what you already know before you begin to read about a topic. Building on what you already know gives you a head start on learning new information. Before you begin a new assignment, think about what you know. You might look at the headings and the visuals to spark your memory. You can list what you know. Then, as you read, consider questions like these.

• How does what you learn relate to what you know?

• How did something you already know help you learn something new?

• Did your original ideas agree with what you have just learned?

Asking Questions

Asking yourself questions is an excellent way to focus on and remember new information in your textbook. For example, you can turn the text headings into questions. Then your questions can guide you to identify the important information as you read. Look at these examples:

   Heading: Using Seismographic Data

   Question: How are seismographic data used?

   Heading: Kinds of Faults

   Question: What are the kinds of faults?

   You do not have to limit your questions to text headings. Ask questions about anything that you need to clarify or that will help you understand the content. *What* and *how* are probably the most common question words, but you may also ask *why, who, when,* or *where* questions.

Previewing Visuals

Visuals are photographs, graphs, tables, diagrams, and illustrations. Visuals contain important information. Before you read, look at visuals and their labels and captions. This preview will help you prepare for what you will be reading.

Often you will be asked what you want to learn about a visual. For example, after you look at the normal fault diagram below, you might ask: What is the movement along a normal fault? Questions about visuals give you a purpose for reading—to answer your questions.

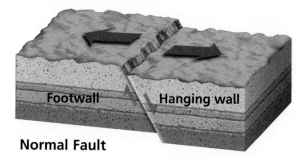

Footwall   **Hanging wall**

Normal Fault

Outlining

An outline shows the relationship between main ideas and supporting ideas. An outline has a formal structure. You write the main ideas, called topics, next to Roman numerals. The supporting ideas, called subtopics, are written under the main ideas and labeled A, B, C, and so on. An outline looks like this:

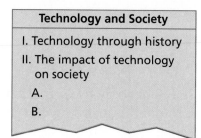

Technology and Society
I. Technology through history
II. The impact of technology on society
A.
B.

Identifying Main Ideas

When you are reading science material, it is important to try to understand the ideas and concepts that are in a passage. Each paragraph has a lot of information and detail. Good readers try to identify the most important—or biggest—idea in every paragraph or section. That's the main idea. The other information in the paragraph supports or further explains the main idea.

Sometimes main ideas are stated directly. In this book, some main ideas are identified for you as key concepts. These are printed in bold-face type. However, you must identify other main ideas yourself. In order to do this, you must identify all the ideas within a paragraph or section. Then ask yourself which idea is big enough to include all the other ideas.

Comparing and Contrasting

When you compare and contrast, you examine the similarities and differences between things. You can compare and contrast in a Venn diagram or in a table.

Venn Diagram A Venn diagram consists of two overlapping circles. In the space where the circles overlap, you write the characteristics that the two items have in common. In one of the circles outside the area of overlap, you write the differing features or characteristics of one of the items. In the other circle outside the area of overlap, you write the differing characteristics of the other item.

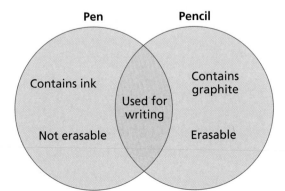

Pen | Pencil
Contains ink
Not erasable
Used for writing
Contains graphite
Erasable

Table In a compare/contrast table, you list the characteristics or features to be compared across the top of the table. Then list the items to be compared in the left column. Complete the table by filling in information about each characteristic or feature.

Blood Vessel	Function	Structure of Wall
Artery	Carries blood away from heart	
Capillary		
Vein		

Identifying Supporting Evidence

A hypothesis is a possible explanation for observations made by scientists or an answer to a scientific question. Scientists must carry out investigations and gather evidence that either supports or disproves the hypothesis.

Identifying the supporting evidence for a hypothesis or theory can help you understand the hypothesis or theory. Evidence consists of facts—information whose accuracy can be confirmed by testing or observation.

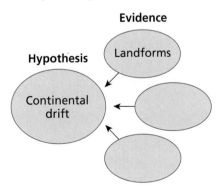

Evidence

Hypothesis | Landforms

Continental drift

Sequencing

A sequence is the order in which a series of events occurs. A flowchart or a cycle diagram can help you visualize a sequence.

Flowchart To make a flowchart, write a brief description of each step or event in a box. Place the boxes in order, with the first event at the top of the chart. Then draw an arrow to connect each step or event to the next.

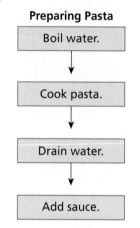

Preparing Pasta

Boil water.

↓

Cook pasta.

↓

Drain water.

↓

Add sauce.

Cycle Diagram A cycle diagram shows a sequence that is continuous, or cyclical. A continuous sequence does not have an end because when the final event is over, the first event begins again. To create a cycle diagram, write the starting event in a box placed at the top of a page in the center. Then, moving in a clockwise direction, write each event in a box in its proper sequence. Draw arrows that connect each event to the one that occurs next.

Seasons of the Year

Winter
Spring
Summer
Fall

Relating Cause and Effect

Science involves many cause-and-effect relationships. A cause makes something happen. An effect is what happens. When you recognize that one event causes another, you are relating cause and effect.

Words like *cause, because, effect, affect,* and *result* often signal a cause or an effect. Sometimes an effect can have more than one cause, or a cause can produce several effects.

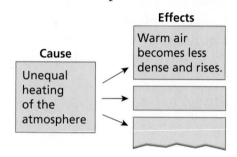

Cause

Unequal heating of the atmosphere

Effects

Warm air becomes less dense and rises.

Concept Mapping

Concept maps are useful tools for organizing information on any topic. A concept map begins with a main idea or core concept and shows how the idea can be subdivided into related subconcepts or smaller ideas.

You construct a concept map by placing concepts (usually nouns) in ovals and connecting them with linking words (usually verbs). The biggest concept or idea is placed in an oval at the top of the map. Related concepts are arranged in ovals below the big idea. The linking words connect the ovals.

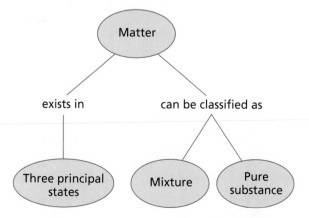

Matter

exists in

can be classified as

Three principal states

Mixture

Pure substance

Building Vocabulary

Knowing the meaning of these prefixes, suffixes, and roots will help you understand the meaning of words you do not recognize.

Word Origins Many science words come to English from other languages, such as Greek and Latin. By learning the meaning of a few common Greek and Latin roots, you can determine the meaning of unfamiliar science words.

Prefixes A prefix is a word part that is added at the beginning of a root or base word to change its meaning.

Suffixes A suffix is a word part that is added at the end of a root word to change the meaning.

Greek and Latin Roots		
Greek Roots	**Meaning**	**Example**
ast-	star	astronaut
geo-	Earth	geology
metron-	measure	kilometer
opt-	eye	optician
photo-	light	photograph
scop-	see	microscope
therm-	heat	thermostat
Latin Roots	**Meaning**	**Example**
aqua-	water	aquarium
aud-	hear	auditorium
duc-, duct-	lead	conduct
flect-	bend	reflect
fract-, frag-	break	fracture
ject-	throw	reject
luc-	light	lucid
spec-	see	inspect

Prefixes and Suffixes		
Prefix	**Meaning**	**Example**
com-, con-	with	communicate, concert
de-	from; down	decay
di-	two	divide
ex-, exo-	out	exhaust
in-, im-	in, into; not	inject, impossible
re-	again; back	reflect, recall
trans-	across	transfer
Suffix	**Meaning**	**Example**
-al	relating to	natural
-er, -or	one who	teacher, doctor
-ist	one who practices	scientist
-ity	state of	equality
-ology	study of	biology
-tion, -sion	state or quality of	reaction, tension

Safety Symbols

These symbols warn of possible dangers in the laboratory and remind you to work carefully.

 Safety Goggles Wear safety goggles to protect your eyes in any activity involving chemicals, flames or heating, or glassware.

 Lab Apron Wear a laboratory apron to protect your skin and clothing from damage.

 Breakage Handle breakable materials, such as glassware, with care. Do not touch broken glassware.

 Heat-Resistant Gloves Use an oven mitt or other hand protection when handling hot materials such as hot plates or hot glassware.

 Plastic Gloves Wear disposable plastic gloves when working with harmful chemicals and organisms. Keep your hands away from your face, and dispose of the gloves according to your teacher's instructions.

 Heating Use a clamp or tongs to pick up hot glassware. Do not touch hot objects with your bare hands.

 Flames Before you work with flames, tie back loose hair and clothing. Follow instructions from your teacher about lighting and extinguishing flames.

 No Flames When using flammable materials, make sure there are no flames, sparks, or other exposed heat sources present.

 Corrosive Chemical Avoid getting acid or other corrosive chemicals on your skin or clothing or in your eyes. Do not inhale the vapors. Wash your hands after the activity.

 Poison Do not let any poisonous chemical come into contact with your skin, and do not inhale its vapors. Wash your hands when you are finished with the activity.

 Fumes Work in a ventilated area when harmful vapors may be involved. Avoid inhaling vapors directly. Only test an odor when directed to do so by your teacher, and use a wafting motion to direct the vapor toward your nose.

 Sharp Object Scissors, scalpels, knives, needles, pins, and tacks can cut your skin. Always direct a sharp edge or point away from yourself and others.

 Animal Safety Treat live or preserved animals or animal parts with care to avoid harming the animals or yourself. Wash your hands when you are finished with the activity.

 Plant Safety Handle plants only as directed by your teacher. If you are allergic to certain plants, tell your teacher; do not do an activity involving those plants. Avoid touching harmful plants such as poison ivy. Wash your hands when you are finished with the activity.

 Electric Shock To avoid electric shock, never use electrical equipment around water, or when the equipment is wet or your hands are wet. Be sure cords are untangled and cannot trip anyone. Unplug equipment not in use.

 Physical Safety When an experiment involves physical activity, avoid injuring yourself or others. Alert your teacher if there is any reason you should not participate.

 Disposal Dispose of chemicals and other laboratory materials safely. Follow the instructions from your teacher.

 Hand Washing Wash your hands thoroughly when finished with the activity. Use soap and warm water. Rinse well.

 General Safety Awareness When this symbol appears, follow the instructions provided. When you are asked to develop your own procedure in a lab, have your teacher approve your plan before you go further.

Science Safety Rules

General Precautions
Follow all instructions. Never perform activities without the approval and supervision of your teacher. Do not engage in horseplay. Never eat or drink in the laboratory. Keep work areas clean and uncluttered.

Dress Code
Wear safety goggles whenever you work with chemicals, glassware, heat sources such as burners, or any substance that might get into your eyes. If you wear contact lenses, notify your teacher.

Wear a lab apron or coat whenever you work with corrosive chemicals or substances that can stain. Wear disposable plastic gloves when working with organisms and harmful chemicals. Tie back long hair. Remove or tie back any article of clothing or jewelry that can hang down and touch chemicals, flames, or equipment. Roll up long sleeves. Never wear open shoes or sandals.

First Aid
Report all accidents, injuries, or fires to your teacher, no matter how minor. Be aware of the location of the first-aid kit, emergency equipment such as the fire extinguisher and fire blanket, and the nearest telephone. Know whom to contact in an emergency.

Heating and Fire Safety
Keep all combustible materials away from flames. When heating a substance in a test tube, make sure that the mouth of the tube is not pointed at you or anyone else. Never heat a liquid in a closed container. Use an oven mitt to pick up a container that has been heated.

Using Chemicals Safely
Never put your face near the mouth of a container that holds chemicals. Never touch, taste, or smell a chemical unless your teacher tells you to.

Use only those chemicals needed in the activity. Keep all containers closed when chemicals are not being used. Pour all chemicals over the sink or a container, not over your work surface. Dispose of excess chemicals as instructed by your teacher.

Be extra careful when working with acids or bases. When mixing an acid and water, always pour the water into the container first and then add the acid to the water. Never pour water into an acid. Wash chemical spills and splashes immediately with plenty of water.

Using Glassware Safely
If glassware is broken or chipped, notify your teacher immediately. Never handle broken or chipped glass with your bare hands.

Never force glass tubing or thermometers into a rubber stopper or rubber tubing. Have your teacher insert the glass tubing or thermometer if required for an activity.

Using Sharp Instruments
Handle sharp instruments with extreme care. Never cut material toward you; cut away from you.

Animal and Plant Safety
Never perform experiments that cause pain, discomfort, or harm to animals. Only handle animals if absolutely necessary. If you know that you are allergic to certain plants, molds, or animals, tell your teacher before doing an activity in which these are used. Wash your hands thoroughly after any activity involving animals, animal parts, plants, plant parts, or soil.

During field work, wear long pants, long sleeves, socks, and closed shoes. Avoid poisonous plants and fungi as well as plants with thorns.

End-of-Experiment Rules
Unplug all electrical equipment. Clean up your work area. Dispose of waste materials as instructed by your teacher. Wash your hands after every experiment.

The laboratory balance is an important tool in scientific investigations. You can use a balance to determine the masses of materials that you study or experiment with in the laboratory.

Different kinds of balances are used in the laboratory. One kind of balance is the triple-beam balance. The balance that you may use in your science class is probably similar to the balance illustrated in this Appendix. To use the balance properly, you should learn the name, location, and function of each part of the balance you are using. What kind of balance do you have in your science class?

The Triple-Beam Balance

The triple-beam balance is a single-pan balance with three beams calibrated in grams. The back, or 100-gram, beam is divided into ten units of 10 grams each. The middle, or 500-gram, beam is divided into five units of 100 grams each. The front, or 10-gram, beam is divided into ten major units of 1 gram each. Each of these units is further divided into units of 0.1 gram. What is the largest mass you could find with a triple-beam balance?

The following procedure can be used to find the mass of an object with a triple-beam balance:

1. Place the object on the pan.
2. Move the rider on the middle beam notch by notch until the horizontal pointer drops below zero. Move the rider back one notch.
3. Move the rider on the back beam notch by notch until the pointer again drops below zero. Move the rider back one notch.
4. Slowly slide the rider along the front beam until the pointer stops at the zero point.
5. The mass of the object is equal to the sum of the readings on the three beams.

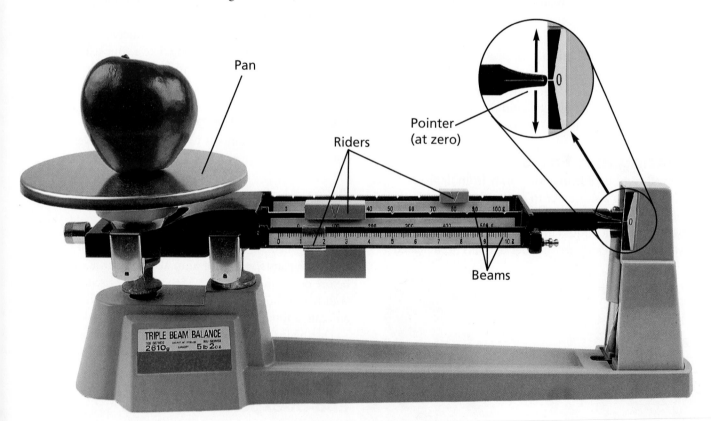

Triple-Beam Balance

Name	Symbol	Atomic Number	Atomic Mass[†]
Actinium	Ac	89	(227)
Aluminum	Al	13	26.982
Americium	Am	95	(243)
Antimony	Sb	51	121.75
Argon	Ar	18	39.948
Arsenic	As	33	74.922
Astatine	At	85	(210)
Barium	Ba	56	137.33
Berkelium	Bk	97	(247)
Beryllium	Be	4	9.0122
Bismuth	Bi	83	208.98
Bohrium	Bh	107	(264)
Boron	B	5	10.81
Bromine	Br	35	79.904
Cadmium	Cd	48	112.41
Calcium	Ca	20	40.08
Californium	Cf	98	(251)
Carbon	C	6	12.011
Cerium	Ce	58	140.12
Cesium	Cs	55	132.91
Chlorine	Cl	17	35.453
Chromium	Cr	24	51.996
Cobalt	Co	27	58.933
Copper	Cu	29	63.546
Curium	Cm	96	(247)
Darmstadtium	Ds	110	(269)
Dubnium	Db	105	(262)
Dysprosium	Dy	66	162.50
Einsteinium	Es	99	(252)
Erbium	Er	68	167.26
Europium	Eu	63	151.96
Fermium	Fm	100	(257)
Fluorine	F	9	18.998
Francium	Fr	87	(223)
Gadolinium	Gd	64	157.25
Gallium	Ga	31	69.72
Germanium	Ge	32	72.59
Gold	Au	79	196.97
Hafnium	Hf	72	178.49
Hassium	Hs	108	(265)
Helium	He	2	4.0026
Holmium	Ho	67	164.93
Hydrogen	H	1	1.0079
Indium	In	49	114.82
Iodine	I	53	126.90
Iridium	Ir	77	192.22
Iron	Fe	26	55.847
Krypton	Kr	36	83.80
Lanthanum	La	57	138.91
Lawrencium	Lr	103	(262)
Lead	Pb	82	207.2
Lithium	Li	3	6.941
Lutetium	Lu	71	174.97
Magnesium	Mg	12	24.305
Manganese	Mn	25	54.938
Meitnerium	Mt	109	(268)
Mendelevium	Md	101	(258)
Mercury	Hg	80	200.59

Name	Symbol	Atomic Number	Atomic Mass[†]
Molybdenum	Mo	42	95.94
Neodymium	Nd	60	144.24
Neon	Ne	10	20.179
Neptunium	Np	93	(237)
Nickel	Ni	28	58.71
Niobium	Nb	41	92.906
Nitrogen	N	7	14.007
Nobelium	No	102	(259)
Osmium	Os	76	190.2
Oxygen	O	8	15.999
Palladium	Pd	46	106.4
Phosphorus	P	15	30.974
Platinum	Pt	78	195.09
Plutonium	Pu	94	(244)
Polonium	Po	84	(209)
Potassium	K	19	39.098
Praseodymium	Pr	59	140.91
Promethium	Pm	61	(145)
Protactinium	Pa	91	231.04
Radium	Ra	88	(226)
Radon	Rn	86	(222)
Rhenium	Re	75	186.21
Rhodium	Rh	45	102.91
Roentgenium	Rg	111	(272)
Rubidium	Rb	37	85.468
Ruthenium	Ru	44	101.07
Rutherfordium	Rf	104	(261)
Samarium	Sm	62	150.4
Scandium	Sc	21	44.956
Seaborgium	Sg	106	(263)
Selenium	Se	34	78.96
Silicon	Si	14	28.086
Silver	Ag	47	107.87
Sodium	Na	11	22.990
Strontium	Sr	38	87.62
Sulfur	S	16	32.06
Tantalum	Ta	73	180.95
Technetium	Tc	43	(98)
Tellurium	Te	52	127.60
Terbium	Tb	65	158.93
Thallium	Tl	81	204.37
Thorium	Th	90	232.04
Thulium	Tm	69	168.93
Tin	Sn	50	118.69
Titanium	Ti	22	47.90
Tungsten	W	74	183.85
Ununbium	Uub*	112	(277)
Ununhexium	Uuh*	116	(292)
Ununoctium	Uuo*	118	(294)
Ununpentium	Uup*	115	(288)
Ununquadium	Uuq*	114	(289)
Ununtrium	Uut*	113	(284)
Uranium	U	92	238.03
Vanadium	V	23	50.941
Xenon	Xe	54	131.30
Ytterbium	Yb	70	173.04
Yttrium	Y	39	88.906
Zinc	Zn	30	65.38
Zirconium	Zr	40	91.22

[†]Numbers in parentheses give the mass number of the most stable isotope.

*Discovery not yet officially confirmed

Key

C	Solid
Br	Liquid
H	Gas
Tc	Not found in nature

	1	2	3	4	5	6	7	8	9
1	1 H Hydrogen 1.0079								
2	3 Li Lithium 6.941	4 Be Beryllium 9.0122							
3	11 Na Sodium 22.990	12 Mg Magnesium 24.305							
4	19 K Potassium 39.098	20 Ca Calcium 40.08	21 Sc Scandium 44.956	22 Ti Titanium 47.90	23 V Vanadium 50.941	24 Cr Chromium 51.996	25 Mn Manganese 54.938	26 Fe Iron 55.847	27 Co Cobalt 58.933
5	37 Rb Rubidium 85.468	38 Sr Strontium 87.62	39 Y Yttrium 88.906	40 Zr Zirconium 91.22	41 Nb Niobium 92.906	42 Mo Molybdenum 95.94	43 Tc Technetium (98)	44 Ru Ruthenium 101.07	45 Rh Rhodium 102.91
6	55 Cs Cesium 132.91	56 Ba Barium 137.33	71 Lu Lutetium 174.97	72 Hf Hafnium 178.49	73 Ta Tantalum 180.95	74 W Tungsten 183.85	75 Re Rhenium 186.21	76 Os Osmium 190.2	77 Ir Iridium 192.22
7	87 Fr Francium (223)	88 Ra Radium (226)	103 Lr Lawrencium (262)	104 Rf Rutherfordium (261)	105 Db Dubnium (262)	106 Sg Seaborgium (263)	107 Bh Bohrium (264)	108 Hs Hassium (265)	109 Mt Meitnerium (268)

Lanthanides

57 La Lanthanum 138.91	58 Ce Cerium 140.12	59 Pr Praseodymium 140.91	60 Nd Neodymium 144.24	61 Pm Promethium (145)	62 Sm Samarium 150.4

Actinides

89 Ac Actinium (227)	90 Th Thorium 232.04	91 Pa Protactinium 231.04	92 U Uranium 238.03	93 Np Neptunium (237)	94 Pu Plutonium (244)

Key

■ Metal

□ Metalloid

■ Nonmetal

■ Properties not established

				13	14	15	16	17	18
									2 **He** Helium 4.0026
				5 **B** Boron 10.81	6 **C** Carbon 12.011	7 **N** Nitrogen 14.007	8 **O** Oxygen 15.999	9 **F** Fluorine 18.998	10 **Ne** Neon 20.179
10	11	12		13 **Al** Aluminum 26.982	14 **Si** Silicon 28.086	15 **P** Phosphorus 30.974	16 **S** Sulfur 32.06	17 **Cl** Chlorine 35.453	18 **Ar** Argon 39.948
28 **Ni** Nickel 58.71	29 **Cu** Copper 63.546	30 **Zn** Zinc 65.38	31 **Ga** Gallium 69.72	32 **Ge** Germanium 72.59	33 **As** Arsenic 74.922	34 **Se** Selenium 78.96	35 **Br** Bromine 79.904	36 **Kr** Krypton 83.80	
46 **Pd** Palladium 106.4	47 **Ag** Silver 107.87	48 **Cd** Cadmium 112.41	49 **In** Indium 114.82	50 **Sn** Tin 118.69	51 **Sb** Antimony 121.75	52 **Te** Tellurium 127.60	53 **I** Iodine 126.90	54 **Xe** Xenon 131.30	
78 **Pt** Platinum 195.09	79 **Au** Gold 196.97	80 **Hg** Mercury 200.59	81 **Tl** Thallium 204.37	82 **Pb** Lead 207.2	83 **Bi** Bismuth 208.98	84 **Po** Polonium (209)	85 **At** Astatine (210)	86 **Rn** Radon (222)	
110 **Ds** Darmstadtium (269)	111 **Rg** Roentgenium (272)	112 ***Uub** Ununbium (277)	113 ***Uut** Ununtrium (284)	114 ***Uuq** Ununquadium (289)	115 ***Uup** Ununpentium (288)	116 ***Uuh** Ununhexium (292)		118 ***Uuo** Ununoctium (294)	

*Discovery not yet officially confirmed

(Atomic masses in parentheses are those of the most stable isotope.)

63 **Eu** Europium 151.96	64 **Gd** Gadolinium 157.25	65 **Tb** Terbium 158.93	66 **Dy** Dysprosium 162.50	67 **Ho** Holmium 164.93	68 **Er** Erbium 167.26	69 **Tm** Thulium 168.93	70 **Yb** Ytterbium 173.04

95 **Am** Americium (243)	96 **Cm** Curium (247)	97 **Bk** Berkelium (247)	98 **Cf** Californium (251)	99 **Es** Einsteinium (252)	100 **Fm** Fermium (257)	101 **Md** Mendelevium (258)	102 **No** Nobelium (259)

English and Spanish Glossary

acid A substance that tastes sour, reacts with metals and carbonates, and turns blue litmus red. (p. 98)
ácido Sustancia de sabor agrio que reacciona con metales y carbonatos, y que vuelve rojo el papel de tornasol azul.

activation energy The minimum amount of energy needed to get a chemical reaction started. (p. 67)
energía de activación Cantidad mínima de energía que se necesita para que empiece una reacción química.

alcohol A substituted hydrocarbon that contains one or more hydroxyl groups. (p. 132)
alcohol Hidrocarburo sustituto que contiene uno o más grupos hidroxilos.

alkali metal An element belonging to Group 1 of the periodic table. (p. 17)
metal alcalino Elemento que pertenece al Grupo 1 de la tabla periódica.

alloy A material made of two or more elements that has the properties of a metal. (p. 37)
aleación Material hecho de dos o más elementos que tiene las propiedades de un metal.

amino acid One of 20 kinds of organic compounds that are the monomers of proteins. (p. 140)
aminoácido Uno de 20 tipos de compuestos orgánicos que son los monómeros de las proteínas.

atom The smallest particle of an element. (p. 7)
átomo Partícula más pequeña de un elemento.

atomic number The number of protons in the nucleus of an atom. (p. 14)
número atómico Número de protones en el núcleo de un átomo.

B

base A substance that tastes bitter, feels slippery, and turns red litmus paper blue. (p. 100)
base Sustancia de sabor amargo, escurridiza y que vuelve azul el papel de tornasol rojo.

C

carbohydrate An energy-rich organic compound made of the elements carbon, hydrogen, and oxygen. (p. 137)
carbohidrato Compuesto orgánico altamente energético hecho de elementos de carbono, hidrógeno y oxígeno.

carboxyl group A —COOH group, found in organic acids. (p. 133)
grupo carboxilo Grupo —COOH, que se haya en los ácidos orgánicos.

catalyst A material that increases the rate of a reaction by lowering the activation energy. (p. 71)
catalítico Material que aumenta la velocidad de una reacción al disminuir la energía de activación.

cellulose A complex carbohydrate found in plant structures. (p. 140)
celulosa Carbohidrato complejo que se haya en las estructuras vegetales.

chemical bond The force that holds atoms together.
enlace químico Fuerza que mantiene unidos a los átomos. (p. 13)

chemical digestion The process that breaks large molecules in food into smaller molecules. (p. 113)
digestión química Proceso que rompe las moléculas grandes en la comida en moléculas más pequeñas.

chemical equation A short, easy way to show a chemical reaction, using symbols. (p. 57)
ecuación química Forma corta y sencilla de mostrar una reacción química, usando símbolos.

chemical formula A combination of symbols that represents the elements in a compound. (p. 25)
fórmula química Combinación de símbolos que representan a los elementos de un compuesto.

chemical property A characteristic of a substance that describes its ability to change into different substances. (p. 47)
propiedad química Característica de una sustancia que describe su capacidad de convertirse en sustancias diferentes.

chemical reaction The process in which substances undergo chemical changes that result in the formation of new substances. (p. 48)
reacción química Proceso por el que las sustancias sufren cambios químicos que dan como resultado la formación de nuevas sustancias.

chemistry The study of the properties of matter and how matter changes. (p. 46)
química Estudio de las propiedades de la materia y de sus cambios.

cholesterol A waxy lipid in animal cells. (p. 142)
colesterol Lípido ceroso que se haya en las células animales.

closed system A system in which no matter is allowed to enter or leave. (p. 59)
sistema cerrado Sistema en el cual la materia no puede entrar ni salir.

coefficient A number in front of a chemical formula in an equation that indicates how many molecules or atoms of each reactant and product are involved in a reaction. (p. 60)
coeficiente En un ecuación, número delante de una fórmula química que indica cuántas moléculas o átomos de cada reactivo y producto participan en una reacción.

colloid A mixture containing small, undissolved particles that do not settle out. (p. 86)
coloide Mezcla que contiene partículas pequeñas y sin disolver que no se depositan.

combustion A rapid reaction between oxygen and fuel that results in fire. (p. 75)
combustión Reacción rápida entre el oxígeno y el combustible que produce fuego.

complex carbohydrate A long chain, or polymer, of simple carbohydrates. (p. 138)
carbohidrato complejo Cadena larga, o polímero, de carbohidratos simples.

compound A substance made of two or more elements chemically combined in a specific ratio, or proportion. (p. 7)
compuesto Sustancia hecha de dos o más elementos combinados químicamente en una razón o proporción específica.

concentrated solution A mixture that has a lot of solute dissolved in it. (p. 92)
solución concentrada Mezcla que tiene muchos solutos disueltos en ella.

concentration The amount of one material in a certain volume of another material. (p. 70)
concentración Cantidad de un material en un cierto volumen de otro material.

conservation of mass The principle stating that matter is not created or destroyed during a chemical reaction. (p. 58)
conservación de la masa Principio que enuncia que la materia no se crea ni se destruye durante una reacción química.

corrosive The way in which acids react with some metals so as to eat away the metal. (p. 99)
corrosivo Forma en que reaccionan los ácidos con algunos metales, como si se comieran el metal.

covalent bond A chemical bond formed when two atoms share electrons. (p. 31)
enlace covalente Enlace químico que se forma cuando dos átomos comparten electrones.

crystal An orderly, three-dimensional pattern of ions or atoms in a solid. (p. 26)
cristal Patrón ordenado tridimensional de iones o átomos en un sólido.

D

decomposition A chemical reaction that breaks down compounds into simpler products. (p. 62)
descomposición Reacción química que descompone los compuestos en productos más simples.

diamond A form of the element carbon in which the atoms are arranged in a crystal structure. (p. 124)
diamante Forma del elemento del carbono en la cual los átomos de carbono están dispuestos en una estructura de cristal.

digestion The process that breaks down complex molecules of food into smaller molecules. (p. 113)
digestión Proceso que rompe las moléculas complejas de comida en moléculas más pequeñas.

dilute solution A mixture that has only a little solute dissolved in it. (p. 92)
solución diluida Mezcla que sólo tiene un poco de soluto disuelto en ella.

DNA Deoxyribonucleic acid, one type of nucleic acid.
ADN Ácido desoxirribonucleico, un tipo de ácido nucleico. (p. 143)

double bond A chemical bond formed when atoms share two pairs of electrons. (p. 32)
enlace doble Enlace químico formado cuando los átomos comparten dos pares de electrones.

ductile A term used to describe a material that can be pulled out into a long wire. (p. 38)
dúctil Término usado para describir un material que se puede estirar hasta crear un alambre largo.

E

electron dot diagram A representation of the valence electrons in an atom, using dots. (p. 13)
diagrama de puntos de electrones Representación del número de electrones de valencia en un átomo, usando puntos.

electrons Negatively charged particles that move around outside the nucleus of an atom. (p. 8)
electrones Partículas con carga negativa que se mueven alrededor del núcleo de un átomo.

element A substance that cannot be broken down into any other substances by chemical or physical means. (p. 6)
elemento Sustancia que no se puede descomponer en otras sustancias por medios químicos o físicos.

endothermic reaction A reaction that absorbs energy in the form of heat. (p. 52)
reacción endotérmica Reacción que absorbe energía en forma de calor.

energy level The specific amount of energy an electron has. (p. 10)
nivel de energía La cantidad específica de energía que tiene un electrón.

enzyme A biological catalyst that lowers the activation energy of reactions in cells. (p. 71)
enzima Catalítico biológico que disminuye la energía de activación de las reacciones en las células.

ester An organic compound made by chemically combining an alcohol and an organic acid. (p. 133)
ester Compuesto orgánico formado químicamente al combinar un alcohol y un ácido orgánico.

exothermic reaction A reaction that releases energy in the form of heat. (p. 53)
reacción exotérmica Reacción que libera energía en forma de calor.

family Elements in the same vertical column of the periodic table; also called a group. (p. 15)
familia Elementos en la misma columna vertical de la tabla periódica; también llamado grupo.

fatty acid An organic compound that is a monomer of a fat or oil. (p. 142)
ácido graso Compuesto orgánico que es un monómero de una grasa o aceite.

fuel A material that releases energy when it burns.
combustible Material que libera energía cuando se quema. (p. 75)

fullerene A form of carbon that consists of atoms arranged in the shape of a hollow sphere. (p. 125)
fullereno Forma del elemento del carbono que consiste en átomos de carbono colocados en forma de esfera hueca.

glucose A simple carbohydrate; the monomer of many complex carbohydrates. (p. 137)
glucosa Carbohidrato simple; monómero de muchos carbohidratos complejos.

graphite A form of the element carbon in which a carbon atom is bonded tightly to three other carbon atoms in flat layers. (p. 124)
grafito Forma del elemento carbono en el cual un átomo de carbono se une estrechamente a otros tres átomos de carbono en capas llanas.

group Elements in the same vertical column of the periodic table; also called a family. (p. 15)
grupo Elementos en la misma columna vertical de la tabla periódica; también llamado familia.

halogen An element belonging to Group 17 of the periodic table. (p. 17)
halógeno Elemento que pertenece al Grupo 17 de la tabla periódica.

hydrocarbon An organic compound that contains only carbon and hydrogen. (p. 128)
hidrocarburo Compuesto orgánico que contiene sólo carbono e hidrógeno.

hydrogen ion A positively charged ion (H^+) formed of a hydrogen atom that has lost its electron. (p. 104)
ión hidrógeno Ión con carga positiva (H^+) formado por un átomo de hidrógeno que ha perdido su electrón.

hydroxide ion A negatively charged ion made of oxygen and hydrogen (OH^-). (p. 105)
ión hidróxido Ión con carga negativa formado de oxígeno e hidrógeno (OH^-).

hydroxyl group An —OH group, found in alcohols.
grupo hidroxilo Grupo —OH, que se haya en los alcoholes. (p. 132)

indicator A compound that changes color in the presence of an acid or a base. (p. 100)
indicador Compuesto que cambia de color en presencia de un ácido o una base.

inhibitor A material that decreases the rate of a reaction. (p. 71)
inhibidor Material que disminuye la velocidad de una reacción.

ion An atom or group of atoms that has become electrically charged. (p. 23)
ión Átomo o grupo de átomos con carga eléctrica.

ionic bond The attraction between oppositely charged ions. (p. 24)
enlace iónico Atracción entre iones con cargas opuestas.

ionic compound A compound that consists of positive and negative ions. (p. 24)
compuesto iónico Compuesto que tiene iones positivos y negativos.

isomers Compounds that have the same chemical formula but different structural formulas. (p. 130)
isómeros Compuestos que tienen la misma fórmula química pero diferentes fórmulas estructurales.

L

lipid An energy-rich organic compound made of carbon, oxygen, and hydrogen. Fats, oils, waxes, and cholesterol are lipids. (p. 141)
lípido Compuesto orgánico rico en energía hecho de carbono, oxígeno e hidrógeno; las grasas, aceites, ceras y colesterol son lípidos.

M

malleable A term used to describe material that can be hammered or rolled into shape. (p. 38)
maleable Término usado para describir el material que se puede golpear o enrollar para darle forma.

matter Anything that has mass and occupies space.
materia Cualquier cosa que tiene masa y ocupa espacio. (p. 6, 46)

mechanical digestion The physical process that tears, grinds, and mashes large pieces of food into smaller ones. (p. 113)
digestión mecánica Proceso físico que rompe, tritura y muele grandes pedazos de comida en pedazos más pequeños.

metallic bond An attraction between a positive metal ion and the electrons surrounding it. (p. 37)
enlace metálico Atracción entre un ión metálico positivo y los electrones que lo rodean.

mixture Two or more substances that are mixed together but not chemically combined. (p. 7)
mezcla Dos o más sustancias que se mezclan, pero que no se combinan químicamente.

model Physical, mental, visual, and other representations of an idea to help people understand a concept that they cannot observe directly. (p. 8)
modelo Representaciones físicas, mentales o visuales de una idea que ayudan a la gente a entender un concepto que no se puede observar directamente.

molecular compound A compound that is composed of molecules. (p. 32)
compuesto molecular Compuesto que contiene moléculas.

molecule A neutral particle made of two or more atoms joined by covalent bonds. (p. 31)
molécula Partícula neutral hecha de dos o más átomos que se unen por enlaces covalentes.

monomer One molecule that makes up the links in a polymer chain. (p. 134)
monómero Molécula que forma los enlaces en una cadena polímera.

N

nanotube A form of carbon that consists of atoms in the form of a long, hollow cylinder. (p. 125)
nanotubo Forma del carbono que consiste en átomos en forma de un cilindro largo y hueco.

neutralization A reaction of an acid with a base, yielding a solution that is not as acidic or basic as the starting solutions were. (p. 108)
neutralización Reacción de un ácido con una base, que produce una solución que no es ácida ni básica, como lo eran las soluciones originales.

neutrons Small, uncharged particles that are found in the nucleus of an atom. (p. 10)
neutrones Partículas pequeñas sin carga que se encuentran en el núcleo de un átomo.

noble gas An element of Group 18 of the periodic table. (p. 16)
gas noble Elemento del Grupo 18 de la tabla periódica.

nonpolar bond A covalent bond in which electrons are shared equally. (p. 34)
enlace no polar Enlace covalente en el que los electrones se comparten por igual.

nucleic acid A very large organic compound made up of carbon, oxygen, hydrogen, nitrogen, and phosphorus; examples are DNA and RNA. (p. 143)
ácido nucleico Compuesto orgánico muy grande hecho de carbono, oxígeno, hidrógeno, nitrógeno y fósforo; ejemplos son ADN and ARN.

nucleotide An organic compound that is one of the monomers of nucleic acids. (p. 144)
nucleótido Compuesto orgánico que es uno de los monómeros de los ácidos nucleicos.

nucleus The central core of the atom, containing protons and usually neutrons. (p. 9)
núcleo Parte central del átomo que contiene protones y normalmente neutrones.

O

open system A system in which matter can enter from or escape to the surroundings. (p. 59)
sistema abierto Sistema en el que la materia puede entrar desde el medio que la rodea o salir hacia él.

English and Spanish Glossary

organic acid A substituted hydrocarbon with one or more of the —COOH group of atoms. (p. 133)
ácido orgánico Hidrocarburo sustituto que tiene uno o más grupos de átomos —COOH.

organic compound Most compounds that contain carbon. (p. 127)
compuesto orgánico La mayoría de los compuestos que contienen carbono.

period Elements in the same horizontal row of the periodic table. (p. 15)
período Elementos en la misma fila horizontal de la tabla periódica.

pH scale A range of values used to express the concentration of hydrogen ions in a solution. (p. 106)
escala pH Rango de valores usados para expresar la concentración de iones de hidrógeno que hay en una solución.

physical change A change that alters the form or appearance of a material but does not make the material into another substance. (p. 48)
cambio físico Cambio que altera la forma o apariencia de un material, pero que no convierte el material en otra sustancia.

physical property A characteristic of a substance that can be observed without changing the substance into another substance. (p. 47)
propiedad física Característica de una sustancia que se puede observar sin convertir la sustancia en otra sustancia.

polar bond A covalent bond in which electrons are shared unequally. (p. 34)
enlace polar Enlace covalente en el que los electrones se comparten de forma desigual.

polyatomic ion An ion that is made of more than one atom. (p. 23)
ión poliatómico Ión que está hecho de más de un átomo.

polymer A large molecule in which many smaller molecules are bonded together. (p. 134)
polímero Molécula grande en la que muchas moléculas más pequeñas están unidas.

precipitate A solid that forms from a solution during a chemical reaction. (p. 50)
precipitado Sólido que se forma de una solución durante una reacción química.

product A substance formed as a result of a chemical reaction. (p. 57)
producto Sustancia formada como resultado de una reacción química.

protein An organic compound that is a polymer of amino acids. (p. 140)
proteína Compuesto orgánico que es un polímero de aminoácidos.

protons Small, positively charged particles that are found in the nucleus of an atom. (p. 9)
protones Partículas pequeñas con carga positiva que se encuentran en el núcleo de un átomo.

reactant A substance that enters into a chemical reaction. (p. 57)
reactante Sustancia que participa en una reacción química.

replacement A reaction in which one element replaces another in a compound or when two elements in different compounds trade places. (p. 62)
sustitución Reacción en la que un elemento reemplaza a otro en un compuesto o dos elementos de diferentes compuestos se intercambian.

RNA Ribonucleic acid, a type of nucleic acid. (p. 143)
ARN Ácido ribonucleico, un tipo de ácido nucleico.

salt An ionic compound made from the neutralization of an acid with a base. (p. 109)
sal Compuesto iónico formado por la neutralización de un ácido con una base.

saturated hydrocarbon A hydrocarbon in which all the bonds between carbon atoms are single bonds. (p. 131)
hidrocarburo saturado Hidrocarburo en el que todos los enlaces entre los átomos de carbono son enlaces simples.

saturated solution A mixture that contains as much dissolved solute as is possible at a given temperature. (p. 93)
solución saturada Mezcla que contiene la mayor cantidad posible de soluto disuelto a una temperatura determinada.

scientific theory A well-tested idea that explains and connects a wide range of observations. (p. 8)
teoría científica Idea bien comprobada que explica y conecta una amplia gama de observaciones.

solubility A measure of how much solute can dissolve in a given solvent at a given temperature.
solubilidad Medida de cuánto soluto se puede disolver en un solvente dada una temperatura determinada. (p. 93)

solute The part of a solution present in a lesser amount and dissolved by the solvent. (p. 84)
soluto Parte de una solución presente en menor cantidad y disuelta por el solvente.

solution A well-mixed mixture containing a solvent and at least one solute that has the same properties throughout. (p. 84)
solución Mezcla homogénea que contiene un solvente y al menos un soluto que tiene las mismas propiedades en toda la solución.

solvent The part of a solution that is present in the largest amount and dissolves a solute. (p. 84)
solvente Parte de una solución que está presente en la mayor cantidad y que disuelve un soluto.

starch A complex carbohydrate in which plants store energy. (p. 139)
almidón Carbohidrato complejo en la que las plantas almacenan la energía.

structural formula A description of a molecule that shows the kind, number, and arrangement of atoms. (p. 129)
fórmula estructural Descripción de una molécula que muestra el tipo, número y posición de los átomos.

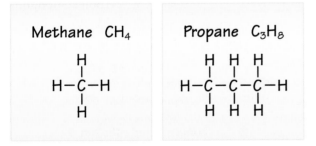

subscript A number in a chemical formula that tells the number of atoms in a molecule or the ratio of elements in a compound. (p. 25)
subíndice Número en una fórmula química que indica el número de átomos que tiene una molécula o la razón de elementos en un compuesto.

substituted hydrocarbon A hydrocarbon in which one or more hydrogen atoms have been replaced by atoms of other elements. (p. 132)
hidrocarburo sustituido Hidrocarburo en el cual uno o más átomos de hidrógeno han sido sustituidos por átomos de otros elementos.

supersaturated solution A mixture that has more dissolved solute than is predicted by its solubility at a given temperature. (p. 97)
solución supersaturada Mezcla que tiene más soluto disuelto de lo que se predice por su solubilidad a una temperatura determinada.

suspension A mixture in which particles can be seen and easily separated by settling or filtration. (p. 86)
suspensión Mezcla en la cual las partículas se pueden ver y separar fácilmente por sedimentación o por filtración.

symbol A one- or two-letter set of characters that is used to identify an element. (p. 14)
símbolo Grupo de caracteres de una o dos letras que se usa para identificar un elemento.

synthesis A chemical reaction in which two or more simple substances combine to form a new, more complex substance. (p. 62)
síntesis Reacción química en la que dos o más sustancias simples se combinan para formar una sustancia nueva más compleja.

triple bond A chemical bond formed when atoms share three pairs of electrons. (p. 32)
enlace triple Enlace químico formado cuando los átomos comparten tres pares de electrones.

unsaturated hydrocarbon A hydrocarbon in which one or more of the bonds between carbon atoms is double or triple. (p. 131)
hidrocarburo no saturado Hidrocarburo en el que uno o más de los enlaces entre átomos de carbono es doble o triple.

unsaturated solution A mixture that contains less dissolved solute than is possible at a given temperature. (p. 93)
solución no saturada Mezcla que contiene menos soluto disuelto de lo que es posible a una temperatura determinada.

V

valence electrons The electrons that are in the highest energy level of an atom and that are involved in chemical reactions. (p. 12)
electrones de valencia Electrones que tienen el más alto nivel de energía de un átomo y participan en reacciones químicas.

Index

Page numbers for key terms are printed in **boldface** type.
Page numbers for illustrations, maps, and charts are printed in *italics*.

Index

Page numbers for key terms are printed in **boldface** type.
Page numbers for illustrations, maps, and charts are printed in *italics*.

Acknowledgments

Grateful acknowledgment is made to the following for copyrighted material:

Acknowledgment for page 159: Excerpt from *The Iron Peacock* by Mary Stetson Clarke. Copyright © 1966 by Mary Stetson Clarke. Reprinted with permission from The Estate of Mary Stetson Clarke.

Note: Every effort has been made to locate the copyright owner of material reproduced in this component. Omissions brought to our attention will be corrected in subsequent editions.

Staff Credits

Diane Alimena, Scott Andrews, Jennifer Angel, Michele Angelucci, Laura Baselice, Carolyn Belanger, Barbara A. Bertell, Suzanne Biron, Peggy Bliss, Stephanie Bradley, James Brady, Anne M. Bray, Sarah M. Carroll, Kerry Cashman, Jonathan Cheney, Joshua D. Clapper, Lisa J. Clark, Bob Craton, Patricia Cully, Patricia M. Dambry, Kathy Dempsey, Leanne Esterly, Emily Ellen, Thomas Ferreira, Jonathan Fisher, Patricia Fromkin, Paul Gagnon, Kathy Gavilanes, Holly Gordon, Robert Graham, Ellen Granter, Diane Grossman, Barbara Hollingdale, Linda Johnson, Anne Jones, John Judge, Kevin Keane, Kelly Kelliher, Toby Klang, Sue Langan, Russ Lappa, Carolyn Lock, Rebecca Loveys, Constance J. McCarty, Carolyn B. McGuire, Ranida Touranont McKneally, Anne McLaughlin, Eve Melnechuk, Natania Mlawer, Janet Morris, Karyl Murray, Francine Neumann, Baljit Nijjar, Marie Opera, Jill Ort, Kim Ortell, Joan Paley, Dorothy Preston, Maureen Raymond, Laura Ross, Rashid Ross, Siri Schwartzman, Melissa Shustyk, Laurel Smith, Emily Soltanoff, Jennifer A. Teece, Elizabeth Torjussen, Amanda M. Watters, Merce Wilczek, Amy Winchester, Char Lyn Yeakley. **Additional Credits:** Tara Alamilla, Louise Gachet, Allen Gold, Andrea Golden, Terence Hegarty, Etta Jacobs, Meg Montgomery, Stephanie Rogers, Kim Schmidt, Adam Teller, Joan Tobin.

Illustration

All art development by Morgan Cain and Associates unless otherwise noted. Annie Bissett: 155–157; **Kerry Cashman:** 143; **John Edwards:** 64, 107; **Barbara Hollingdale:** 16; **Rich McMahon:** 18–19, 138; **Fran Milner:** 114; **All charts and graphs by Matt Mayerchak.**

Photography

Photo Research John Judge

Cover Image top, Jeff Hunter/Getty Images, Inc.; **bottom,** Phil Degginger/Color-Pic, Inc.

Page vi, Russ Lappa; **vii l,** LWA-Dann Tardif/Corbis; **vii r,** Richard Haynes; **viii l,** 2004 Estate of Alexander Calder/Artists Rights Society (ARS), New York/Art Resource, NY; **viii r,** Russ Lappa; **ix,** Richard Haynes; **x t,** George D. Lepp/Corbis; **x b,** Ken O'Donoghue; **1,** Leonard Lessin/Peter Arnold, Inc.; **2 all,** NASA/Goddard Space Flight Center Scientific Visualization Studio; **3,** Ken O'Donoghue.

Chapter 1

Pages 4–5, Kenneth Eward/BioGrafx/Photo Researchers, Inc; **5r,** Richard Haynes; **7,** Andre Jenny/Focus Group/PictureQuest; **8t,** Royalty-Free/Corbis; **8b,** Russ Lappa; **9,** Dorling Kindersley; **10t,** ©Stockbyte; **10b,** Frank Cezus/Getty Images, Inc.; **11,** Paul Johnson/Index Stock Imagery, Inc.; **12–13,** Jump Run Productions/Getty Images, Inc.; **16,** Terry W. Eggers/Corbis; **17l,** Richard Megna/Fundamental Photographs; **17m,** Fundamental Photographs; **17r,** Andrew Lambert Photography/SPL/ Photo Researchers, Inc.; **18l,** Lester V. Bergman/Corbis; **18m,** Cecile Brunswick/Peter Arnold, Inc.; **18r,** The Granger Collection, NY; **19t,** Alexander Tsiaras/Stock Boston; **19b,** AP/Wide World Photos; **20l,** George Payne; **20r,** Sheila Terry/SPL/Photo Researchers, Inc.; **21,** Russ Lappa; **22t,** Russ Lappa; **22b,** Richard Haynes; **22b inset,** Russ Lappa; **24tl,** Lawrence Migdale/Photo Researchers, Inc.; **24tr,** Stephen Frisch/Stock Boston; **24b,** Barry Runk/Grant Heilman Photography; **25,** Ric Ergenbright/Corbis; **26,** M. Claye/Jacana/Photo Researchers, Inc.; **27,** Richard Megna/Fundamental Photographs; **28,** Richard Haynes; **29,** Richard Haynes; **30,** Richard Haynes; **35,** Richard Hutchings/Photo Researchers, Inc.; **36,** Andrea Pistolesi/Getty Images, Inc.; **37,** Russ Lappa; **38bl,** Helene Rogers/Art Directors; **38br,** 2004 Estate of Alexander Calder/Artists Rights Society (ARS), New York/Art Resource, NY; **38–39t,** NASA; **39r,** Dorling Kindersley; **40,** Jump Run Productions/Getty Images, Inc.

Chapter 2

Pages 44–45, Richard Megna/Fundamental Photographs; **45r,** Russ Lappa; **46,** Ariel Skelley/Corbis; **47,** Tim Hauf/Visuals Unlimited; **48l,** Richard Haynes; **48r,** Russ Lappa; **49 both,** Richard Megna/Fundamental Photographs; **50tl,** John Serrao/Photo Researchers, Inc.; **50tm,** Charles D. Winters/Photo Researchers, Inc.; **50tr,** Russ Lappa; **50b,** Michael P. Gadomski/Photo Researchers, Inc.; **51 both,** Russ Lappa; **52,** David Young-Wolff/PhotoEdit; **53,** Aero Graphics, Inc./Corbis; **55,** Richard Haynes; **56,** Russ Lappa; **58 all,** Russ Lappa; **59t,** John D. Cummingham/Visuals Unlimited; **59 both,** Dorling Kindersley; **66,** Aaron Horowitz/Corbis; **69,** Charlie Neibergall/AP/Wide World Photos; **70 both,** Richard Megna/Fundamental Photographs; **72,** Russ Lappa; **73,** Russ Lappa; **74t,** Richard Haynes; **74b,** Melanie Duncan Thortis/The Vicksburg Post/AP/Wide World Photos; **75,** Kevin Keane; **77 all,** Russ Lappa; **78t,** John Serrao/Photo Researchers, Inc.; **78b both,** Richard Megna/Fundamental Photographs.

Chapter 3

Pages 82–83, Richard Megna/Fundamental Photographs; **83r,** Richard Haynes; **85,** Digital Vision/Getty Images, Inc.; **86,** Richard Haynes; **88t,** Layne Kennedy/Corbis; **88b,** Onne van der Wal/Corbis; **89,** Paul Barton/Corbis; **90,** Russ Lappa; **91,** Richard Haynes; **92l,** Tim Laman/Index Stock Imagery, Inc.; **92m,** Randy Ury/Corbis; **92r,** Mike & Carol Werner/Stock Boston; **93,** Richard Haynes; **94,** Russ Lappa; **95 all,** Richard Haynes; **96,** Tony Freeman/PhotoEdit; **97 all,** Russ Lappa; **98t,** Russ Lappa; **98b,** Lawrence Migdale/Photo Researchers, Inc.; **99 both,** Russ Lappa; **100 both,** Russ Lappa; **101,** LWA-Dann Tardif/Corbis; **102t,** Mark C. Burnett/Stock Boston; **102bl,** Russ Lappa; **102br,** Russ Lappa; **103tl,** B. Daemmrich/The Image Works; **103tr,** Russ Lappa; **103b,** Russ Lappa; **104,** Russ Lappa; **105,** Tom Pantages; **107,** Richard Haynes; **110,** Russ Lappa; **111,** Richard Haynes; **112,** Cleo Photography/Photo Researchers, Inc.; **113,** Russ Lappa; **114,** Richard Haynes; **116,** Richard Haynes.

Chapter 4

Pages 120–121, Gerald D. Tang; **121r,** Richard Haynes; **122l,** Volker Steger/SPL/Photo Researchers, Inc.; **122r,** SIU/Peter Arnold, Inc.; **124l,** Cary Wolinsky/carywolinksy.com; **124r,** Barry Runk/Grant Heilman Photography; **125,** Richard Pasley/Stock Boston; **126,** Richard Haynes; **127tl,** Tom Vezo/Minden Pictures; **127tr,** Russ Lappa; **127b,** Getty Images, Inc.; **128t,** Amana America, Inc.; **128b,** Tony Craddock/SPL/Photo Researchers, Inc.; **130t,** Russ Lappa; **130b,** Richard Haynes; **131l,** Michael J. Doolittle/The Image Works; **131r,** Grant Heilman Photography, Inc.; **132,** Roberto Borea/AP/Wide World Photos; **133t,** R.J. Erwin/Photo Researchers, Inc.; **133b,** Russ Lappa; **134,** Richard Haynes; **135t,** Russ Lappa; **135b,** Russ Lappa; **136t,** Russ Lappa; **136–137b,** Richard Haynes; **137t,** E.S. Ross/Visuals Unlimited; **138l,** Library of Congress; **138m,** Science Museum/Science & Society Picture Library; **138r,** Gim Media/Gemological Institute of America; **139t,** Mauro Fermariello/SPL/Photo Researchers, Inc.; **139b,** Richard Haynes; **140 both,** Richard Haynes; **141,** Richard Haynes; **142,** ISM/Phototake; **144,** Erich Lessing/Art Resource, NY; **146–147,** Richard Haynes; **148,** Richard Haynes; **149,** Russ Lappa; **150,** Erich Lessing/Art Resource, NY.

Page 154, Robert Llewellyn/Corbis; **155t,** Spencer Grant/PhotoEdit; **155b,** PhotoDisc/Getty Images, Inc.; **157,** Russell Gordon/Aurora; **158t,** Mary Evans Picture Library; **158b,** Corbis; **159t,** Bettmann/Corbis; **159b,** PhotoDisc/Getty Images, Inc.; **160–161,** Russ Lappa; **161t,** LWA-Dann Tardif/Corbis; **162,** Tony Freeman/PhotoEdit; **163t,** Russ Lappa; **163m,** Richard Haynes; **163b,** Russ Lappa; **164,** Richard Haynes; **166,** Richard Haynes; **168,** Tanton Yachts; **169,** Richard Haynes; **171t,** Dorling Kindersley; **171b,** Richard Haynes; **173,** Image Stop/Phototake; **176,** Richard Haynes; **183,** Richard Haynes; **192,** Richard Haynes.